YOU CAN'T SHOOT THE ENGLISH

YOU CAN'T SHOOT
THE ENGLISH

by

Coralie Kinahan

VANTAGE PRESS
New York / Washington / Atlanta
Los Angeles / Chicago

FIRST EDITION

Copyright © 1981 by Coralie Kinahan

Published by Vantage Press, Inc.
516 West 34th Street, New York, New York 10001

Manufactured in the United States of America
Standard Book Number 533-04570-3

Library of Congress Catalog Card No.: 79-57545

AUTHOR'S NOTE

The main characters in this book are entirely fictitious, but the subsidiary characters and all the events and occasions are accurate, with the exception of the fire in Galway, which is based on one that was perpetrated in Cork the previous year, 1912.

The year 1913 was (in marked contrast to 1912) free from arson and bloodshed, but I did not want my heroine to gain all her information from hearsay, so I altered the date of this fire.

I write this book because I was sad that so few of the grandchildren of these people know anything about the thrilling adventures they had. The First World War, coming so soon after the end of this book, wiped out all interest in any other subject, and when the Ulster Volunteer Force volunteered to go to France as the Ulster Division, they were wiped out almost to a man at the Battle of the Somme, suffering seventy percent casualties in their gallant stand.

The complete secrecy of the gun-running and the training of the Volunteers meant that hardly any records of their times exist, and most of the people concerned are now dead. I am most grateful, therefore, to Commander Henderson, who put the copies of the *Belfast News Letter* of that period at my disposal, and also to the many people who reminisced for me and gave me the idea for the story. Also to the people who helped me to find books and articles of that period.

With five small children to look after, I could not attempt to write a history of those times, but I hope this simple romance may arouse enough interest in the period for readers to do their own research if they want to know more about it.

CORALIE KINAHAN
Castle Upton,
Templepatrick,
Northern Ireland
June 1966

YOU CAN'T SHOOT THE ENGLISH

Chapter 1

AUTUMN 1912

Bruised pride, a desire for vengeance, and a longing for love are not good sleeping companions, but coupled with the tramp and thump of many footsteps on the steel roof of her cabin, they did away with even the possibility of sleep and Ellen began to long for the stewardess to arrive with the cup of thin, scalding tea and terrible early morning cheerfulness designed to make passengers vacate their cabins as early as possible.

She looked at her watch: six-thirty. They couldn't possibly be in yet, but she was sure the engines had stopped.

Then a dull groan filled the air, sounding so exactly like she felt that despite herself she gave a small grin. Fog—of course!

No doubt Belfast was constantly wrapped in fog. After all those ghastly factory towns the train had passed through on the way up last night she could believe anything of the North—and wasn't Ulster known as "the Black North"?

She supposed there must be some country not given over to factories as her uncle seemed to spend his whole time shooting grouse and pheasants, but there would probably still be a pall of dirt hanging over it from all the mills.

She lay in her bunk and allowed her mind to dwell dismally on the events leading up to this visit to an unknown aunt.

Putting it baldly, she had been properly led up the garden path and it wasn't as if she were an inexperienced young thing.

1

She was twenty-one and had been living in London for quite long enough to know the form. She knew all about the rich, and "hard to catch" Desmond Campion's reputation with girls and had in fact felt no particular interest in him, considering him at thirty-five to be quite out of her circle, until one day when she had been assigned to play with him at a tennis match.

Ellen rather prided herself on her tennis and was therefore justifiably annoyed when he assured her beforehand not to worry about difficult shots but to "leave them to him" and then rushed around at the net poaching all her balls despite her warning shouts of "mine!"

Very well then, he could just manage on his own, she decided, and let the next few shots go without making any effort to hit them, and added insult to injury by smiling bewitchingly at him as they crossed to the other end.

He glanced crossly at her cool face and said, "You know you *could* have got some of those shots—I can't do *everything!*"

Ellen opened her eyes wide. "But, Captain Campion, you said just to leave it to you!" His eyes met and held hers and, despite herself, a saucy smile broke over her face.

"What a horrid girl you are!" he exclaimed, but his voice was full of amusement and his eyes gleamed. She felt her heart beat faster as she retorted, "What a horrid poacher you are!"

Then they both burst out laughing and the damage was done. The vital spark had been lit and they saw each other constantly all through the summer.

He was fascinated by her resistance and sharp wit; so many girls collapsed like pricked balloons and lost all their attraction. Ellen really wasn't particularly interested in him apart from the flattery of his attention and the amusement of sparring with him. She was still enjoying life too much to take it seriously and was blissfully unaware of how little she really knew about it.

She didn't like the way Desmond held her when they were dancing; it made her uncomfortable to be held so close. One time she was sure he had kissed her—oh so lightly—on the ear, but when she had pulled away he had teased her.

"What are you blushing about?"

2

She hadn't known what to answer. So she put the episode out of her mind and thought no more of it than she did of him; there were too many other things to think about.

Then one night—she had been dancing the Lancers and was still flushed and short of breath when he came to claim her for the next dance—he fetched her a glass of Cup and suggested, "Why not come and drink it outside? It's so hot in here." He pulled back the curtains on the French window. It was the most gorgeous night; a nightingale was singing faintly in the wood at the bottom of the garden.

Silver trees swept down to silver lawns. Two swans swam across the path of the moon on the river, appearing jet black one moment and then ghostly pale as they passed into the shadows.

Ellen was drinking in this beauty when she suddenly became aware that Campion had moved to stand close beside her. A thrill of premonition made her start away from him.

"Don't go." He pulled her back. "You're always so surrounded. I can never get a chance to speak to you alone."

"Oh!" She caught her breath. "What do you want to speak to me about?"

For answer he slid his right hand under her arm and then up to cup her breast, and before she had recovered from the sudden tumult of emotion, his left hand tilted her head back on his shoulder and he kissed her softly all over her forehead and eyes while she lay supine against him.

She couldn't move a muscle: she was drained of all will-power. *This must be what it means to swoon with delight,* she thought in amazement, her whole body thrilling with sensation.

Then suddenly he drew away, almost letting her fall onto the stone seat, her mind in a whirl. Pleasure, amazement, a twinge of shame—she had never been touched like that before. She hadn't known there could be so many conflicting emotions.

He sat down beside her and took out his cigarette case. "May I?" and started calmly to smoke.

She was trembling all over. Suddenly she dropped her face into her hands and burst into tears.

3

"Good Lord! What's all the fuss about?" he exclaimed in surprise. "Surely you have been kissed before!"

Speechlessly Ellen blew her nose and tried to pull herself together.

"Didn't you like it?" he asked curiously, holding his cigarette away and studying her face.

"No—yes—I mean— I don't know—you had no right to—" stammered poor Ellen, all her poise gone.

"Most girls like it. You surely don't think anyone as adorable as you can go through life without being kissed?" he reasoned.

"I don't know . . . I don't know—you make everything seem wrong. I wish you hadn't done it!" she exclaimed confusedly. "Please take me back" and she jumped up and walked quickly into the house, her mind whirling, deeply conscious of his resigned sigh as he stubbed his cagarette out and followed her. Fortunately she found her next partner waiting for her and was able to put the whole incident out of her mind for most of the dance and afterwards fell asleep, much to her surprise, the moment her head touched the pillow.

Next morning she had wakened slowly, with a dragging sense of guilt. The brilliance of the light behind her curtains bespoke another glorious day. Why then, this horrid feeling?

The warning cry of a blackbird as the kitchen cat sauntered lazily down the garden path cut across the warm air and suddenly she remembered. A shock ran through her and her breast tingled as it had done when he touched it, suffusing her in blushes. Her whole body had sprung to life and she lay torn between shame and thrilling sensation.

Then she remembered that she would be meeting him at the garden fete that afternoon. There was to be tennis and she had been so looking forward to it. Now it would be dreadful—she couldn't meet him.

What could she do? She thought of feigning a headache. No—that was too obvious. He would be so triumphant at his power over her. She would have to go—and pray that they would not be put to play together.

4

For the first part of the afternoon she had managed to avoid him—beyond a chilly smile—and was thankful that he took the hint and stayed away from her. After tea her luck changed and she was sent off to partner him against a very expert couple. At first the pace was so hot she had no time to think of her feelings and was exulting in playing her very best when they changed sides and in her excitement she forgot to keep the court between them and suddenly found Campion by her side. He bent over, all admiration for her play, and whispered, "Wonderful what a kiss can do for a girl, isn't it?"

All the sensations of the previous night poured over her again like a flood and a great weakness seized her so that her game collapsed and she bungled shot after shot.

Overcome with chagrin, she was near to tears and was thankful when they finally lost the set and she was able, with perfect truth, to plead a headache and go home.

It was not, she thought, as she brushed her hair that night, that it was so dreadfully wrong to have been kissed, but it was the horrid way he had made it seem as if she had been wanting it—had come into the garden with that intention. It made it all so cheap when it should have been so wonderful! Her cheeks blazed at the memory. The only thing to do was to avoid him completely in the future. It was not as if she really liked him anyway—yet—that kiss had stirred her deeper than she realised.

It turned out to be easier to avoid him than she had expected. Unflatteringly so. Though he was at all the autumn parties he did not do more than return her chilly smile and kept away, dancing assiduously with other girls and never so much as looking her way until she began to wonder if perhaps she had made too much of the episode. Wouldn't it be more grown-up to pretend that it didn't matter at all, at the same time taking good care not to let it happen again?

Inevitable they met in a small party and he was put beside her at dinner.

He laid himself out to charm her as though nothing had happened—and she responded—only slightly aloof. He tried to pierce this new defence and was intrigued to find questions skilfully parried. There was something very piquant about this little Ellen Tristram, and he settled down in earnest to flirt with her.

Ellen was prepared now. She treated his attention as a delightful joke and took care never to be alone with him. Her spirits rose—she could cope with the situation and it was fun.

She found him enormously attractive despite the basic feeling of mistrust.

Gradually people began to notice and wonder had Campion, the notorious flirt, been caught at last. He had never remained constant to any other girl as long as this. Perhaps the pretty Tristram girl, with her cosmopolitan background, was better able to handle him than others. Her mother was surprised and gratified. She had been a little anxious at first, knowing his reputation, but, of course, none of the other girls could hold a candle to Ellen so it would not be strange if he were really in love this time. That young Markham was obviously mad about her, too, but he had no money to go with his title and Campion would be a far more brilliant match. She hoped something would be fixed up soon as her husband's time at the Admiralty was almost up and Heaven knew where they would be sent after this.

But summer came and went, the first frosts crystallised the grass, and nothing was settled.

Looking back, Ellen wondered just when it was that the sun seemed to go in. At first it had been a sparkling affair, a game of quick wit and admiration for each other. Then gradually she had found herself comparing his experienced attentions with the other men's less polished methods and revelling in his masterly handling of any situation to his advantage. She neither noticed nor cared about the gradual falling of her other admirers, nor the look of hurt in Markham's eyes. She had to confess that she, the clever would-be deflater, had fallen into her own trap and was now head over ears in love.

The wonder of this filled her mind completely. She felt she had gained a new understanding and deeper meaning in everything she did and she longed to share this feeling with Desmond; but he was bored with serious things. She longed for him to kiss her again but could not let him know and was ashamed of the longing. She was afraid that if he did kiss her she would only fall deeper into his web. Kisses were such a casual thing to him.

She knew he was only too ready to oblige; indeed several times he had suggested, jokingly, that she must have grown up since the Slowe House Dance and did she still think he was such a Bad Man? Did she not realise it was quite a normal thing to do; other girls liked it—why not Ellen? Underneath her passionate longing she remained quite certain that in real love it should be a joy to yield oneself utterly to the man one loved. It was this constant dragging her down to (existing or imaginary) other girls' levels that hurt so much. There was never a word of real love, only banter; surely, if he did love her, he would show it— say something; think more highly of her.

She was so afraid of showing the depth of her own feelings that she could hear herself becoming stiff and dull. Gradually he seemed to draw away from her as if now that he realised he had won, he had lost interest. He no longer made plans ahead for their enjoyment nor asked her to keep dances for him. Every now and then he would come back in his easy way and tease and charm her until she felt sure he must really love her after all. Then he would disappear for weeks and she would hear that he had been at balls in Scotland, parties somewhere else.

She would be plunged into despondence and make her mind up to be done with him. Then back he would come, seeking her out, having little secrets with her, dancing all the tangos with her as if nothing had changed.

To make matters worse, her father's new appointment had come through. They could hardly be sent farther away. He was appointed to Flag Rank and was to take over command of one of the new battle cruisers due to join the China Squadron before Christmas. Her father, overjoyed at the prospect of going to sea again, was full of plans for closing their house in London and busy making enquiries from sailors recently back from Hong Kong about accommodation for his wife and daughter.

Mrs. Tristram was in rather a quandary; she had whiled away many happy hours planning a wedding and picturing her daughter happily settled as mistress of Campion's lovely house in Northumberland, while she followed her own husband out East.

Now things seemed to be going wrong. Ellen was obviously unhappy, alternating between fits of depression and a wild, brittle gaiety. Kind friends reported Campion dancing attendance on some girl in the North and she was constantly reminded of all that she had previously heard against him. She was not going to have her beautiful daughter the subject of every gossiping cat in town. Her husband must speak to him. They must become engaged or else he must leave her alone. Fortunately for the Admiral, who was a shy man and did not relish this task at all (though he was prepared to do his duty when it had been established beyond all doubt that it *was* his duty) Ellen overheard part of the discussion and was so horrified at the thought of her parents' interference that she immediately resolved to tell Campion herself, at the first opportunity, that she was going away. Surely, if he loved her, he would say something then.

She really knew in her heart that the affair was over but she was determined to hear it from his own lips. She would not then, in future, be inventing excuses for him. At the back of her subconscious mind was always the hope that when he realised he was going to lose her he might find that he really loved her.

At the dance that night she waited apprehensively for him to seek her out. As usual, she had almost given up hope when he sauntered up and led her on to the floor. They danced in silence and she marvelled anew that the thrill she felt at his touch could fail to awaken some answering feeling in him. But evidently it could, for presently he said in a bantering tone, "You are very quiet tonight, Ellen, are you not enjoying the dance? Shall I return you to your admirers?"

He made as if to release her but she stood her ground bravely, saying with a sang-froid, which she was far from feeling, "No. There is something I want to tell you so I shall try to make the best of it . . . shall we go outside for a moment?"

He looked at her in amazement and then laughingly took her in his arms again, whispering as they danced, "Now it is my turn to worry. Do you think my character will stand up to being seen going into the garden with the notorious Miss Tristram? No-o-o! I think we had better stay safely on the floor."

It was the last straw to have him mocking exactly those fears which so beset her and as for ascribing the danger to her . . . She was goaded to folly and retorted hotly, "You didn't seem to be so much troubled by the conventions a year ago!"

He danced the full length of the room before answering cryptically, "Neither was your mother, then!"

Sudden fear clutched Ellen's heart. Surely her father had not had time. No, it was impossible.

"Wh . . . what do you mean?" she stammered incredulously. "Mother has not said anything to you, has she?"

"No," he laughed shortly, "but I can see a glint in her eye that tells me that she very soon will. I don't think that she likes me very much."

From a dry throat Ellen said, "You could make her like you . . . you've never tried." She pleaded.

"Why should I?" he answered abruptly. "It's not her I want to dance with. Perhaps you are right; we should finish this discussion in a less public place." He promptly led the way out of the house. They walked in silence down a path of clipped yews deep in shadows, across the grass where the still heavy-leafed trees stood black against the frosty sky and cast sombre pools of darkness over the old walled garden. It was too cold a night to have tempted anyone else out but Ellen was so worried she did not notice.

Now that they were alone she did not know how to begin, so they walked without speaking, uncomfortably constrained to Ellen but not apparently to Campion, who must have had a change of mood for presently he observed whimsically, "You know this is an unexpected privilege. I quite thought that you and I were never going gardening again!"

"But this is quite different . . ." she started nervously, her heart going like a hammer, "that isn't why . . . I mean . . . I . . . I . . . wanted to tell you something." She clenched her hands together and turned to face him as they reached the gate at the

9

end of the path, looking beseechingly at him as she sought for words.

He laughed down at her. "But I would much rather kiss you. Beautiful girls are made to be kissed in beautiful gardens." He took a step towards her, his face dark in the shadow of the trees.

"No . . . no . . . please don't. Please go away. I don't want to be kissed now." She backed away and was brought up sharp by the gate behind her. He rested one hand on it and with the other carelessly tipped her face up and bending down touched her lips with his—so softly. "I . . . just . . . don't . . . believe . . . you." He kissed her between each word.

Ellen's knees turned to water and there was a rushing in her ears. She could not have moved if the angel with the fiery sword himself had appeared before her. She gazed up at Campion, her eyes swimming with tears.

"Isn't that nicer than talking?" he asked softly, and began to kiss her again, lightly, warmly, expertly—on her neck, her cheeks, eyelids, tip of her nose, and back to her lips again.

"Darling," he murmured, as her lips clung to his, "you have such a lot to learn." He slipped his arm round her and turned her deftly to lean against his shoulder, kissing and murmuring endearments until she was entirely supine, enthralled with love, a plaything in his hands.

Then he kissed her more fiercely, his lips hard against hers. She could feel his teeth through them and his hands pressing into her shoulders. She gave herself up to the strange, pulsing sensation and kissed him back, all concentration in her mouth. She was dimly aware of a moment of shock when his hands slid inside her dress to cradle her breast, but her body yearned towards him and her mind was whirling. *So this is love . . . he loves me . . . this is what it means to be loved.* Her body strained to his. *It's alright after all, he loves me . . . he loves me,* sang her heart in a crescendo of joy.

She scarcely knew that he had turned her around to face him and that his thigh was pressing hers against the gate. She could hardly breathe. She was like a person drowning. But suddenly it wasn't lovely any more. A tiny cold shaft of doubt pierced her thraldom; there was a rushing in her ears; and when he suddenly shot his tongue between her parted lips it was as though an icy sword cut through the mists, galvanising her into life. Struggling and pushing to get out of his grasp she turned her head wildly from side to side, fighting with all her strength. All at once he let her go and she fell back, shuddering, against the gate, staring up at him speechlessly. There was a strange expression on his face, almost anger, and he seemed to have nearly as much difficulty in finding his voice as Ellen.

A full minute passed before he said in his normal dry tone, "You silly child, it wouldn't have hurt you!" He touched her frozen cheek. "I'm sorry if I frightened you. Here, come and sit on this bench and I will help you tidy yourself."

Ellen sank down thankfully; her legs would not have supported her another minute. Then suddenly she became aware of her dress pushed down far over her arms and breasts and was engulfed in burning waves of shame as she feverishly jerked it up to cover them. She could not raise her eyes. She was so appalled with herself that she was barely conscious of him speaking.

"You looked so lovely like that," he leaned towards her but she pulled away, her legs still shaking too much to stand. "Have I shocked you? Surely not! You must not be puritanical—everybody kisses nowadays . . ." and so he talked on while she fought for composure and when she did not answer he finally lit a cigarette.

She could not say a word. All her world had collapsed and only a sick, choking sense of shame overwhelmed her. He didn't love her; this meant nothing to him, it was just another episode. His only emotion was anger at being frustrated. It was also clear to her now that there was no point in talking. She felt absolutely numb.

Gradually, as her head cleared, she realised that he was asking her what she had been going to tell him.

She made a tiny, futile gesture with her hands. What was the point of telling him now?

He leant back, drawing on his cigarette. "Don't tell me

11

there was nothing . . . just a ruse to lure me into the garden!" he teased.

She gasped. If she had had a gun in her hand she would have shot him there and then. She jumped to her feet. "You insufferable beast! You drag everything down to your own level . . . how could I have been such a fool . . . such a blind, pig-headed fool as to think you cared for me when all you have been doing was to amuse yourself at my expense?" She drew a long uneven breath and whispered to herself, "Thank God, we are going away and I hope I never, never see you again."

She made as if to leave him and then turned back again to say, quivering with remorse as she stood over him, "That was what I was going to tell you . . . that we are going away. I was so unhappy—I couldn't bear not to see you again. I thought . . . I thought . . ." she could not go on.

"What did you think?" he asked curiously.

"Oh!" she exclaimed bitterly. "I was a damn fool; I thought you loved me."

He threw away his cigarette. "But, Ellen darling, I do . . ." he expostulated. "I think you're a sweet girl and when you've grown up a bit you'll make some lucky dog a most beautiful wife."

"But not you?" she blurted out despite herself.

"Me?" he paused, returning his cigarette case to his pocket, and said wearily, "Why do all you young girls want to rush into marriage? Why can't you just enjoy the moment?"

At this heartless confirmation of all her shipwrecked hopes she finally lost her temper. "I'll tell you why," she cried furiously, "it's because we have decent standards—and hearts—and I only wish I had realised a bit sooner that you have neither!"

She turned on her heel and rushed across the grass, a pale, valiant ghost in the shadowed garden.

He watched her go. Reluctant admiration, annoyance, and a slight sense of guilt played on his face. He lit another cigarette and sat for a long time there until, finally stubbing it out, he stood up, shrugged his shoulders as if throwing off an unwelcome burden and walked back to the ballroom.

Chapter 2

For the next week Ellen drifted listlessly about the house, making excuses to avoid meeting people and spending a great deal of time in her room. In a sense she was relieved to have the affaire over. She had at last seen right through Campion; and if it had not been for the physical ache in her newly-awakened body she would have been able to rise above her misfortune.

She felt a growing reluctance to the thought of going to Hong Kong. She could just hear people laughing and saying how lucky it was that having failed to catch the richest man in London, she could now go and try her luck with the girl-starved Far Eastern Forces. The more she thought about it, the more she hated the idea—and her mother, watching the circles growing under her eyes, began to wonder if it would be wise to take Ellen in this state to the heat of Hong Kong. There was so little time to make any other arrangements. Then a letter came from her sister one morning with the perfect solution.

Mrs. Tristram looked up at her husband, explaining in relief, "Listen, Aubrey, this is the very thing. You know I had written to Marion to ask her to have Harry up for some shooting when he gets leave from the Curragh? Well, she writes back saying she will be delighted to have him but asks also would I not send Ellen as well, at least for part of the time we are away." She laid the letter on the table and waited for his answer, which came with reluctance.

The Admiral loved his pretty daughter and felt that he had not seen so much of her that he would easily agree to losing her for two whole years. But she could always come out later on if

13

she were not happy, and her brother Harry would be near her. Maybe it was a good idea . . . for a time, anyway. He walked to the door, nearly colliding with Ellen coming down to breakfast.

"Well, you two talk it over together and do whatever you think best—only make up your minds quickly, for I'm not going to change the tickets every other day." He paused thoughtfully, his hand on the doorknob. "I suppose it's quite safe over there or Marion would not have asked her to stay. I think I will have a word with Arthur at the club before we make up our minds. They are so damned excitable, these Irish." He came back and kissed his family rather absently and then hurried off.

"What on earth was father talking about?" Ellen asked.

Her mother gave her the letter to read and dismissed her husband's anxiety somewhat airily. "They're always fighting about something in Ireland. This time it's the Home Rule Bill," she explained. "They are never satisfied . . . they don't like being governed by England and think they can do it much better themselves and pester the life out of everyone to do away with the Viceroy. Then as soon as the bill is ready to go through Parliament, they change their minds and start pestering everyone again to stop it. They are really quite mad but quite amusing, if you can keep them off politics."

She added, "Your Aunt Marion adores them and has become more Irish than the Irish ever since she married one of them."

So they discussed the prospect of Ellen going for a long visit to her Aunt Marion in County Antrim. Ellen felt that she did not much care where she went and that Ireland was as good a place as any to take her sore heart until it recovered.

She was very fond of her brother Harry, a year older than herself, in the Army, and newly stationed at the Curragh Camp in the South of Ireland. It would be lovely to see more of him and her aunt sounded kind and friendly.

So here she was three weeks later on the S.S. *Patriotic*, wrapped in fog and gloom.

The thump of the engines starting again and a sudden activity of feet on the iron plating over her head made Ellen sit up and look at her watch. It was already past ten o'clock. "Heavens! I suppose we are already in Belfast and I am not even dressed!" She hurriedly pulled aside the little curtain hiding the porthole and sat blinking in amazement at the scene before her. They were nowhere near Belfast—that was quite sure. The sea stretched opalescent beneath a clear blue sky, and in the distance park-like green fields stretched down to the very edge of the water from an escarpment of grey rock-faced hills: a formation that reached as far as the eye could see. The whole scene shimmered in translucent light with little tendrils of morning mist still clinging to the tops of the hills.

It was all unbelievably beautiful. She was so surprised at this transformation from the dreary industrial gloom of the night before that she wondered momentarily if she could have got onto the wrong ship. She jumped onto the floor and hustled into her grey suit, coiled her hair around her head, locked her cases and, seizing her hat, ran up on deck, eager to find out more about this place.

As she hurried towards the bows, the breeze whipped fresh pink into her cheeks and her eyes sparkled as she gazed around. It was all so beautiful that the bad night in the stuffy cabin with her sorrowful memories was quite forgotten.

They were in a wide channel with green fields and hills on either side and directly ahead lay the harbour in the hollow of the hills. The last of the mist lifted slowly over the buildings forming mysterious shapes with the gantries and scaffolding in the shipyards as the blue haze mingled with the smoke.

"The 'Emerald Isle' of course!" Ellen murmured to herself as she looked. "Only, emerald is too hard a colour, this is more like a dark opal, there is a . . ." she sought in her mind for a suitable description "I know—a lambency, a limpidity about this colour. It could never be as cold or exotic as an emerald. I wonder if the people are like their country, soft and mysterious. Father said they were always fighting, which doesn't sound very soft or mysterious, but I think I can understand already a little bit why Aunt Marion loves it so much."

Slowly they drew nearer to the harbour, the distance across

the water narrowed and Ellen could see, with great interest, that many of the green fields were in fact parkland. All along either bank of the Lough, at intervals of a mile or less, were large houses set amongst great trees with gardens and parkland sweeping right down to the shore. One or two of the houses were beautiful old buildings, but most of them seemed to be Victorian and heavily ornate with a tendency to turrets. However, as they were half-screened by trees and in such exquisite surroundings, the architecture did not strike too discordant a note.

Ellen wondered if the people were all very rich; there did not seem to be any other kind of dwelling except a few scattered, whitewashed cottages, hardly any higher than the hedges surrounding them. Farther back there had been a small town on the Lough edge, huddled behind an imposing square-towered castle. She wished she were not travelling alone and could ask someone all the questions that leapt to mind.

People were standing about in groups all along the deck and she got the impression that a large proportion of the travellers seemed to know each other. They moved from one group to another, hailing each other and stopping to talk, unlike the anonymous behaviour of travellers from the Continent arriving in England. She sensed, also, a kind of suppressed excitement in the people that was very intriguing.

She was too busy taking in all these impressions to realise that a number of people were taking an equal interest in her. A very pretty, sophisticated looking girl cannot appear in a provincial boat without being immediately noticed and wondered about. In many ways the Liverpool steamer was very like a small provincial town; few people travelled to Ulster unless they already had business or family connections there, in which case they already knew many of the local inhabitants by sight at least. One tall young man, in particular, was most interested in Ellen's appearance. He also seemed to be travelling by himself, though he had exchanged greetings and paused to talk to a large number of people on the boat.

He was sure that Ellen was a stranger to the North. Her smartly tailored coat and skirt, indeed her whole air, breathed

London, so it was with particular pleasure that he watched the expression of enchantment on her face as she surveyed his country for the first time. He wondered very much who she could be and where she was going to stay. But he was not going to try to brush acquaintance with her by offering to carry her cases for a number of reasons.

Firstly, being a true Ulsterman, he was in the habit of thinking before acting, and having reached the age of thirty, he realised that young men who claimed acquaintance with nice young ladies by such impetuous methods did themselves very little lasting good in the eyes of either the lady or her family. If he had thought that this was his only chance of meeting her he might not have been so high-minded about it but he could afford to stand back, safe in the knowledge that in the course of the autumn round of parties and dances there was no house in the province to which he would not be invited at some time and so find out who she was.

Secondly, this 28th day of September was a day of supreme importance to him as to all other Ulstermen—a day on which even the most beautiful girls could only take second place in his interests. This pretty girl merely added a pleasant feeling of anticipation to his existing sense of exuberance.

He went below to collect his bag, which he had left conveniently placed for a quick disembarkation. However, it was nowhere to be seen and some considerable time elapsed before he managed to discover it beneath a huge pile of boxes destined for Omagh, a small town at least sixty miles away from his home. He was intrigued by the sight of a woman, heavily draped in black crepe, sitting beside what was obviously a coffin in the deck area cordoned off for third-class passengers. He could not repress a slight feeling of guilt when he compared her lonely sorrow with the frivolous thoughts that had been passing through his own mind.

By the time he had retrieved his bag and hurried down the gangway to the waiting line of cabs Ellen had already discovered her aunt and was being installed, with considerable fuss and talk, in a very high, very bright blue motor car with an immense

17

amount of gleaming brasswork, while a chauffeur piled her luggage on the back and an impish looking boy of about fourteen climbed into the driver's seat and made a great show of familiarity with the mechanism, to the delight of the onlookers and the amusement of his mother.

As the tall young man hurried past the car he smiled at the boy, calling, "You make me feel very staid going in a cab, Michael. I hope you won't frighten my horse too much when you overtake me!"

Michael grinned enthusiastically. "You'll have to come over and see her properly, sir. She's the fastest car in the country. Father can hardly bear to let her out of his sight."

At this moment Lady Richardson gave up supervising the bestowal of the baggage and sat down, revealing Ellen sitting beyond her. The young man raised his hat and, smiling, walked on to the cab-line, well pleased at having found out so quickly where the pretty girl was staying and that it should be not only with people he liked very much but who lived quite close.

"I wonder where James Melville has been.. He looks very pleased with life," remarked Lady Richardson. "He is one of the nicest men over here, Ellen. People forecast a great future for him."

The chauffeur tucked the rug in around their knees and climbed into the driving seat and they set off through some very shabby streets.

"I'm afraid you will get a very bad impression of Ulster, starting like this," observed her aunt, divining her thoughts, "but Belfast is not beautiful. It has been built in such a hurry, trying to keep up with all the new industry, that no one has troubled about the look of it. Such a pity when the setting is so beautiful."

"Yes, I know. Coming up the Lough it looked perfectly exquisite . . . all misty with the sun shining through. But it's not a big town, is it? and don't you live quite a long way outside, Aunt Marion?" Then she added mischievously, "Mummy always talks as if Kilwater was halfway to Africa!" Her aunt was so attractive and so much younger than Ellen had expected that she felt completely at ease with her already.

Lady Richardson laughed. "It's quite extraordinary—people either understand and love us or don't understand and hate us. I'm afraid your mother falls into the last category and refuses to allow us any good points at all. I hope you won't feel the same, but you will have to postpone your verdict on the house for a while. This is a very special day for us over here. We have decided to fight for our right to be governed by England, and Sir Edward Carson has drawn up a Covenant that is to be signed by him and James Craig, and all of us who feel as they do, at the City Hall today. Your uncle is signing it and there is one for women, too, which I intend to sign. The town will be absolutely crowded out, so we have decided to stay in all day and have taken a room at the Grand Central Hotel and will go home this evening when it is all over."

Most of this might just as well have been spoken in Greek to Ellen, who only read the "Engagement" column in *The Times* and never listened to any political discussions. However the look of the already thronged streets through which the car was now scarcely making any progress at all, and the fact that a charming, gay person like her aunt was taking part in whatever it was, made her feel a stir of interest and ask rather humbly, "But I thought Ireland *was* ruled by England?"

"Yes, it is; that's just it; but now the southern counties want to change and have their own government, while we in the North wish to remain under England."

"Well, what's wrong with that? Why on earth do you have to fight for that?" asked Ellen, now thoroughly muddled. Before her aunt had time to explain their car was brought to a complete standstill by a large number of policemen forming themselves into a chain across the road where it was traversed by what looked like a main shopping street. The crowd surged around them. Up till now they had been quite quiet but now they went mad, all yelling and throwing their hats in the air and pushing forward against the linked arms of the police. The occupants of the car jumped to their feet and craned forward to see what it was all about.

"By Jove, Mother, it's Sir Edward himself and Captain Craig! They must be on their way to the Ulster Hall now. Oh, Mother, isn't that wonderful! Oh, Neill, do hurry! Can you not push a way through the people? We'll never get there at this rate!"

Michael was hopping up and down on the seat, urging the chauffeur on, but he remained quite unmoved, merely saying dourly, "I'd be afeared to push them, Master Michael, they're that excited they'd maybe take us fer Fenians. There's the Polis comin' now. They'll make way for us!" The landau having passed, the police quickly cleared the roads again and the crowd broke up into excited groups, allowing the big blue car to drive on to the hotel.

Ellen noticed a number of well-dressed men standing on a balcony, looking down at the crowd, and one or two waved back.

"There's Father. I do hope he joins us soon. I'm longing to hear all the news and I'm starving with hunger, too—it must be ages since breakfast."

"Well, here we are, so you won't have to starve much longer," said Lady Richardson as the car drew up under the portico of a big hotel in the main street.

The usual crowd thronged the doorway but made room for them to pass inside, many admiring glances following their progress.

Sir Charles joined them shortly before morning coffee was served and was immediately charmed by his pretty niece.

"I hope you will enjoy being with us and maybe stay as long as your aunt in the end! What do you think, Marion? Would you say that we had sufficiently attractive men nowadays to persuade such a pretty girl to stay over here for good?"

He glanced quizzically at his wife who laughed back. "I don't know about attractive, but after driving through the streets this morning she can have no doubts about the sufficiency of men in this province! I remember when I first came over

20

I thought they were the ugliest lot of men I'd ever seen—
except, of course, for yourself!" She gave her husband a happy
smile.

"Dear me," said Sir Charles, with a comical look. "I hope
we have made a better impression on you than that, Ellen."

Poor Ellen, who besides being in a very unsusceptible frame
of mind, had thought exactly that, gave a beautiful blush, to the
undisguised joy of her cousin, and cast about in her mind for
some way of softening the blow.

"Well, not . . . um . . . exactly ugly, but they struck me as
being very hard looking . . . very . . . well . . . determined and
they all look as if they live in the country, not in the town."

"She means all their faces are red," put in Michael helpfully.

"No, I don't," contradicted Ellen, getting into her stride.
"I mean they all look very fit and—well—hard!" Her voice trailed
off and she met her uncle's teasing eyes rather defiantly.

He beamed at her. "Well, Ellen, you must be very clever as
well as pretty, for that is a very accurate description of an
Ulsterman; they are hard, as Mr. Asquith will discover if he goes
on trying to push us out of the Empire," he concluded in rather
a grim voice.

He turned to tell his wife the latest gossip from the club
and Ellen tried to remember what one talked about to young
cousins aged fourteen.

"Do you go to school in England?" she asked politely.
Any topic was better than sitting under his clear, considering
look.

"Yes, I go to Harrow, but father says that either the school
has gone down or I'm a fool and I have to have a tutor here for
a year."

"Oh dear!" exclaimed Ellen, slightly shaken by this engaging
candour. "Does that mean you have to work awfully hard all
the time?"

"Oh Lord, no," he answered happily. "Mr. Grantham is a
splendid fellow. I've taught him a lot about Ulster and he's so
keen now he's joined the Volunteers and we hardly have any
time for lessons!"

21

Ellen broke into helpless laughter; she was coming rapidly 'round to her mother's point of view that the Irish were all mad. "And doesn't Uncle Charles mind?" she asked.

"Well, he says we'll need every man we can get and Mr. Grantham is a cracking good shot."

Ellen felt herself sinking deeper and deeper into the mists of madness. "But what is he going to shoot?"

"The English, of course . . . or the Fenians . . . whoever attacks us first. 'Not an Inch'—that's our motto!"

"But you can't shoot the English!" objected Ellen. She spoke in a voice of gentle reason suitable for use with dangerous lunatics. *Mother might have told me*, she thought, but continued out loud, "I'm English and you're half-English. I don't know who the Fenians are but wouldn't it be better to stick to fighting them and not us?"

Michael leaned back in his chair and looked at her in comical dismay.

"Poor Cousin Ellen, you really are very, very ignorant, aren't you? I suppose girls never talk about anything but dances and dresses and love. Thank goodness I shall be safely out of the way in the army before my sisters reach that stage."

Then he sat up with a disarming grin just as she was deciding that she really didn't like him, and nodded his head at her across the table. "But I'll teach you. You're really rather nice and I'm sure it will be fun having you to stay."

Fortunately for Ellen, who could think of no suitable rejoinder to this gallant promise, her uncle and aunt now began plying her with questions about the family, which lasted until coffee was finished and it was time for them to fetch their coats and climb into the car again for the short distance to the City Hall. Even in the car, if it had not been for the efforts of many police controlling the crowds, they could never have reached their objective, for the people in the main street and around the square in which the City Hall was set were now packed solid from end to end.

As they reached the square a group of men and clergy came onto the lawn in front of the portico of the City Hall and the band struck up the hymn "Oh God, Our Help in Ages Past," the whole crowd joining in with a deep-voiced sincerity that brought tears to Ellen's eyes even though she did not understand the cause. The hymn was followed by prayers and then after a short pause, cheers were heard in the distance and a procession was seen coming around the side of the City Hall, headed by a man carrying an old, yellow flag.

"That's the flag that was carried before King Billy at the Battle of the Boyne!" hissed Michael in Ellen's ear. "And those men marching 'round it are some of the Volunteers to see that nobody destroys it."

"Oh," said Ellen, more mystified than ever, but trying very hard to say something intelligent. "Who are those men walking behind it? Surely one of them is a bishop, isn't he?"

"Yes, that's the Bishop of Down and the Dean of Belfast with him, the tall one with the beard. The very big man in the front with the long chin—that's our leader, Sir Edward Carson. You should hear him speak. He's terrific! And those are the Orange Lodges coming behind. Don't they look splendid? You'll see James Melville soon—the fellow who was on the boat this morning—he's in one of the first Lodges. Look, there he is! They are going in now to sign. Oh how I wish I was old enough! They say some of them are going to sign with their own blood," he continued with relish. "I'd love to do that!"

At this point Sir Charles and Lady Richardson climbed down to join the rapidly moving queue of would-be signatories.

When they had gone, Sir Charles pushing his way through the crowd with Lady Richardson holding firmly on to his coat to prevent herself being cut off, Ellen turned to Michael and said eagerly, "Oh, Michael, do try to explain to me what it is all about; nobody in England talked about anything like this. They just say, 'Oh the Irish are never satisfied, they are always fighting' and shrug their shoulders, but this is a huge thing. Look, there are more and more men coming and they all look such decent, sensible people."

"Well," said Michael, heaving an enormous, portentous sigh, "it's all religion, really; that's why the English don't understand. In Ireland the Roman Catholics and the Protestants have always fought—it's a kind of permanent vendetta. It's the result of people being sent over to populate the country for whichever king of England happened to be reigning. If it was a Protestant king he sent over lots of Protestants with grants of land to 'make' the country for him. Then the next thing would be a Roman Catholic king and he would do the same and give them full permission to wipe out the Protestants. Then it would happen all over again, only with the Protestants in power, so naturally they have all got something to fight about. Now in the whole of Ireland there are more Roman Catholic than Protestants, but in this corner it is the other way 'round—I say, this is a fearful lecture—are you sure you want to hear more?"

"Oh yes; if I am going to live here I'll have to understand, and the quicker the better," she assured him.

"All right. To continue, if the whole of Ireland breaks away from England and has Home Rule—governs itself—that will be 'Rome Rule,' which means that we don't think the Roman Catholic majority would treat us fairly, so we have asked to remain under England."

"Yes, I understand that. I should have thought England would be glad to keep you."

"Well, she's not! There's a whole lot of political clap-trap and the long and the short of it is that she means to force us in under the South and we don't intend to go. That's why Sir Edward Carson has raised the Ulster Volunteers Force, and if the army is sent against us, we will fight. Mr. Grantham thinks I could be a messenger boy. I've got a jolly good bike and I'm tophole at finding my way about in the dark."

"Really," said Ellen returning to something she found easier to understand, "I think Mr. Grantham sounds an awfully bad tutor. What do your sisters do—are they learning to be messengers, too?"

"Oh, no! They're mad with rage because Mr. Grantham and I won't tell them anything. Cynthia thinks she is in love with him anyway—she's always mooning around getting in his way. Half the time she imagines she is grown-up and is awfully dull and prissy, and then she forgets and is really quite fun. But Alice is the girl! She can climb any tree on the place—she'll do *anything*."

So by the time her uncle and aunt returned to the car, Ellen had learned a good deal, not only about "The Cause" but also about the cousins she was to make her home with. Her head was positively reeling with information and she was beginning to wish she had had a slightly better night and was more able to take it all in.

She looked forward with great interest to seeing Kilwater and her two cousins, not less Mr. Grantham, who seemed totally different from any of the dried-up and pompous tutors who had been imported to help her brother Harry make a reasonable entry into Sandhurst. She thought her aunt was beautiful, and so smartly turned out she could not believe her home would emerge to be the bog dwelling her mother had made it out to be. Aunt Marion seemed so unaffected and happy that she found it hard to remember that she was only a few years younger than Mrs. Tristram.

The whole atmosphere already seemed so different from London that she felt as if she had been transported into another world entirely. She had not even had a moment to remember her unhappiness of the night before; she felt a little bit like a person does after an accident who had recovered consciousness and suddenly realises that they are not going to die after all and will in fact soon recover completely. It was such a wonderful feeling that for her the rest of that momentous twenty-eighth of September passed in a daze.

Belfast was like a superactive anthill. During their lunch in the hotel people were continually coming and going, exchanging comments on the morning's achievements and swapping stories. Ellen was able to sit back in a haze of sleepiness and content, letting the world go by her.

The accumulated excitement and strain of the past few weeks suddenly seemed to overwhelm her so that she had only a vague memory of the drive out to the house that evening. She retained an impression of wide, rolling hills—the hills she had seen from the boat, sweeping so greenly down to the Lough—over which the tall, blue car had climbed, through a broad valley and eventually into the woodland surrounding her uncle's house.

It had been too dark to see the building except as a heavy grey shape, with a fanlight over the halldoor from which golden light streamed. Then a blinding glow as the door opened and Lady Richardson swept her up the wide stairs to her room, leaving her with a warm embrace and the comforting words, "My dear, I know you are far too tired to come down and face a whole houseful of strangers. Here is Bridget to unpack for you. You just get straight into bed and I will have supper sent up to you on a tray in a few minutes."

So here she was, tucked up in bed, hot water bottle at her feet and the soft light of the fire flickering over the room that was to be hers for the next two years. White panelling reached quarter-way up the walls and a regiment of daisies, tied with blue bows, marched diagonally from the panelling to the ceiling; in the firelight they wavered and fused into horses galloping with wildly flowing manes and tails. But if she looked at them sideways they became sinister witches with tousled hair and waving broomsticks.

Good wallpaper for putting one to sleep! she thought. The same daisies, now disbanded, peeped frivolously from the frills of her dressing table and 'round the pelmet of her small four-poster bed, and the blue bows reappeared to tie back the curtains and on the lampshades.

Outside the rising wind had disturbed the rooks and she could hear them squawking as they shifted about in the treetops. But inside it was absolutely still except for the faint breathing of the curtains and the hiss of the fire.

She began to count the daisies, scrunching her toes to keep the score—or were they horses?—it really didn't matter. She slid off into a deep, refreshing sleep with the soft Irish air drifting into the room like balm.

Chapter 3

The days passed so happily that Ellen was amazed one day to find, as she put the date at the top of a letter to her mother, that she had been over a month at Kilwater, though in many ways she felt as if she had never lived anywhere else.

Her cousins were charming; it was the sort of house where there was something nice always happening, in either the children's sphere or the grown-ups', and there was a continuous feeling of gaiety and activity.

Mr. Grantham had turned out to be a tall, slim, aesthetic looking youth with a tremendous zest for life hidden under a very shy exterior. He had nearly died of embarrassment that first morning when Ellen had been introduced to him and had said, smilingly, "I really am quite nervous at the thought of living in the same house as you, Mr. Grantham. Michael tells me you are a crack shot and are going to shoot all the English! I sincerely hope you will think it over and spare some of the women and children at least!"

The tutor had felt much more like going out to shoot Michael, at once, and finally plucked up enough courage to say so, which was greeted with such a chorus of approval, led by the sisters, that he had been able to finish his breakfast quite comfortably after all.

He was a much more effective tutor than Michael admitted, and not only did they spend a certain portion of every day swotting in the library, but his conversation generally was on a sufficiently high level for Michael to be constantly absorbing knowledge and devoloping his reasoning powers without realising it, which was the only way to get Michael to learn anything.

He had a pleasant sense of the ridiculous and got much amusement from the picture of himself chatting away about the ancient Greeks and their philosophy while he and Michael dammed a stream to make a watermill, or blocked up holes in the old punt preparatory to making a fishing expedition on the Six-Mile Water.

The Six-Mile Water was a lovely river, flowing through the grounds in a variety of moods. It entered the park in a very excited state, tumbling through a narrow glen, down a steep and mossy waterfall overhung by beech trees, and then broadening out into a dignified salmon stream; flowing over and between huge grey stones, forming deep pools, and gradually slowing its pace as it approached the flat meadows in front of the house until it stretched out into a smooth sheet of shining water drifting between grassy banks and shaded in places by a stately oak or lime tree.

The long front windows of the house looked out across the river to a distant line of low hills, startlingly blue on a wet day but lost in a haze when the sun shone. The house itself was rather a confusion of styles, a previous owner having added turrets in all the most unsuitable places, at sad variance with the attractive Georgian front. However the general effect was of informality and friendliness. It was well settled into the ground and the walls were covered with various climbing plants, such as japonica, ceanothus, and clematis, and a beautiful Gloire de Dijon rose reached right up to the bedroom windows, with still a few late heads shining pale amongst the bright leaves.

Inside the rooms were light and sunny. Large vases of flowers and exquisite pieces of china and furniture intermingled with rather shabby chintzes, littered writing desks, revolving bookcases full of novels, and every sign of lively habitation.

At the back of the house was a square stableyard with a clock tower, and behind that again were the farm buildings, complete with duck pond and huge Dutch barn. The buildings were all protected from the north winds by lovely beechwoods, artifically cleared in many places and planted with rhododendrons and flowering shrubs.

Each of the cousins had taken Ellen under their wing. Indeed, they had almost torn her limb from limb in their desire to be the first to do the honours and introduce her to their special haunts. Alice's interests were almost exclusively centred in the woods and the farmyard. She was a fragile nymph of incredible toughness, with masses of pale, perfectly straight hair, a very pale skin and large sad, brown eyes. Her clothes, crisp and colourful at breakfast would be limp and dull by lunch, and bedraggled beyond recognition by teatime, her boots caked with mud and dust. She looked as if a puff of wind would blow her down, but there wasn't a tree on the place that she failed to climb, no bird built a nest that Alice did not know about, and she had a special communion with all the animals to whom she talked exactly as if they were human. She knew where the stable cat had hidden her kittens in the hay right up at the top of the barn and was the only person whom the cat would allow to touch them. Ellen had climbed up the hay, made the acquaintance of the kittens, had her hand reduced almost to a jelly by the loving licking of the baby calves, and very much enjoyed going out riding with all the children, but she had drawn the line at going up the trees and contented herself with picking blackberries below while Alice demonstrated her skill in the branches above.

Cynthia had "put away childish things" but not entirely successfully. She was very pretty in a more usual style, with laughing blue eyes, a tiptilted nose and curly brown hair. She was very like her mother and copied her sedulously in every way. Her special haunts were the walled garden—where she helped her mother pick and arrange flowers, except for occasional lapses when she strayed into the hothouses and stuffed herself with peaches and grapes—the summer house, with a book, and scampers through the woods to various hiding places where she could sit and dream of being a beautiful lady without fear of interruption.

Ellen was exactly her idea of a beautiful romantic young lady and Cynthia spent much time in her room, studying her clothes and the way she did her hair and asking questions about grown-up things.

It was the ideal place for Ellen to have come. There was too much going on for her to dwell on her unrequited love, and although she had had one or two bad nights, on the whole she spent so much time dashing about on the ponies with the children that she fell into bed at night and slept the moment her head touched the pillow. Only sometimes some chance word or phrase would remind her of Campion and she would be overcome with longing for him, only to be plunged in shame to think that after the way he had behaved she could still go on longing for him. Even so, she could almost feel a thin crust forming between the Now and the Then and her prayers at night were a curious muddle of gratitude for this protection and yearning for a chance to express all these new desires and emotions which had been awakened in her. She really did not know what she wanted, but she found a tremendous relief in pouring out her muddled feelings, for she was determined not to let her aunt know anything about it. Sometimes she felt positively sorry for God having to listen to and try to make sense out of it all, but she had pledged herself never to get into a similar mess again and to try to be less occupied with herself and she thought that was some small recompense for all the listening.

Life was so peaceful that Ellen had temporarily forgotten all about the talk of fighting and the Covenant until one day when it was all brought abruptly to her notice. Alice had said that she had discovered a simply wonderful field of mushrooms a few miles away and suggested going out very early one morning on the ponies to gather a huge basket of them for their mother as a surprise. The early start essential for the surprise element had been too much for Cynthia, who dearly loved her bed and always stayed in it until the last possible moment. Michael was busy constructing his watermill and needed every moment before lessons began to work on it. Poor Alice was so downcast at the lack of enthusiasm for her marvellous idea that

Ellen offered to go with her, knowing that the children were not allowed to go on long rides alone.

So together they crept out in old riding habits, saddled the ponies themselves, tied fishing creels to the saddles to put the mushrooms in, and rode off through the dripping trees. Once out of the woods they raced across the fields in the sheer joy of having such a lovely morning to themselves, the ponies just as excited as they were, until they came to the mushroom field, semi-circular in shape and sheltered all down one side by a thin wood strangled with undergrowth.

They tied the ponies to the fence by the wood and proceeded to search the field where there were indeed quantities of little, firm, white mushrooms. They had nearly filled their baskets when Ellen became aware of loud shouts and the roar of engines coming from the other side of the trees.

"What on earth can that noise be about, Alice?" she exclaimed in amazement. So far as she knew they were miles from habitation and it could not be a market in the middle of nowhere.

"I don't know . . . but do let's go and look. We can easily squeeze through the bushes and see without being seen."

Ellen was very sure that they should not. Suppose it was something dangerous? But curiosity overcame her scruples, and anyway Alice had already vanished into the undergrowth, so after fastening the mushroom baskets to the saddles in case they had to make a quick getaway, she forced her way through the ragged hedge and struggled after Alice to the other side of the wood.

The child turned with shining eyes to her and said, "Oh, Ellen, just look! It's the Volunteers drilling. Oh, what luck! I wonder is there anyone we know there?"

Ellen, peering through a young holly bush, saw over a hundred men drawn up in straight lines, and to one side half-a-dozen motor cars with small guns mounted on the back seats. A group of men were inspecting the ranks and another group were on guard round a covered lorry at the back of the field.

Two sides of the field were protected by an estate wall and

31

the fourth was open onto a succession of poor, uncultivated fields, full of rushes. There was no habitation in sight and the place had obviously been chosen for its secluded position.

While they watched the inspection was completed and the leader called all the men closer together to deliver an address, which the girls, hidden in the bushes, could not hear. The inspecting party then withdrew towards the lorry, to be shortly followed by all the men in double file.

It was only as the men returned to their positions that Ellen realised the full significance of what she was seeing.

"Why, they are being given guns! Alice, who are these men? I'm sure we should go home before we are discovered."

"Oh no! I think it is quite safe. All the best people are Volunteers—only they don't talk about it because it is supposed to be a secret. I did see them once before, but not here, and they didn't have guns then. They must have just got them today. Oh gosh, this is exciting! Won't Michael be mad with rage at missing it all!" exclaimed Alice, almost falling out of her bush in her efforts not to miss a single move.

Ellen, torn between fear of being discovered and a curiosity almost greater than Alice's, now noticed a move away from the field.

"Look, they are dispersing. Most of them are going back through the gate in the wall. Who lives there?"

Alice, as usual, knew all the answers.

"That's the local Lord's house, Lord Templeton. I expect he's out there with them. I tell you what, Ellen . . ." she said with inspiration, "if we go back and get the ponies quickly we can ride back a different way and probably pass most of them going home—accidently on purpose, you know."

With which words Alice was already beating her way back and Ellen perforce followed, half expecting to find the ponies being ridden off by a couple of Volunteer spies and themselves stranded miles from home. However, the ponies were there, still safely tied to the fence, looking very bored, and showing their resentment by fidgeting about so much that it took the girls all their time to get into the saddles.

Alice knew every inch of the country and they were soon making a wide detour of the wood, which brought them out at a country road crossing some boggy fields. They rode slowly along down this in the autumn sunshine and, to Alice's huge delight, were soon overtaken by the hooded lorry they had seen in the field and from which the guns had been distributed. It passed them at a brisk rate, but not too fast for Alice to spot the man on the near side.

"Oh how gorgeous!" She pushed her pony alongside Ellen, her eyes brimming with mischief, "It's James Melville! He always affects to know nothing about the Volunteers when I ask him. How I shall enjoy telling him I have actually seen him handing out the guns. And just wait until Michael hears what he has missed!"

Ellen just got a glimpse of a pair of amused eyes glancing at her out of the window as the lorry whirled past, and immediately became very conscious of her face and riding habit all stained with green from the undergrowth, and wisps of hair coming down under her felt hat. It was silly of her to have let Alice bring them out on a road in this state, and yet, how could she have prevented it when she had no idea where she was or how to get home.

They jogged along in silence, each occupied with her own thoughts until, turning in at the park gates, they overtook Mr. Grantham pedalling along like mad on his bicycle. He looked very surprised to see them, and then remembered. "Oh, yes! You have been out looking for mushrooms. I do hope you have been successful for I am ravenously hungry!"

"And you think we are going to give you some of our mushrooms, do you, Mr. Grantham?" said Alice in silken tones. "I'll strike a bargain with you: I'll give you half my basket if you tell me where you have been so early in the day."

"Oh," stuttered her victim, "just for a bicycle run, you know—studying the flora and fauna."

"Really!" said Alice, in tones of incredulity. "And did you discover anything interesting? We saw something *very* interesting, didn't we, Ellen?" with great emphasis.

"Yes indeed," agreed Ellen, entering into the spirit of the game. "A most interesting kind of fauna I have never seen before!"

"Perhaps it is not too late to appeal to you, Miss Tristram," pleaded Mr. Grantham in desperation, "for some of *your* mushrooms, or have yours got strings attached to them, too?"

"Oh, yes," said Ellen, all smiles, "I shall be delighted to share mine with you; they are a special stringless variety. But I feel sure, after such a display of generosity, you will want to help us discover the identity of the strange phenomenon we have just seen. I rather thought it was a skein of the lesser black-backed gunmen, but Alice seems to think it was a covey of Ulster Volunteer birds?"

Mr. Grantham groaned, his worst fears confirmed.

"What on earth possessed Alice to take you in that direction today of all days?"

"Oh, we were just looking innocently for mushrooms when we heard all those odd noises and went to see what it was," said Ellen.

"You may have been just innocently looking for mushrooms, Miss Tristram, indeed, I am sure you were, but I very much doubt if Alice has ever 'just innocently' looked for anything in her life! I believe that she has a better information service than the whole Ulster Volunteer Force put together."

Alice took this as a very high compliment and did not deny her knowledge, though, in fact, she had only overheard Neill the chauffeur saying to one of the gardeners that he would see him in the field at the back of Castle Upton at six o'clock the next day, and when she had pestered him to know what they were going to do, he had in desperation produced the story about the mushrooms, which she did not for a moment believe and had only used as a blind for her own plans. She reflected that it was lucky there had been some mushrooms or there might have been some awkward questions to answer.

By this time they had reached the house, and as Alice and Cynthia took their breakfast in the old nursery, under the doting eye of their ex-nanny, there was still no mention of what they

34

had seen on their ride as far as the dining-room party was concerned, although the mushrooms were much appreciated by the grown-ups. But as soon as Mr. Grantham had finished his morning's lessons and lunch was over, Ellen waylaid him going out of the front door.

"Are you going for a walk, Mr. Grantham? May I come with you, please. There are all sorts of things I want to ask and I'm sure you know all the answers."

He was delighted, if apprehensive, at the thought of her company, and waited while she fetched her coat. Then they set off, down the side of the river.

"My poor brain, for what it is worth, is at your service, Miss Tristram. I only wish I thought I was the subject of such attention!" he said, smiling.

"Well, you know, in a way you are. I mean I can understand people fighting for the cause of their own country, but why does it appeal to someone like you? You don't live over here. You are not a soldier, and I should have thought it would not further whatever profession you intend to grace later to become known as a Revolutionary, a joiner of local wars or lost causes. And yet I don't think you are the sort of person who rushes into a thing without a good reason."

"So you want to know how the great mind of Eric Grantham works, or, more probably, if it works?"

"Exactly so, 'say on McGrantham.'"

Mr. Grantham winced. "If I bare my soul to you, you must promise never, never to misquote the classics."

Ellen laughed. "Very well, I promise. It is no great hardship for that is the only classic I know. We did it at school and although I was terribly bored at the time, I have since found the occassional quote lends considerably to the 'ton' of the conversation!"

"Sacrilege! The classics should not be wasted on girls, but we will say no more on the subject lest we fall out."

"Well then, tell me your reasons for joining the Ulster Volunteers, please."

"There are so many reasons really," he said seriously, taking a long breath. "I suppose the main one is the appeal of a minority fighting for its rights. There is no doubt they are right. Why should they be denied the protection and government they have always had? England spends most of her time conquering countries and subjecting them to her rule, and beating her chest and saying how beneficial it is for them, and then when she has a country which realises and appreciates its benefits, and wants to keep them she decides to throw it to its natural enemies in order to gain a few miserable votes in Parliament. It's against all the rules, as well as being completely inconsistent."

"Is it really just to get votes that Parliament is doing this?" asked Ellen incredulously.

"Yes, pure and simple. The Liberals are almost certain to lose the next election; their only hope of winning is to get the support of the sixty or so Southern Irish members of Parliament, and so they are prepared to sacrifice almost anything to buy their votes. On the other hand, the Southern members see their last chance of getting what they have wanted for years and are pressing as hard as they can."

"I see . . . it's not very noble behaviour, is it?"

"No, but it is fairly average politics. The only snag is that on these occasions the minority usually gives in and then the government puts out a tremendous propaganda to support what they are doing, and everybody forgets all about the pros and cons except the poor minority, which just fades away. But this time the minority says it is going to fight, and I believe they will. That is why I admire them so much and am proud to have joined them."

"Well, I must say England sounds to be behaving very badly; but suppose it comes to war? It would be dreadful, you would be fighting against all your friends. What about your parents, what would they think?" she asked.

"Oh, I think father would understand. He has always been in a minority himself. He is the seventh child of a seventh child, which is a very unlucrative thing to be, and life has always been rather hard for him, so he would appreciate the feelings of the underdog."

36

"And your mother?"

"Yes, she would mind dreadfully, but more because I was endangering my life than anything else."

"Oh dear, it all sounds so terribly stupid!" exclaimed Ellen. Eric Grantham looked rather hurt. "No, you mustn't say that. This is not a wild student rising; it is the solemn decision of a large number of steady, reliable citizens who see their way of living being seriously threatened in the future."

"But they could not possibly win," she expostulated. "I mean, the whole British army would be against them, and it would not matter how brave they were, in the end you would be beaten. I wonder what people in the army think about it. There must be quite a lot of Ulstermen in the army anyway, what would they do?"

"That's what remains to be seen," he replied. "If we had to fight, it would mean civil war and the government would certainly be put out before much harm was done; and the Opposition are with us, against Home Rule, so that is what we are playing for." He shook back his hair from his forehead, as if tossing off his worries, and smiled engagingly at her. "Must we ruin a lovely walk by talking politics? Let us take a leaf out of Omar Khayyam and say, 'Why fret ye if today be sweet?' "

"Very well," she laughed, falling in with his change of mood, "that is escapism, but I have heard enough to keep my little brain busy for some time. We really need a bottle of wine if we are to follow the poet's advice properly!"

"I don't believe your aunt would approve, Miss Tristram," he said primly. "Family tutor sacked for drunken revels with employer's niece—that would be a nice finish to my career! No, I fear we must make do with blackberries instead. Are you coming out for the shoot next weekend? Perhaps you would bring me a bottle of beer up for lunch and remind us not to talk politics. All conversations seem to lead to 'Rome Rule'—that is what Ulster calls government by the South—these days, but it would be a poor compliment to you and Lady Richardson after bringing up our lunch for us."

"Oh, yes, Aunt Marion said we were to join you for lunch.

I do love picnics at shoots. The open air always seems to bring out the best in people, as well as making the food taste delicious."

And so the conversation veered away to lighter subjects as they turned into one of the paths leading through the beech-woods, now seemingly filled with sunshine, the effect of the ruddy glow of fallen leaves forming a thick russet carpet beneath their feet, and the thin gold veil of leaves overhead through which the October light poured with redoubled strength.

It became the first of many walks. For each of them the other's company was ideal for the present state of their feelings. Eric was not in a position to ask any girl to marry him and was well aware of this fact; but he would have been less than human if he had not enjoyed the company of the only member of the household anywhere near his age, especially when that member was an enchantingly pretty girl, full of gaiety and intelligence. Eric was an idealist and inclined to think of himself as one of a very small group of thinking people; he was therefore surprised to find that this pretty society girl had also got a mind—and used it. As for Ellen, who had found herself tending to look upon all men as double-dyed villains, to distrust their intentions, it was a most valuable lesson for her to have this friendship with an intelligent, amusing man who did not try to flirt with her and was not prepared to let pass her pungent criticisms of his sex; indeed, he did much to soften her attitude to the whole human race and obviously enjoyed her company enormously.

She found herself gradually coming to realise that the section of society in which she had moved was a very small one and by no means representative. London was a melting pot in which many different varieties of people who would not normally have met were thrown together, with the obvious result that some of them would be absorbed into it, others would be rejected and disappear into a different life more compatible to themselves, and still more would pass through the melting pot as a valuable experience and come out with a deeper insight into life and a desire for a more worthwhile existence. Ellen fell into this latter category though she had not realised, as yet, anything but a sense of emptiness in the life she had been leading.

She understood that it was something like this feeling of hers which compelled other girls to join the suffragette movement, but she could not find any real sympathy for that. She had heard the comments of all types of men on the suffragettes and their activities and was convinced that nothing would be gained by women making themselves appear hysterical and unattractive: it only made them so easy to ridicule, and she had a sneaking feeling that if one was really a success as a woman, one ought to be able to get one's way by more attractive methods. Though she had to admit that as far as Desmond Campion had been concerned, she had not proved her theory very well. But that was not a very fair comparison. She still smarted from the snub to her pride, but she had begun to think that perhaps her judgement had been at fault and the prize she had set herself to win had not been worth the effort after all.

Meanwhile, she was kept busy by the demands of her young cousins; she enjoyed her walks and talks with Eric, and her aunt had mapped out an exceedingly pleasant round of parties to keep her amused, including having Harry up to stay as soon as he could get leave. And there was always this fascinating problem of Ulster's future and the way it affected everyone.

Eric had been quite right when he said that nobody talked of anything else; at least, they talked of very little else. When a civil war is pending there are not many facets of one's life which it does not affect. The main difficulty now was to make England realise that Ulster meant what she said about fighting, not to be forced under the Republic of Ireland, and to remain part of Great Britain. All the talk centred round this point.

At the picnic party for the shoot she met James Melville. She had almost dreaded this meeting as her cousins had talked so much about him she felt there could be nothing left to know; he could only be a disappointment after such a build-up and she was very conscious of all the children watching, with great interest, to see her reactions. The men had gathered together at nine in the morning, and been driven about ten miles up onto one of the mountains in a huge old navy blue shooting brake with bench seats and a canvas top. All the dogs, Spaniels and

Labradors, sitting haughtily at their masters' feet, pretending they didn't know each other, except when the brake lurched violently over a bump and they fell in a heap together.

Ellen and her aunt and the girls followed in the car, driven by Neill, the chauffeur, three hours later, with hampers of food and drink, and a heap of rugs to sit on. They had arranged to meet at an old sheep shelter, in case it rained. This shelter was a ring of stone wall with a small grove of beech trees and some posts over which a tarpaulin could have been thrown if it were wet. But it was a glorious day, bright sun after the rain, with the valley below them sparkling with little rivers hurrying down by loughs and pools to the distant sea.

James was removing the cartridges and propping up his gun against the wall as Ellen surrepticiously studied him.

He wasn't really good looking, she decided. It was too clever a face to be so simply classed: too thin, with too high a forehead and a thin, sensitive mouth, giving a withdrawn expression that made you feel it was terribly nice of him to notice you at all and put you in his debt immediately. He was further armoured with a pair of remarkably beautiful grey eyes, long brown eyelashes and a smile of blinding sweetness. There was a quiet confidence about him that appealed to her.

The other men were still standing about discussing their luck during the morning, wrangling over whose shot had killed a bird that had flown the whole length of the line, apparently unscathed, only to drop dead five or six hundred yards behind them. Half of the party were convinced that it had dropped dead from shock at having passed through such a formidable barrage alive.

While they were all thus engaged, James Melville simply appeared at Ellen's side with two steaming platefuls of game pie and hot potatoes, and said, "I have reserved the two best seats over there," nodding towards the bank, "with backrests, south elevation, dry, sandy soil, and close to the hamper. I hope you will give me the pleasure of your company?" and just in case there was any doubt about her complying, he gave one of his charming smiles, and Ellen found herself seated comfortably on

40

a heap of rugs, eating a delicious meal and talking away as if she had known him all her life.

"How is it," he queried, "that Lady Richardson can have been one of my best friends for years and yet fail to have mentioned the existence of a charming niece? A nephew has been referred to but never a niece!"

"Well, you see, my mother considers that only savages live in Ireland and that it is therefore not a fit place for young ladies, and as I had never met Aunt Marion or Uncle Charles I was in no position to argue."

"I see. And what has happened to bring about this wonderful volte-face?"

"I think Mother came to the conclusion that there were more savages in London, and still more in Hong Kong, where Daddy has been sent, and so the only alternative was to send me to Aunt Marion and hope for the best." She laughed up at him. "We seem to have very few relations, so it was a desperate situation and called for desperate measures!"

"Yes, indeed; so it seems. I am so glad you took the plunge. Do you find us so very savage now that you have been here for some time?" he asked seriously.

"But of course not!" She looked him very straight in the eye with a provocative twinkle. "Savages rush around all the time with arrows and tomahawks—you are much more up to date with armoured cars, rifles, and suchlike!"

He grinned. "Touché. I had temporarily forgotten about that episode and was hoping for some charming little tribute to our obvious culture!"

"Well, I suppose if I had not arrived on the day you were all signing your Covenant, and had not gone out mushrooming with Alice one morning in the middle of a military manoeuvre, and was stone deaf into the bargain, I expect your culture *would* have been the most striking thing about you. But after that, the thing which strikes me most is that a civilised community can't get its way without behaving like . . ."

"Savages?" he finished for her. "Yes, I see your point of view, but I shall hope to convert you to mine before too long.

41

We badly need intelligent friends in England," he said seriously, and then noticing that the rest of them had finished their lunch, he rose to his feet. "I must go and wield a gun again. I hope you don't mind me keeping my eye in, in this way," he added wickedly, strapping on his cartridge belt again. "When your brother comes up on leave next month, I hope you and he will join our party for the Hunt Ball. It is generally one of the best parties of the winter." He moved over to thank Lady Richardson for the delicious lunch and, at the same time, to claim her and her party to dine with him before the Hunt Ball.

"I will get my mother to write to you but I know you are always in such demand one has to stake one's claim early," he said with his sweet smile.

"James dear, I may look senile but I am qiute able to form my own opinion as to why you are so anxious to book us up now," Lady Richardson assured him comfortably. "Anyway, we will be delighted to come with you. Now you must hurry or Charles will say that 'women ruin shoots—always talking, etc., etc.' . . ." she smiled as he hurried off.

"Well, Ellen, you seem to have been doing some quite successful shooting, too. You will enjoy the dance, James is one of the best hosts I know. Now, come and let us help Neill to stack all these things in the car or it will be dark before we get home."

On the way back, in the open car, her aunt gave Ellen a thumbnail sketch of the company at the shoot.

The short, fat man with the very red face had made a fortune in shipbuilding in Glasgow. He had started as a messenger boy in one of the big firms and had risen not only to own his own firm but to marry the very pretty daughter of a local impoverished but impeccably bred family. They had then moved to Ulster, bought an enormous estate and proceeded to forget their past as quickly as possible. On the whole, they were a popular pair; she could be charming and he had the good sense not to leave his native wit behind him during his meteoric rise and could be relied upon to give a shrewd and witty turn to any conversation. They also had two very attractive daughters for whom they entertained a great deal and very lavishly.

The very thin and wrinkled old man was the exact opposite; he was the head of one of the oldest families in Ireland, a fount of wisdom on points of fairy law and Celtic customs; indeed, he was more than half fey himself and came out shooting with much more interest in the animals and country than in the number of birds shot. He had recently horrified his family by turning Roman Catholic because, he said, the Protestant faith was incompatible with Irish folklore. His wife said that the only difference it made was that he now went to church with the servants instead of with the family! The young man with the moustache was his son and had lately left the Indian Army and was trying to learn something about the management of his lands in which his father had lost all interest since he had become so immersed in ancient Irish history. He had, in fact, been only too eager to give it all away to the ever hungry Roman church to save himself the trouble of administering it, quite regardless of the welfare of the Protestant families still living in its small farms.

Then there were the two pleasant soldiers from the West Kent Regiment, stationed at Victoria Barracks in Belfast.

A stout, old man, with a white moustache, who was a deputy lieutenant of the County Antrim, had a lovely estate in the south of the county, a downtrodden wife, and a very conceited son in the Irish Guards who seldom bothered to come home. There was also a sensible daughter who had married, very young, a linen magnate of just as ancient but less overbearing genealogy.

Lastly, there was James, the only son of a charming old man who had found his family wine business being squeezed out by the bigger Roman Catholic businesses in Dublin. He had taken fortune in both hands and moved up to the industrial and Protestant North, married the bishop's daughter, and sat back, following her advice ever since. James had entered the business twelve years previously, foregoing his three years at Oxford in order to redress the firm's not very firm balance. This he had

43

done most successfully and was now able to take time off to enjoy himself and dabble more than a little in politics. He had travelled abroad a good deal in the interests of his trade but lately his activities had been somewhat curtailed by his mother contracting a crippling illness. Everyone had thought that she was going to die but she had made a wonderful recovery and now was perfectly healthy except that she was obliged to go everywhere in a bath-chair. The dinner party to which he had just invited Ellen and her aunt would be the first party they had held since his mother's illness.

An ardent Loyalist, many people thought James was one of the key organisers of the Volunteer Force, but he disclaimed more than a keen interest.

"I admire him particularly," concluded Aunt Marion, "because of the way he buckled to and made his business into a success when all his contemporaries were still amusing themselves at universities and taking life easy. It has made him a little apart from the others even though most of them are now running their own linen mills or estates. He didn't have that carefree start to his life which they had, and now he is such a responsible and wise young man he gets more and more responsibility heaped on his head. I would love to see him marry some nice light-hearted girl who would supply all the fun that he has missed . . . Unfortunately, Alice and Cynthia are too young: I only wish I saw some sign of a similar young man growing up for them." She made a ludicrous face. "Sometimes when I look at Michael's friends I wonder if I should not be training my daughters to keep house on a rifle range or in the treetops! I cannot picture any of them ever leading normal lives in houses!"

Chapter 4

Harry duly arrived on leave in November. Ellen drove down to the station in the horse and trap to meet him and surprised herself with the surge of affection she felt on seeing him again. She had forgotten how long it was since she had been with one of her immediate family. He looked terribly fit and much older than when she had last seen him. All the coltish youthfulness had gone and he was now a personality with definite opinions of his own. She felt quite shy when she thought of all the experiences he must have been through in the eighteen months since they last met and which had added up to this new grown-up man of the world. But Harry had no inhibitions about his sister if he had noticed any great change in her. After enveloping her in a bearlike hug he stood back and exlaimed, "Well, you *have* improved in the Irish air—you are quite a beauty now. Last time I saw you, you were just as pale and peaky as all the other young London misses."

"Speak for yourself!" she retorted. "I shall have to write a long letter to mother and reassure her that you are obviously not being either starved or maltreated at the Curragh."

"Yes, and I hope that I shall be able to tell her that your manners have not become too provincial and hearty with living so long in the bogs," he teased. "Come along now and let us meet these ferocious cousins of ours. I am sure your letters lose nothing in the writing and I can't wait to see what they are really like."

He had not long to wait. Before they were halfway home

the sound of galloping hooves in the next field made their horse prick up his ears and begin to sidle along, tossing its head as the drumming hooves soon resolved themselves into the three cousins on their ponies. They gave a loud cheer at the sight of the trap and put their ponies over a low bank onto the road in front of the shocked and horrified carriage horse, who was suffering already from the ignominy of having to pull the trap, and proceeded to canter cheerfully along the road on either side of him, plying Harry with questions and making his task of driving the horse well-nigh impossible.

Ellen watched his rapid transition from a cool young soldier into a hot and bothered young man with some amusement and only intervened when it began to look as if the horse was really getting the upper hand. Telling the children to finish their ride across country or she would tell Uncle Charles that they had been galloping their ponies on the tarmac in absolute defiance of his orders.

By the time the trap turned in at the drive gates Harry had recovered his composure and Ellen was very proud of her brother as she introduced him to her uncle and aunt, and looked forward to showing him off to all her new friends at the dance that evening.

The dance was to be at the Taggarts, the rich shipbuilder's house, and was in honour of his second pretty daughter who was just seventeen.

Lady Richardson was resplendent in rose-coloured satin, with a fragile diamond tiara in her hair. Ellen wore white chiffon with large grey coin dots scattered over it and the skirt lightly draped and caught with small bows. With it she wore long pearl earrings, and when she and her aunt duly paraded before the children they were obviously hard put to decide who looked the most beautiful. Groans and sighs and longings to be grown-up followed the ladies down the stairs to the drawing-room where the rest of the family were waiting to receive the dinner guests.

This was the first dance Ellen had been to since her arrival in Ireland and she felt as excited as before any of the grand balls in London.

At dinner she had a charming soldier on one side and the captain in charge of the naval base on the other. The captain had three daughters who were rationed out between Harry, Eric Grantham, and the land agent from a nearby estate—a very gay young man with a great reputation as a cricketer and a terrible stutter.

The naval captain knew Ellen's father well and had endless reminiscences about him, to the irritation of the soldier who was longing to hold Ellen's attention with tales from the Boer War, in which, she felt sure, he must have been the youngest participants, as he still looked scarcely any older than herself.

The competition for her attention was so great that Ellen could not fail to be flattered, and her uncle, looking at her sparkling eyes and flushed cheeks, made a mental resolution to increase his usual quota of one dance with each of the married ladies in his party to include one with his lovely niece.

When they arrived at the dance they found everything done on the most lavish scale. There were flowers all the way up the stairs and in every imaginable corner of the rooms. The ballroom had three exquisite chandeliers holding not less than forty candles each and shedding their soft light on the lovely dresses and the pale blue velvet curtains draping the long windows.

Harry lost no time in obtaining the maximum number of dances with each of the pretty Miss Taggarts, claiming that a soldier on leave could not afford to waste his time. Ellen hoped for their sakes that his dancing had improved for otherwise she saw visions of yards and yards of their billowing net dresses being torn off during Harry's wild cavalry charges.

Ellen's own programme was soon filled. She already knew quite a number of the men in the room and her radiant appearance quickly brought far more introductions than she could spare dances for. James came up rather formally and asked for a waltz, which she gave him with not the best grace in the world for she had set aside the two dances (which was all society allowed a young lady to have with the same young man in one evening), for him and was a bit piqued at this apparent lack of enthusiasm after such special treatment at the shoot. *Just Des-*

mond all over again, she thought rather sadly, *Well, anyway, that is a mistake I am not going to make twice!* and she proceeded to flirt like mad with the soldier who had sat beside her at dinner.

Her hasty judgement of James was hardly justified, as his seeming diffidence was caused merely by the knowledge that having secured her for the supper dance he was in no doubt that they would have supper together, and there was also an extra dance after supper that he saw no reason why they should not have, too. Also it was his policy never to rush his fences: he had been completely captivated by her at the shoot, and tonight she certainly took the shine out of every other girl in the room. But he reasoned that an outstanding girl like this, fresh from London, was almost certain to have formed an attachment already for someone over there, and if that was the case he, James, would be well advised to proceed at a decorous pace and not make a fool of himself at this stage and age over a girl who must have had the pick of much more exciting fellows than him. So he contented himself with enlisting the aid of the butler in keeping a table for two in a corner of the dining room and persuading him to bring from one of the other tables an exquisite bowl of golden tea roses to put in the centre. Then he returned to the ballroom to work his way through the programme until their dance came 'round.

This was not really a very great penance for there were a number of girls at the dance who would willingly have become Mrs. James Melville and laid themselves out to be as charming as possible. Although he did not return their feelings and took refuge behind his veil of formality, it was nevertheless very pleasant and flattering for him.

Ellen noticed that he danced every dance and the only person he danced twice with was her aunt, with whom he obviously "got on" terribly well. She watched his head bent as he listened to some amusing story, and then his delightful smile, and thought how nice it must be to be happily married and not have to bother all the time about what people were thinking of you.

When their dance eventually came 'round she had intended to be very sophisticated and rather distant, but she found the sincerity of those grey eyes at close quarters undermined her act completely. Besides, he danced divinely so that she gave herself up to the bliss of a perfectly matched waltz, and by the time they had dined together and danced the "extra" she admitted to herself that perhaps she had judged too hastily, and, further, that she had not spent such a happy, harmonious time since the earliest days of her friendship with Desmond.

Harry was having a most successful evening flirting outrageously with at least six different girls whose names he had got into a complete muddle, so that most of the drive home was taken up with the others trying to attach a name to his descriptions so that he would not cause undying offence the next time he met the young ladies in question. He never seemed to notice anything unusual or different about the girls, such as the colour of their hair or dresses, but had his programme covered with scrawls, "big eyes," "pearls," or "fluffy," each of which might have belonged to several different girls, so it became a battle of wits to place the rightful owners and Aunt Marion only hoped he had not accepted too many invitations since they seemed unlikely ever to find out from whom they came.

The Hunt Ball the following week followed much the same pattern, as far as Harry was concerned, but was indelibly marked on Ellen's mind because of the conversation, which took place in the Melville's house at dinner beforehand.

They were all seated 'round the big mahogany table, a party of about sixteen including various county families and the inevitable soldiers from the large military headquarters at Victoria Barracks. The talk amongst the older people turned on to politics as always, and Ellen heard her uncle saying to Mrs. Melville, "I see that devil Redmond is pressing Asquith again to have Home Rule brought up in the House after Christmas." There was an unusually serious note in his voice that caught Ellen's attention so that she found herself listening to the older conversation while keeping up an appearance of interest in the chatter immediately around her.

49

"I know," she heard Mrs. Melville answer in a worried voice. "If Asquith only had the courage to go to the country he would find out that it is not what the people want at all; but then, of course, he would have to go back on his promise to Redmond and Redmond would see to it that he lost the support of the sixty Irish members of Parliament."

"Exactly. And then Asquith would have lost his majority and he knows once his party goes out they will never get in again, and he cares a great deal more about that than the good of the loyal people of Ulster."

Then the lady on Sir Charles's right joined in. "What I cannot understand is how he can turn a deaf ear to Carson. If ever there was a man who does what he says he is going to do, that is Carson, and yet Asquith persists in treating him as a tiresome child."

One of the soldiers who had been listening across the table with considerable interest here interpolated, "I think, perhaps, Mr. Asquith is just not as confident as he would like to appear. I understand we are to receive reinforcements very shortly in case of 'trouble.' I think the general feeling is that we soldiers have been treated so well by the Ulster people that we might be very reluctant to fire on them, which, of course, is perfectly true, and that a new lot of men would not have the same scruples."

"Good Lord! What a mix-up it is," exclaimed Sir Charles. "These politicians need their heads examined! But they will have to look out; we are in a much stronger position to defend ourselves than we were a few months ago. Then we had only a few guns and very little organisation; now everyone is interested." He laughed reminiscently and looked around the table at which everyone was now listening. "The other night I had to go to a meeting in a church hall, which shall be nameless, down in the country, and it was so damned cold I went out to have a look at the boiler to see if the fire had gone out, and what do you think I found? The sexton sitting there as cosy as you please, with a huge fire going, and surrounded with trays of bullet cases. When I said it was damn cold in the hall, he was dreadfully

50

sorry and said, 'the throuble is, sor, I have to keep opening the door of the fire to take the bullets out and that looses the heat to the hall.' "

"And what did you do?" asked the company in one voice.

"Oh, I told him to carry on, it was a good cause," smiled Sir Charles. "It meant the meeting ran through very quickly for it was too cold to delay."

Ellen could hardly believe her ears. Here they were all sitting happily together at dinner discussing the manufacture of bullets to shoot each other with. Even Harry had paused in his dalliance to listen as James took up the text of another story.

"Oddly enough, the last time I was coming over in the *Patriotic* I noticed a poor widow sitting beside a coffin in the third class, and I remember thinking what a terrible journey it must be for her and hoping the authorities would make it as easy as possible for her. I heard afterwards that they *were* especially kind and I need not have worried anyway, for the coffin was full of guns!"

"Did she get caught?" asked Harry.

"Oh no! She got every possible assistance on to the train and the story never got out until the guns had all safely reached their destination. She must be a very brave woman."

"Yes, indeed," exclaimed Lady Richardson. "In more ways than one, I would feel I was tempting Providence to make use of a solemn thing like that, but it certainly shows the degree of feeling there is for someone to do a thing like that."

The conversation then became general, everyone wondering how brave they would be in similar circumstances, but Ellen returned to it later when she was sitting out a square dance with James. They had both been dancing hard all evening and preferred to sit and talk than hold a scrappy conversation through the separations of the Lancers.

"Mr. Melville, do tell me, where do the guns come from?" she asked suddenly.

He looked sad. "I really could not tell you that even if I did know. It all has to be done with the utmost secrecy. There is no law against the importation of firearms into the country, but naturally no customs officer in his senses could fail to report their passage and then the government would impound them, so it all has to be done with the utmost secrecy and only the people immediately concerned know any of the details."

"But you *must* be concerned," she insisted. "I saw you myself handing out guns to the men that morning at Castle Upton."

"Good heavens! Did you really?" he exclaimed, with a comical lift of his eyebrows. "Our security must be getting terribly slack."

"Oh, it was all Alice's doing. I thought we were looking for mushrooms but I think she knew about the drilling all along. You never know with Alice."

He picked up her fan and began fanning himself gently with it, leaning back in his corner of the sofa.

"Miss Tristram, I am beginning to be seriously alarmed," he said. "I am not at all sure that you are not turning out to be one of these beautiful English spies about whom one reads in novels—sent to ensnare simple fellows like me and discover all our secret plans."

Ellen smiled back impishly. "But of course I am, only the trouble is that you are turning out not to be a simple fellow at all, but a double-dyed villain with a secret and deadly purpose and I am not finding out anything at all." She sighed melodramatically. "Indeed, I fear that if I cannot send back a satisfactory report soon to headquarters I may be recalled. But I suppose that is what you want?"

He laid down the fan and sat up in well-feigned alarm. "Good gracious no! It is not what we want at all. It is my sacred duty to convert you to our cause and then discover who all your accomplices are."

"And do you think you will succeed?" she asked, looking straight into his eyes in the manner of an arch-siren. She was very surprised to feel her heart give a great lurch as she met his grey gaze, suddenly quite serious. She looked down quickly, confused at the nonsensical conversation taking such a turn and the strange behaviour of her heart so that she only half heard his reply. "I shall leave no stone unturned to try to make you love this country as I do," he said. "I thought that morning on the boat when you were arriving that you were well on the way to liking it then."

She looked up quickly. "Were you on the boat that day? I didn't see you."

"No, you were so busy looking at the view and you seemed so enthralled with it I felt we had a very promising convert coming along." His tone had changed and was pleasantly bantering again. "But I am afraid since then we have shocked you with our goings-on, and now you are beginning to think that maybe England is nicer and safer after all?"

"I wouldn't say shocked exactly," she said, knitting her brows, "but you are so very different from what I expected. Who was it said the Irish were 'lazy, dishonest, and utterly charming'?"

"I know," he chimed in, amused, "and we in Ulster are the exact opposite—hardworking, honest, and utterly without charm!" He heaved a dolorous sigh. "The trouble is that we are not Irish at all; our ancestors were Scottish people, whole villages and families, who were given money and grants of land by the English government to come and settle down and make the country peaceful and prosperous. Before that the native Irish were always so busy feuding and fighting that the big landlords had never been able to make anything of it and so James the first started what is called the 'Plantation of Ulster' with sober, respectable Scottish Protestants."

"And did it work?" asked Ellen.

"Well, it worked in the sense that the land was farmed well and the country became more or less civilised, but the Irish, who were driven out of the fertile valleys and were largely Roman Catholic, never forgot or forgave. They retired into the poor land in the hills and bogs and have been nursing a grievance ever since. Hence the continuous vendettas. While we have an impartial government in England things run fairly smoothly, but if that goes there will be the most appalling outburst of bloodshed . . . people who don't live here don't realise what a thin skin of restraint there still is between the two races."

Ellen was so interested that James went on telling her anecdotes for some time. She could understand so clearly now how the Irish must resent being driven out of the rich land, and, even more, the prosperity that had come to the North through the hard-working Scotsmen's efforts. She could understand, too, how the Scots, having put so much time, work, and money into the land that they had been asked by their Sovereign to take over—not to mention having lived there for close on four hundred years—must feel. They, too, deserved consideration and recognition. At last Ellen thought of her neglected partners in the ballroom and rising hurriedly to her feet, exclaimed, "How awful! I must have missed nearly the whole of Captain Beauchamp's dance—I must fly!"

James rose more slowly, reluctant to lose her when she seemed so much in heart with him. "I will come with you and if he has given up, may I not finish the dance with you?" When they reached the ballroom James was delighted to see that the gallant captain had obviously given up looking for Ellen and was now dancing with a plain girl in a pink frilly dress. He gave Ellen a most speaking glance and she had the grace to look slightly ashamed of herself before forgetting him completely in the pleasure of the Dolores waltz.

Lady Richardson had also noticed Ellen's absence and her return with James, and was secretly very pleased to notice how well they seemed to be getting on. She adored matchmaking and could think of nothing nicer than that her charming niece and her favourite young man should fall in love. But she wisely gave no sign of having noticed anything and it was left to Harry, later in the evening having a cooling drink with his sister after a long, hot, Dashing-White-Sergeant to comment on Ellen's partiality for James's company.

"Seems a nice fellow, Melville," he observed. "A great improvement on that Hussar you were going everywhere with last summer. What was his name?"

"Harry," she cried with annoyance, "where do you get your information from, you never even saw him?"

"Oh, I heard all about it from a chap in the regiment. He

didn't like him at all. Said he was always sneering at everyone and behaving as if he'd bought the world."

Ellen was silent. She really did not know what to say. Although she was now inclined to agree with her brother about Desmond, she did not like to admit having been in love with someone so disparaged and rightly so. She would rather forget about it, as she had been succeeding very well in doing, and it was irritating to have Harry reminding her. Also, she was not pleased at having her apparent partiality for James taken for granted like this when she was by no means sure of it herself. She had no intention of getting herself hurt again and had been rather shaken to find that her feelings could attempt to go contrary to her intentions so soon again.

Fortunately, Harry did not seem to expect an answer and was quite happy, rattling on about the various girls he had danced with and the company in general. His leave was up in two days' time but he expected to come North again to spend a brief Christmas with the Richardsons, and as far as Ellen could judge from his conversation, his activities in the interval would be mainly confined to "huntin', shootin', and dancin'." Harry was certainly blissfully happy in the army; many of the senior officers talked of troubles in the Balkans and prophesied war in the fairly near future. Others staked their reputation that wars were a thing of the past, that the world was now too civilised to attempt to solve its problems that way. To Harry, who did not read newspapers except for the racing news, this talk of war gave a pleasant feeling of purpose to his life in the army without ever seeming to touch it too closely.

The occasional Sinn Feinn attacks on country houses in the remoter districts of Ireland, and an even more occasional demonstration or attack against a small group of British soldiers, provided a spice to their life without in any way interfering with their amusements.

The doors of all the big houses were open to the officers at the Curragh and the people seemed delightful. Carefree and gay, they all talked politics all the time but in the most witty and lighthearted way that made them seem no more important than the next race meeting. It was not until he went North that he heard them spoken about seriously and he had been amazed to find sensible, serious-minded men like his uncle and James, and even the tutor, taking an active part in preparing for what seemed like a civil war.

Ellen had asked him what on earth he would do if he was ordered to march North and fight against their uncle and he had been completely at a loss to think of an answer, or even to envisage such a situation arising. He was far too busy thinking what a pretty little thing Mabel Taggart was and how lightly she danced. When she looked up into his eyes he felt enormously protective and a strong desire rose in him to prevent anything ever happening to hurt her. Pity she was so rich. Her father probably had some fat and steady linen merchant lined up for her and would not be pleased to have her carried off by a not very rich young man in an expensive regiment. It would not help either if he was to find himself fighting on opposite sides. Promotion gained that way, however gallantly, would hardly help his prospects. For an amused moment, he tried to imagine which would be the best or worst—to carry out a heroic and victorious attack on the Taggart's house and then with pistol at her father's throat demand her hand in marriage, or to be wounded in a glorious defence of the Taggart's house against his own regiment and have her broken father offer his lovely daughter's hand as the only possible return for such gallantry. Certainly there was scope for a variety of piquant situations. He grinned to himself at the thought and ambled off to see if there was any chance of getting an "extra" with the fair Mabel.

Ellen, meanwhile, was claimed for her dance by Eric, who did not excel on the dance floor but made up for it by talking, so that it was not until she got home that she was able to turn over in her mind the events of the evening. Then she found herself in a somewhat muddled frame of mind. It had been a lovely evening and she had danced almost every dance. She had made the exciting discovery that her heart was no longer completely numb, and although her feelings towards James were very hazy still, it made her feel most wonderfully alive again to think that there was someone she would be meeting constantly and whom she found very definitely attractive.

It was even more intriguing because she could not decide if he was merely making sure of another political recruit and enjoying himself at the same time, or whether he was genuinely falling in love with her in a cautious and adult manner that she had not hitherto experienced.

There was no doubt that he was the most sought-after of all the young men over here, and that he exerted himself to be liked by all ages, but she thought that that was just part of his character and not vanity. He liked to see people happy and automatically did his best to make them so. She had watched him talking to other girls and noticed that even the shyest ones opened up to him. It was very flattering that he wanted her to share his feelings for his country, but it might easily be that he wanted all pretty female visitors to share this feeling and that once converted he would have no further personal interest in them.

Anyway, she decided, as she fell asleep, there could be no harm in flirting a little bit. It was balm to her hurt pride to be singled out for such distinguished attention, and a man of James's age should be old enough to look after himself.

Chapter 5

The next four months seemed to fly by—remarkable in the world of politics for the Home Rule Bill to allow Ireland to have a separate government passing its second reading in the House of Parliament, and the consequent stimulant to the recruiting campaign of the Ulster Volunteer Force raised to defend Ulster's interests. Eric Grantham reported jubilantly that their numbers had now increased from fifty-six thousand to nearly eighty-five thousand, and that now more than half of them possessed guns and ammunition.

Surely the English must realise that this was not just bluff!

But the government was now torn with worry about the impending possibility of war with Germany. If this happened, the Irish ports would be vital to the defence of England, but if the government decided to keep those ports for England and drop the Home Rule Bill it would immediately lose the votes of the sixty southern Irish members upon whom it depended for its majority and would then get out of power. The only thing it could do was to stick its head in the sand and hope that war would not materialise.

Ellen's affairs were going rather better than the government's were. She had been seeing a good deal of James. First there had been a number of dinners and dances over Christmas. She had discovered that he played the piano, and as she sang very sweetly herself this had brought them together at more parties. But they did not often meet in the daytime, as he kept conscientious office hours and this was new and intriguing to Ellen, who found herself comparing him very favourably with

Desmond, who had never hesitated to push his duties onto someone else if he wanted to get leave for any particular occasion.

During the latter end of January there was a very hard spell of frost and they had several days of skating on the artificial lake at the Taggarts that were tremendous fun. All ages joined in with varying degrees of skill and over the weekend ice hockey matches were organised. James led the home team against the soldiers and honours were fairly evenly divided until Michael, in a desperate attempt to extract the puck from between the legs of Captain Beaumont, had not only tripped the captain and brought him crashing to the ice with a severe blow on the back of the head, but had then lost his balance, swerving madly around with arms flailing the air, and caught James such a whack on the knee with his hockey stick that James had been obliged to sit with his eyes tight shut for three whole minutes on the rapidly melting ice, reminding himself that Michael was a close relation of the girl he admired so much, in order not to say what he felt like saying. When he did open them, Ellen was standing in front of him, exclaiming, "Poor, Mr. Melville! Did my uncouth cousin catch you a most frightful whack?" And then, as he got quickly to his feet, she caught sight of a dark patch on the knee of his breeches and cried, "Look, it's bleeding—how dreadful!" and dropped on her knees to look more closely. "You really ought to let me tie it up for you." She raised her eyes to James's, full of sympathy, and for a moment he thought he would have to sit down again; it gave him the most extraordinary sensation to have this beautiful girl, with frost-whipped cheeks and shining eyes on her knees in front of him. Suddenly he knew, quite irrevocably, that this was the girl he must marry. He had never felt so sure of anything in his life and he felt quite dazed with the torrent of new feeling sweeping through him. Ellen watched his bewildered expression and wondered if he had been hit on the head as well as the knee, and was about to summon aid when he came to himself, and, holding out his hands, said, "This is all wrong. I should be sitting at your feet. Please don't embarrass me any further . . ." and pulled her up to his own level. If there

59

had not been so many people around he would have liked to have asked her to marry him straight away, so strong were his feelings, but Michael was hopping around them so horrified at having laid out the captains of both teams with one blow that he was nearly in tears, and spent the rest of the afternoon fussing around like an old hen, never leaving James alone for a minute.

Despite the protests of the two men that they were not too badly injured to go on with the match, it was generally felt that enough damage had been done for one day and they all adjourned to the house for an enormous tea of hot scones, soda bread, muffins, and cakes, with fresh salty butter from the farm, honey, clotted cream, and strawberry jam, which was set on a low table in front of a huge wood fire. They all sat or lay on cushions and chairs in attitudes of complete relaxation as the heat seeped into their frozen limbs and they glowed with contentment.

James refused to be tied up and swore that he was alright, though Captain Beaumont was much less gallant and nursing a colossal lump on the back of his head, said he would rather fight the Germans any day than take part in a friendly match with an Irishman. However, when someone suggested that if he played his cards carefully he might get sick leave, he brightened up a lot and put on a great act of forgiving Michael until the party finally broke up.

A thick fall of snow put an end to the skating and the roads for some time were so treacherous that neither horse nor car could travel with any pleasure and families had to fall back on their own resources for amusement. Ellen practised a number of new songs, finished a silk scarf she had been knitting for Harry for the past two years, and embarked on a set of petit-point chair seats as a present for her aunt. She felt she had plenty to think about and it was extremely pleasant to sit in one of the big chairs in the long drawing room, filled with pots of cyclamen and azalea, watching the artificial roses growing beneath her fingers, while her aunt wrote letters and caught up on the countless small household jobs which were always shelved in good weather.

60

Sir Charles strolled in and out, discussing with his wife various arrangements for house and estate and the children were always on the move. Though really banished to the use of the back staircase only, they could sometimes be heard coming down the broad front flight. First the house would shake as they took off, then there would be a tortured squeak from the bannisters and a tremendous thump followed by a victorious yell. "I got right down to the bottom in one jump, Michael!" Usually Lady Richardson just paused in her writing while a look of resignation passed over her face, but occasionally she would snap her pen down on the desk and rush out of the room into the hall whence would be heard what the family called "sounds off." She always looked a little ashamed of herself when she came back from one of these forays with the children, who were quick to turn their mother's repentant mood to good account by tiptoeing around the house in the most ostentatious manner, speaking in whispers, until at last she would be obliged to laugh and exclaim, "There's no need to go on behaving as if someone were dying; do just try to behave sensibly when you are in my end of the house. After all, we don't want it all to look as if bears lived in it, like the nursery wing, do we?"

Ellen thought this was a slightly overdrawn picture of the nursery, though it was indeed rather scratched about the paint-work, and the cushions were more often on the floor than on the chairs. The chair covers had usually climbed halfway up the back, exposing torn whipcord and bulging horsehair from bygone days, while they hung in festoons on the front. The table was always littered deep in books and paper, chewed pencils, and boxes of paints. It was hard to believe that every morning the nursery began the day as tidily as any other room in the house! In the summer it was not so bad, as the children spent most of the day outside, but in wet weather the room, indeed, looked lived in.

Still, it was structurally so pleasant in its rectangular shape and deep bay windows that no amount of mess could really spoil its appearance, and Ellen spent quite a lot of time there, learning to play backgammon with the children, strumming on the old piano or joining in noisy sessions of Old Maid and Racing Demon.

When the weather improved, Ellen went on two occasions to the theatre in Belfast, in small parties organised by James. On each occasion she returned home with a sense of real happiness, which she had never experienced with Desmond. With him she had always known wild beatings of the heart, dryness of the throat (which she supposed now must have been partly fear of his ability to hurt her), thrills to his nearness, and heights of joy when he had been in one of his good moods, kind and almost loving. None of this did she experience with James; just a steady feeling of deep pleasure in his company, almost a sense of homecoming, which left her with a warm glow after each encounter.

She wondered which of these different emotions was really love. It would not, at this moment, break her heart if she was never to see James again, but she would miss him dreadfully; a richness would have gone out of her life. Perhaps it really was that her heart was still numb since she had given it so wholly to Desmond only to have it tossed aside, and now she was feeling only with her mind.

Whatever it was, she felt like the burnt child who is being very cautious of the fire though irresistibly drawn by its warmth, and James felt through all her friendly, sympathetic chatter a strong sense of reserve and this worried him. It made him hold back from saying anything that might jeopardise their friendship.

Sometimes he wondered if she was just putting in time with him and was really fond of someone in England, only waiting for her parents return to announce an engagement. Then he would feel that this was an unworthy thought, Ellen had too open a nature to cover her feelings so well—perhaps she was shy, not sure of herself. He could wait. At thirty he had learnt that the best things are worth waiting for and he was not going to ruin a chance that meant so much to him by rushing in too soon.

Nevertheless, it was such an unusual thing for him not to be sure if his feelings were reciprocated that he suffered considerable anxiety; Ellen was continually in his thoughts and his love for her grew in leaps and bounds. He had yet to know about absence making the heart grow fonder, but definitely, anxiety did. He wished that the same could be said for Ellen.

His instinct to hold back was exactly right, for as Ellen worked over her petit-point chair seats before the fire on the cold winter evenings, she was worried, too. She was sure now that James loved her, and while one-half of her mind whispered, "Take care . . . you thought this before and look what happened!" the other half recognised that James was quite a different type of man from Desmond. She was afraid that he would propose soon and she would not know what to say. He was not the kind of man who would ask her twice. If she accepted him simply on the rebound from Desmond and was not really in love with him that would only lead to unhappiness and he was a man who would take it very hard. Also, her aunt would never forgive her. Yet, if she were to refuse him because she did not feel sure if she really loved him, she would lose him as she had lost Markham and she could not possibly continue to stay over here. Where, then, could she go?

"Dear me," she sighed, "why is love so very complicated, or am I just terribly stupid about it?"

Cynthia was also going through a bad patch emotionally. A new governess had arrived after Christmas; a gentle, shy girl, whose efforts to control her charges aroused the most protective instincts in Eric Grantham and the deepest disgust in Michael. She had never taught before and was keenly aware of the narrow margin between her own age and that of her pupils, which, while it helped her to understand their high spirits, made her task doubly difficult in other ways. She was perfectly confident of her ability to teach and eventually control the girls, but was terribly worried in case the delay should be too great and Lady Richardson pack her off home before she had a chance to prove herself. She was one of a large family of a country clergyman in Armagh, and with five brothers—three still at school—she felt she simply had to make a success of her first venture to independence.

She need not have worried so much if she had realised how

well aware of the situation the grown-ups were, and Ellen and Mr. Grantham gave her all the support they could. Ellen realised that much of the trouble in the schoolroom was caused by Cynthia's unconscious jealousy. She cherished an adolescent hero worship for Eric Grantham and the rapidly maturing side of her character recognised an instinctive rival in Miss McInnis. So she felt unsettled and played up in a way of which she would have been ashamed if she had been old enough to realise what she was doing. Alice tagged along with her for the fun of it, though she would have been the first to repent if she had suspected how unhappy the little governess was. Of course, the more they played up, the more Eric tried to help Miss McInnis (no one had ever seemed to see him as a big, strong man before and it was a role he found himself enjoying very much) and the more he helped, the more difficult Cynthia became. Finally, after about two weeks skirmishing, Ellen came into the nursery one morning just before lunch to find the governess in tears, no sign of Cynthia, and Alice, looking very ashamed of herself, tidying up the lesson books.

It seemed that Cynthia had simply got up in the middle of the arithmetic lesson, announced that she was bored and that she was going for a ride. Miss McInnis had told her to get on with her lessons, and all had been peace for a moment while she explained a point to Alice. When she looked up, Cynthia had gone.

Alice's sense of fair play recognised that this was too much and did everything that she could to make amends, being truly ashamed of all the mean things she had done, but Margaret McInnis felt she had been proved an utter failure and the only course left open to her was to go and admit defeat to Lady Richardson at once.

It was at this point that Ellen walked in.

"But this is absolutely ridiculous!" she exclaimed, after extracting the story between sniffs and sobs from Alice and the governess. "Honestly, Alice, I don't know how you could be so stupid and unkind. You know perfectly well Cynthia is only

being beastly because she is jealous of Miss McInnis. She is just
working it out of her system and why you have to join her in
being so unkind to a stranger in your house I can't think."

Alice promptly burst into redoubled tears, and if Ellen had
not been so bothered she would have had to laugh at the flood
of tears before her.

Well, anyway, there would be no more trouble from Alice;
so she assured the weeping little governess that Lady Richardson
was perfectly aware of what had been going on and was not a
dragon but a very understanding and kind woman; also that she
was quite sure Cynthia would have already realised that she had
gone too far and that everything would be alright from now on.

"Come along, Miss McInnis . . . may I call you Margaret?
It's so much easier. This isn't 'Jane Eyre'! I truly promise, if
you'll only stop crying and come to lunch, everything will go
smoothly from now on."

Lunch was a somewhat strained meal, Ellen, Eric, and Lady
Richardson doing all they could to disregard the woebegone
faces 'round the table. Luckily Sir Charles was out for lunch
and Cynthia was rather frightened and consequently very silent.

After lunch a long walk was organised for everyone except
Cynthia, whom her mother took into her room and explained
how selfish and unkind she had been. She did it so kindly, for
she understood that Cynthia was in an unhappy and mixed-up
frame of mind, that Cynthia burst into tears and, throwing her
arms 'round her mother's neck, sat on her knee and gave way to
such an orgy of strangled sobs, sniffs and shudders that Lady
Richardson eventually put her to bed with the great luxury of
a fire in her room, a new book, and supper on a tray.

So ended what was later referred to as "the great flood!"
Sir Charles was at a loss to understand the outburst of giggles
that came from everyone at breakfast when he innocently
remarked, "How nice it is to see the sun again!"

In April, Ellen received an invitation from an aunt of
James's to go to stay at her house in Galway for a few days and
attend the Galway Blazer's Point to Point and a dance the
following night. As she had never met the aunt, she realised that

the invitation must have been organised by James, and with a speeding pulse, wrote her acceptance.

The arrangement was that she was to join James and the major of the Dorset Regiment, at present stationed in Belfast, and his newly acquired wife, and that they should all travel down by train.

Ellen's local train arrived in Belfast about an hour before the other one was due to depart to Dublin, en route to Galway, with many changes and halts on the line. James was already waiting on the platform and carried her off to have some coffee in the station hotel while they waited for the others to join them. Ellen was looking bewitchingly pretty in a little chinchilla toque, cocked over one eye, and a grey tweed coat and skirt trimmed with maroon velvet. James surveyed her with such pride and approval that she felt quite embarrassed and hastily began to chatter about the journey and to ask questions about Galway.

He explained that the express train only took them as far as Portadown where they would have to change into a very slow and inferior train, which rambled westwards, stopping at every station on the line.

"It is ages since I was down there," he said, "but I never go through Portadown without thinking of the time I was with my mother and the Boer War was on. I expect you were too young to be interested in it, but there was a Boer general called 'de Wet' who gained considerable fame as a fighter but even more for the number of times he was captured by the British and yet managed to escape. He became a national character and I remember this time my mother was waiting for the train at Portadown when a small urchin came along, shouting 'deeWet, deeWet, photies of deeWet. Buy one for a penny!' Well, mother was bored and she thought it would be interesting to see what he looked like, so she persuaded my father to buy one. He opened the envelope given to him by the boy and was naturally annoyed to find nothing in it. The boy, by this time, was some way down the platform and my father strode after him, seized him by the arm and said, 'Look here, you young rascal, there was nothing in that envelope you sold me.' Whereupon the lad rapped back as quick as lightning, 'Mother of God! don't tell me he's escaped again!' and fled off down the platform as fast as his legs would carry him. My father was so delighted with this that he forbore to chase him. Somehow, whenever I go there I still expect to see that urchin plying his trade."

James went on to explain how there was no food on the train so his mother had provided a large hamper of lunch that should help to while away the time on the slow train; though he added a private rider to himself that no train could be slow enough if he was sharing it wtih Ellen.

At this moment Major and Mrs. Balfour arrived, and after making the necessary introductions they all went out to board the train.

Major Balfour was a nice big man, with a tremendous fair moustache that rivetted Ellen's attention and made her inclined to forget what he was talking about. His wife was probably younger than Ellen, but looked older, having a dark, rather hard style of beauty, and a very definite manner of speaking. She expressed herself as dying to see this famous "Galway Blazer" country and was obviously saddened to find that neither James nor Ellen hunted and were not therefore a suitable audience for her favourite topic of conversation. However, she could be very amusing, slightly at the expense of others, and the time passed very quickly.

They were in the slow train, unpacking the luncheon hamper, when she turned to Ellen in her direct way and said, "You know, I feel sure I have seen you somewhere before. Have you always lived over here?"

Ellen explained that she had only come over eight months before and had been living in London previous to that.

Valerie Balfour's eyes lit up. "Of course, now I remember! You were a great friend of Desmond Campion's, weren't you? I remember coming up against you two at the Slowe Hall Tennis Tournament."

Poor Ellen felt her face go crimson at this unexpected mention of Desmond and her heart missed a beat. She was aware that James was watching her with keen attention as she murmured, "Yes, we did play together, but I'm afraid I don't remember meeting you."

"Oh no," rushed on the tactless Valerie, "I'm sure you would not have noticed; I had an absolute mouse of a partner and Desmond is so frightfully good; you were most unfairly matched and we hadn't a chance."

Ellen murmured something noncommittal about tennis being her favourite game and sought to change the conversation by handing 'round a selection of cold meats out of the hamper, but the wretched girl babbled on.

"My goodness, he is an attractive man, isn't he? If I had not just got engaged to dear old Robert here, I would have been madly jealous of you." She rolled her eyes at "dear old Robert" who gazed at her devotedly. Ellen shot a look at James and noticed his eyebrows had risen in a look of most comical dismay, while he fixed his attention on the sandwich he was eating. She wondered what he was thinking and was surprised to find how much she minded.

Fortunately Valerie seemed to have lost interest in that topic and Ellen was able to steer the conversation onto the shows that had been on in London last summer and which they had both seen.

James, she noticed, did not join in and she felt his eyes resting on her speculatively from time to time.

Presently the talk turned to racing. Valerie asked if there was much racing and did Ellen go often to it? Ellen admitted, rather ruefully, that the last meeting she had been to had been Royal Ascot the previous year and she could not really remember if she had noticed the horses at all. She laughed, as she went on, "It was the first time ladies appeared in the new hobble skirts and I really think there was far more interest taken in their progress than in that of the horses. I know a friend of mine made five pounds on a most elegant female swathed in coffee-coloured chiffon who reached the other side of the enclosure about six inches ahead of another gorgeous creature in an equally tight hemline!"

James and Major Balfour were delighted with this disclosure, but Mrs. Balfour was rather put out.

"But you must admit they are terribly smart," she expostulated, having two or three in her trousseau, and nourishing secret dreams of the furore she would create when she appeared in them for the first time.

"No, I don't honestly think they are smart," remarked Ellen thoughtfully. "I don't think anything that is completely ridiculous is ever smart. You must be able to move gracefully to look smart . . . but perhaps this is just the result of having a very critical brother to influence me."

"For which small mercy we must be sincerely thankful," murmured James. "If you had elected to appear in a hobble, no matter how chic, at the races tomorrow, I think I should have had to make the car break down on the way. Galway is about as far a cry from Ascot as it would be possible to find and the natives have a highly developed wit."

"They sound rather bad mixers," observed Major Balfour. "Maxwell, of our regiment, has entered his horse for the Adjacent Hunts Race. It is a very good horse but he has been warned that the locals generally have the outcome of the race decided sometime before it begins. I hope he survives the course!"

"Oh, I should think he will be all right in the Adjacent Hunts," said James easily. "They have to encourage outsiders in one race, otherwise the meeting would never pay, and also they have beautiful manners. I doubt if they will let him win . . . but it will be done in the nicest possible way."

And so it transpired.

The day of the races was one of those exquisitely soft, sunny days that the west of Ireland can turn out at almost any time of the year from February to December but seldom does. The previous day had been soft, drizzling rain, so that Ellen got little impression of the country on their way, but the house was a rare gem in Ireland, being low built, in gracefully laid out gardens. The panelling throughout the interior was white, picked out in gilt in the main rooms. The glow of numerous fires reflected in the highly polished dark oak floors, and the gentle scent of turf hung in the air. James's aunt obviously loved flowers and every available corner was filled with a profusion of tulips, almond blossom, and starry white magnolia.

There was no house party except for the Balfours and Ellen and James, and Valerie would have voted it not worth the trouble of the long train journey if she had not been so impressed with the beauty of the house and the gentle dignity of its chatelaine.

Major Balfour was less party minded and more inclined to congratulate himself on having found such comfortable surroundings from which to watch "Old Maxwell" ride his race. He was blissfully unaware that his presence there was solely due to him and his wife being a reasonably pleasant and amusing cover under which James could introduce to his favourite aunt, the girl he had set his heart on and who, if possible, he intended to find an opportunity to ask to marry him.

James was by now reasonably sure of the answer being "yes," though, he reflected, she had looked very conscious in the train when Mrs. Balfour mentioned that fellow's name. Possibly it would be wiser to wait a little longer . . . These thoughts flitted through his mind as he sat in the softly lighted drawing room after dinner and played the throbbing accompaniments to the Spanish love songs Ellen sang so charmingly. It was very pleasant, this period of waiting; he had no ugly sense of premonition or fearful urgency. He had waited years to find this girl and it would be senseless to spoil his chance with her by rushing in with a proposal at the wrong moment when she was not yet sure of her own mind.

He watched her across the top of the piano as she sang, charmed anew with the graceful turn of her neck under the thick, piled up hair, and the appeal of her dark eyes as she turned to include him with the others in the plaintive words of the song.

He was filled with such deep contentment in the contemplation of her that all unwittingly his eyes carried the message of his love with such depths of sincerity that Ellen felt her voice tremble as she encountered his gaze. She hoped the rest of the company would attribute it to an artistic tremulo ascribable to the douleur of the song and not to the real reason.

Next morning, after breakfast in bed, with the sun streaming in, James's aunt, Mrs. Hamilton, had taken Ellen and Valerie around the garden, explaining to them how in the soft climate of the West many rare flowers flourished, and it was not uncommon to have camellias and bushes of scented rhododendrons growing out of doors. They were told, too, how the fuschias grew wild all over the country and produced the brilliant scarlet dye used in making the traditional Galway petticoat.

General Hamilton had spent most of his life in the Indian Army and had retired only five years previously to his lovely home, to enjoy the fishing and forget the sorrow that his only son had been killed at the very end of the South African War and would never be able to share it with him. The Hamilton family had lived here for years though many of his own years had been spent far away, and with the present unsettled state in Ireland maybe his son was not missing so much, after all.

Mrs. Hamilton had not achieved such a comfortable philosophy. She took little interest in politics and busied herself in love of her house and garden after so many years on the move, and her care of the soft spoken people in the village.

They did not go out very much but loved to have people to stay, their nephew James in particular.

Mrs. Melville had written some time ago to say that she thought James had fallen at last, and as he had never shown such a degree of interest in any girl before, Mrs. Hamilton had been simply delighted when he wrote suggesting a house party for the local races and dance and given her a chance to meet the young lady.

What she saw she very much approved of and watched the young party go off to the races in the afternoon with an ache in her heart for all the happiness her own son had missed.

It was such a lovely day they had all chosen to go in the open landau and James had been given strict instructions not to allow Doyle, the groom, to enter either of the horses for any races, no matter what the provocation might be.

71

All the way to the hill around which the races were held the roads were crowded with happy, ragged bands of children and grown-ups; the children, for the most part, barefooted, and the girls in filthy black shawls, generally with a baby cunningly tucked into the folds, and Ellen was horrified to see even the babies in arms holding out their dirty little hands and making a very good imitation of the beggar's whine. "Ah . . . give us a penny an' may the good Virgin bless you and bring you luck at the races today . . ." rising to a shrill squeal . . . "Sure a lovely lady like yourself would never miss a copper . . ., etc., etc." which was the invariable reaction of all and sundry at the sight of the carriage.

Yet, despite the dirt and the rags, and the way the Virgin's blessing quickly turned into a vituperative curse when the pennies were not forthcoming, Ellen could not but be struck by the extreme beauty of the children's faces: small and delicately boned, with enormous eyes and thick, long lashes, peering out through elf locks of dark hair. Unfortunately, this beauty seemed but transitory for although most of the elders retained the magnificent eyes, in almost all cases the effect was ruined by broad noses and rotten teeth, and a simplicity of expression bordering on vacancy. Although repelled by such mass methods of begging and the lavish misuse of the Trinity's blessing, and a natural distaste for the ostentation of throwing money to other less fortunate human beings, Ellen could not bear to see such poverty on such a glorious day, so beckoning one small urchin as the carriage paused at the entrance to the course she handed him a sixpenny piece and was both dismayed and alarmed by the reaction. Before she could draw breath the carriage was surrounded on all sides with all ages, shapes and smells of beggars, climbing up the wheels, hanging over the doors, leaning across the occupants, and of the original small boy there was nothing to be seen but a mass of writhing, yelling, fighting humanity in the dust by the side of the road.

Luckily the dogcart ahead of them had moved on, so Doyle was able to whip up the horses and escape before the carriage and all inside were torn to pieces; though one or two of the tougher little beggars hung on for several hundred yards before dropping off and rejoining their friends.

"My goodness . . ." gasped Ellen, straightening her hat, "I had no idea anything like that would happen. I'm most awfully sorry, Valerie, I do hope you are not ruined."

"Almost, but not quite," returned Valerie somewhat tartly, removing pieces of mud and sticks from her coat.

James restored an odd glove to Ellen and said, with a broad grin, "Well, now, let that be a lesson to you. When in Rome, do as the Romans, they generally have good reasons for their doings or not-doings. Every visitor to Ireland makes that mistake once but few of them make it again. The trouble is that if you are recognised on the course, you will be mobbed everywhere you go. I think you had better wear your hat back to front or something."

Ellen began to look really worried, so he laughed and said, "Never mind, I'm only teasing—the chances of being recognised in this mob are pretty slender."

He waved his hand in the direction of the hill, which was, indeed, teaming with humanity, like an anthill with the top lifted off. It was the largest area of high ground for miles around and the valley stretched brilliantly green on all sides, only sparsely dotted with clumps of trees and crisscrossed with stone walls and narrow stone-faced banks, some with straggling hedges along their tops or ditches beneath. In the far distance a range of sapphire hills shimmered in the heat.

"What are all those black things on that mound over there?" Ellen asked, pointing to the far side of the course, as they took up their stand near the last jump.

"Looks like a lot of outsize crows," commented Major Balfour helpfully, raising his field glasses.

James followed the direction of his gaze and exclaimed with delight, "They wouldn't thank you for that description! Those are the priests from the college near here. They are not allowed to disgrace the cloth by attending race meetings and mixing with the betting crowd, so they sit on that hill, which commands a magnificent view of the course and the local urchins make their fortunes running backwards and forwards placing their bets for them."

The three English people were much impressed by this delightfully open way of getting around an awkward situation.

"Though I'm surprised the priests trust the little boys with the money, after what happened to us this morning!" laughed Ellen.

"Oh, it would be a bad boy indeed who would steal from a priest!" exclaimed James. "They have definite standards and are very proud of living up to them though to an outsider they may seem rather curious."

The horses appeared at this moment going down to the start; rather a motley collection, some dock-tailed and some smartly turned out; others unclipped and stragglemaned and their jockeys little better, but one and all surrounded by a bevy of advisers gabbling away last minute instructions to the riders who were far too busy waving and calling out jokes to the crowd to listen to what they were saying. Finally, they beat up their horses and raced helter-skelter down to the start, scattering people in all directions and with great difficulty preventing their horses from completing the course the wrong way around before the race began.

The last jump was also the fourth, being a low wall composed of the round white lichened stones that litter the ground in that part of Galway. It came after a number of small banks and was half way up the side of a hill, which was steep enough to check the horses, before plunging down the other side to a tall narrow bank set on a slight turn and generally reckoned to be one of the nastiest jumps on the course.

"I'm going to back that horse with the enormous head and the teeny-weeny boy on him," murmured Ellen, after some thought.

Valerie was rather critical of her choice so she explained that it was because he was so very ugly no one else would back him and she didn't want him to feel unloved. Valerie was unmoved by such altruism and selected a rather flashy looking big chestnut, with a jockey in glaring squares of pink and orange knitting.

The Major rejoined them at this moment with the news that oddly enough Ellen's coffin-head was a hot favourite and Valerie's chestnut out at ten-to-one. Speculation on the betting was interrupted by a loud screech from the crowd and the race had begun.

A Roman-nosed grey was running away in front of the others who were riding very jealously in a tight bunch with their hands almost on each other's reins. The grey hit the bank below the hill with a tremendous slap, nearly falling, and obviously had no intention of risking its legs again on the stone wall. The lad on top had lost both stirrups and looked equally irresolute as they approached, but the crowd rushed forward with sticks and stones and yells of encouragement so that the horrified horse shot over the jump with the jockey following at the full stretch of the reins, and went rocketing away down the hill to the stone-faced bank. This, however, was quite too much for their rattled nerves and at sight of the onlookers preparing to close in again, the grey swerved quickly to the right and headed for the hills on its own, with the boy clinging 'round its neck as best he could.

Meanwhile, the remaining seven horses rode so close together that Ellen could only pray that none would fall, otherwise the whole lot must surely pile up on top of each other in the most awful carnage. However, as they vanished into the clump of trees beyond the priests' hill, they had begun to thin out a bit, and on emerging Ellen's coffin-head was in the lead, galloping steadily along with its head on its knees and an air of utter dejection. A dock-tailed bay followed with Valerie's chestnut hard on his heels. The murmuring speculation of the crowd swelled to a roar as coffin-head toiled up the slope, and the pink and orange jacket suddenly began to ride, almost drawing level as they approached the last jump. He was quite obviously the fresher of the two horses, and as this fact dawned on the spectators they closed in as one man behind coffin-head, almost lifting him over the stones and completely knocking pink jacket out of his stride so that he only cleared the wall by a miracle and was unable to regain his pace and get within a length of coffin-head as he passed the winning post to the accompaniment of tumultuous cheering.

The Balfours were dumbfounded, and Ellen was torn between sympathy for the horses racing under such conditions and amusement at the Balfours' inability to adapt themselves to such racemanship. The Major twisted his moustache and muttered about objections and clerks of the course, while Valerie, in her high, artificial drawl, kept comparing this with Sandown Park and other better run race meetings she had attended in England.

Finally, James, getting rather bored with the subject, said, "My dear fellow, all the crowd were doing was cheering on the winner, and if the second horse couldn't get over the jump that's all there is to it. There is no law against the crowd trespassing, and they know it, so no point in making an objection; but you will understand now why I don't expect your friend will win his race today." And he proceeded to lead the party off to further their education by introducing them to the side shows—the orange sellers, the copper alleys—and explained the intricacies and dangers of becoming involved in a game of "Find the Lady."

The rest of the meeting passed in much the same way. James and his party returned to the carriage for a picnic tea after the fourth race. He thought there was something odd about Doyle's manner: he looked rather shame-faced and seemed anxious not to be drawn into conversation, though he hovered around ready to give any help if it was needed. James put this down to the possibility of his having been interrupted on the verge of some nefarious scheme to ride one of the general's carriage horses in the Farmers' Race, and decided to say nothing but keep within sight of the horses for the last two races.

Accordingly, they decided to stand by the stone-faced bank at the bottom of the hill for the next race, as it was not only nearer the carriage but would make it easier to get away before the crowds afterwards.

With James's help Ellen climbed onto the top of the bank some yards to the left of the flag and balanced herself against a sapling growing up from the ditch on the other side; James went back to suggest to the Balfours that they might see better from the top of the bank, too, but at that moment the horses suddenly came ino sight thundering down the slope to the jump.

Ellen, slightly scared but exhilarated, was thinking *No wonder cavalry charges are always such a success in wars*, as she couldn't imagine anyone being brave enough to stay at their post with a solid mass of foaming, pounding horses coming straight towards them, when she suddenly saw a horse slightly ahead on the far side shy right across the whole bunch, diverting them so that the whole cavalry charge was now coming directly at her.

Her heart did an enormous sommersault into her boots as she gazed wildly 'round for something to hide behind. Where a moment before there had been a scattered group of spectators between her and the race, suddenly there was no one. Indeed, the last man to leap past her as she clung to the sapling gave himself a good push-off from her shoulder in his haste, almost knocking her down, and while she strove to regain her balance to leap into the cover of the ditch, a hot, hard body flung past her and she was hurled into the mud and covered in a shower of earthclods and small stones as the first three horses thundered over her head. The rest came to a grinding halt, flung against each other, on the near side of the bank, exactly where she had been standing a moment before, and stood or knelt with their heads hanging over, dropping flecks of foam on top of Ellen in the ditch. One jockey was astride the sapling and the rest were nowhere to be seen.

James turned around at the warning shout from the crowd, just in time to see the girl he loved being apparently ground to powder under the hooves of about a dozen horses—for he could not see where she had fallen.

With every drop of blood drained from his face, he tore down the hill and fought his way through the horses on the bank, closely followed by Major Balfour and a section of the crowd athirst for some gory spectacle. As he leapt onto the other side, Ellen sat up in the ditch and met in his eyes such a blazing look of love and concern that she felt quite dizzy and was only too thankful to lean against his shoulder for a moment and pretend it was the fall which had made her giddy and listen to the tumultuous pounding of his heart under her ear.

"Oh, Ellen!" he blurted out, trying to control his voice, "thank God you're safe! Are you quite sure you aren't hurt? I couldn't see how you could escape their hooves and I couldn't get near you!" He paused for breath, his voice still uneven, and his hands touched her gently to see if there were any bones broken.

Ellen felt only the strongest desire to be taken wholly into his arms and kissed within an inch of her life instead of this gentle attention. She felt almost drunken with shock and desire, and closed her eyes in the most abandoned way, from which James immediately decided that she must be seriously hurt and had fainted with pain, and laid her carefully down on the grass while he murmured distractedly, "Oh, Lord! She's fainted . . . for God's sake, Balfour, fetch a doctor . . . she must be badly hurt!"

Ellen forced herself reluctantly out of her stupor. "No, really, I am alright . . . I'll be quite alright in a moment . . . it all happened so quickly . . . !" She became aware that the crowd was gathering and that not only was she covered in mud from head to foot but her hair was hanging in festoons 'round her shoulders.

"Oh, dear!" she exclaimed shakily, "I must look awful . . . and I can't see my hat anywhere . . . perhaps one of the horses is wearing it," she giggled feebly.

"Never mind your hat, dar . . . I mean . . ." hastily correcting himself, "as long as you are sure you are alright who cares about a hat! Do you think you could stand if I helped you?" Then, changing his mind, he picked her up in his arms, like a child, and carried her down the field, through a gateway to the waiting carriage. He fussed over her and propped her feet up on the picnic basket and wrapped her up in rugs as if it was midwinter. All this was done with such solicitude that Ellen felt her face crimson and was overcome with a desire to laugh and cry at the same time, and hoped that James would put down her strange behaviour to shock, which, being a modest man, he did. Though he felt very heartened by the way she had held her arms around his neck and had been severely tempted to declare himself there and then, had not Valerie and her husband come rushing up, full of questions and exclamations and suggestions, which put an end to all privacy.

"Never mind, I shall ask her at the dance tonight," he consoled himself. "Faint heart never won fair maid and nothing venture, nothing win." He felt sure of himself and reasonably sure of her, and looked forward with impatience to the evening.

Doyle was found and the horses put to, and they made off home at a spanking pace, before even the race had finished or the crowd had begun to disperse.

Ellen was really very shaken and relapsed into silence, only smiling shyly when she met James's eyes fixed on her while he answered Valerie's voluble questions as briefly as he politely could.

As the carriage drew up at the front of the house, James jumped down and was just preparing to lift Ellen out when the hall door opened and his uncle and aunt came out onto the step. One look at their faces told James that some terrible shock had come to them since they had left them after lunch. "Keep the horses walking up and down, please, Doyle. We may need them again," called the General, and not even noticing Ellen's dishevelled appearance as James lifted her up the steps, he put his hand on James's shoulder and followed them into the hall.

Chapter 6

With an almost trance-like expression Mrs. Hamilton led them into the drawing room. She told the little maid who was tending the fire to bring tea for them all, and plainly never noticed Ellen's state at all as James helped her onto a sofa. His aunt looked so strange he wondered if she did not need his help more than Ellen and the General didn't look too good either as he closed the door. James could almost sense him giving himself the order to cross the floor without giving way.

What on earth could have happened to make them both look so shocked . . . yes, that was it . . . shocked. They couldn't both have had strokes, and even if one had and the other had been shaken by it, then one of them would be in bed.

All this passed through his mind very rapidly as he helped Ellen. She was really too shaken to be more than aware of the tension, and the Balfours were by now so conditioned to strange goings on in Ireland that they were not inclined to be unduly surprised about anything that happened.

Balfour was very disappointed at not seeing the finish of the race, nor having had a chance to discuss it all with his friend Maxwell, but he quite realised they could not have kept Ellen waiting about after her fall. Valerie realised this, too, but was rather grieved and hoped that if Ellen was not well enough, at least she and her husband and James would be able to go to the Hunt Ball without her. It would be too bad to have to miss that. She had no idea what the plans were . . . whether they were to join another party or were to have a dinner party here—whichever it was, they could hardly expect three of them to sit here all evening with nothing to do just because Ellen had not got out of the way of the horses in time. Anyone with two eyes in their head could have seen what was going to happen, and she was a bit fed up with the whole visit so far. James, obviously, had no eyes for anyone but Ellen, and then the races had not been at all what she had expected. Certainly they had been amusing and she would be able to make a good story out of them but there had not been a single soul she knew . . . there didn't seem to be anything but country people there and then with Ellen's accident they had been dragged back before they had even said good-bye to John Maxwell. Of course, they obviously couldn't have done anything else with only one carriage but it had been a pretty disappointing day and it would be too bad if the dance was off, too.

So her mind ran on, immersed in her own troubles, until she suddenly became aware of old Mrs. Hamilton talking in a rapid, trembling voice.

". . . . and I came in here to deal with some letters at my writing desk . . ." She looked to where it stood by the window as if she could hardly believe that it was still there, and went on: "Suddenly I saw Paddy, our old gardener, pulling up some rose bushes under the French windows. I couldn't at first believe my eyes for he is a very good gardener and loves the roses and nothing would more surely kill them than to be transplanted at this time of year—besides, I had not told him to move them. So I wondered if he had suddenly gone mad and I went out to speak to him."

She paused to steady her voice. The General, who had sunk into a chair beside her, laid his hand on hers.

As soon as I saw his face I realised that something was wrong. The tears were streaming down his cheeks and before I could speak he whispered 'don't say a word, Mem, we're being watched all the time . . . pretend to give me orders what to do and I'll tell ye the trouble' . . . So I directed him, pointing at different flowers with my stick, and he told me that he 'had it for certain' in the town that the Fenians were to burn the house down tonight

81

and shoot anyone who escaped!" She held up her hand for silence, as they all exclaimed in horror.

"You must hear me out . . . and then we must all decide what to do."

Valerie could see that she was fighting for composure though her voice went on in the same quiet, drained, monotone.

"At first I could not believe him . . . but he was absolutely insistent and sure that we were being watched. He would not say who his informant was but he urged me to make haste and pack everything we could and he would put it on the dogcart and take it to the station without anyone knowing, pretending it was boxes of flowers for the shops. And then he said—dear Paddy—he had it all worked out . . ." Mrs. Hamilton brushed the corner of her eye, "he said the General and I were to take the dogs out for their walk before supper, just as we always do and he would meet us some distance away with the dogcart and carry us into town."

There was a short, stupified silence as she finished her story. Then everyone began to talk at once. Valerie kept saying, "How ghastly . . . how ghastly! It can't be true!" for once completely shaken out of her self-centred self.

Ellen suddenly felt she could bear no more; this exquisite house and these dear old people to have such a terrible tragedy happen! After all the upsets of the afternoon she collapsed, weeping quietly into the cushions of the sofa.

Major Balfour burst out, "But, good heavens, Mrs. Hamilton, surely if you know the house is going to be burnt you can alert the police and the fire brigade—then nothing can happen and the men will be caught."

The General interposed dryly, "Unfortunately it does not happen that way in Ireland. Though we tried to telephone immediately he told us the line had been cut already. These men are strangers, sent from another part of the country altogether. It is always like this; the local people would never be used. Although they would all vote against us in an election, they would never hurt us, but these men are trained in this filthy game and are quite ruthless. The local people are terrified of recriminations and they wouldn't dare to lift a finger. In the past ghastly atrocities have been committed on faithful servants, and the news travels. It is most unusual to get even a warning and we must see to it that old Paddy does not suffer for his part."

James was sitting with his hands over his eyes, trying desperately to formulate a plan. Old Paddy's was good, but it must be possible to do more. He racked his brains while Valerie asked curiously, "How do you mean, suffer? What would they do to him?"

"Usually they just disappear," the General answered simply, with an expressive movement of his hands. "Sometimes the bodies are found, but not often. That is why the country folk are so terrified. Nothing is more frightening than something you can't account for."

At this moment the maid entered with the tea tray and they all made an effort not to look stupified and to behave naturally.

Mrs. Hamliton suddenly noticed Ellen's bedraggled state and exclaimed in concern, "My dear Ellen, are you alright? Whatever has happened to you? How dreadful of me not to have asked sooner . . . but all this . . ." She made a pathetic gesture and left the sentence unfinished.

Ellen, helped out by James, gave a brief account of all that had happened, which tided them sucessfully over until tea was laid and the little maid had gone out again.

"How dreadful . . . how dreadful . . . you must be very shaken—and now all this on top of it . . . What shall we do?" she appealed to the men as she poured out tea with an unsteady hand from the silver pot.

"It is so difficult because if we do anything out of the ordinary they will realise that we have been warned and will not only murder old Paddy but will prevent us leaving tonight." She put her hands over her eyes in a gesture of despair, and the General was just clearing his throat to speak when up jumped James and stood in front of the fire, talking rapidly.

"Aunt Lucia, I think I have a plan which would help us to get away a few more things. I can't really believe this is going to happen, but we must do everything possible to prevent it and save the house, in any case. We certainly can't afford to wait and see. This is what I suggest: we pretend that Ellen is much worse hurt—delayed shock or something—and must be got home at once. Therefore the Hunt Ball party is cancelled and Major and Mrs. Balfour escort her home. No, wait a moment," as Balfour began to protest at so inactive a role. "That way you can fill as many suitcases as you dare and pretend they are all theirs, and send them off in the carriage with Doyle as soon as possible. He won't remember how much luggage they arrived with. How about the rest of the servants?"

"They have all gone to the races. Betha is the only maid in the house and she does not work upstairs, so she would not know about the luggage either," Mrs. Hamilton said, eagerly, only too happy to save even a few things.

"Well then," continued James, turning to the girls, "could you travel to Belfast by yourselves if Balfour puts you on the train? I know it's a lot to ask, especially when you have had such a dreadful day, Ellen, but the evening train is a through one and you wouldn't have to change and we need every man we can get here . . . I wish you could go, too, auntie. I can't bear you to have to go through all this strain; but . . ." as she shook her head mutely, "I think you are right; it would be too suspicious if you all left."

Ellen hastened to assure them that she would be perfectly alright, and Major Balfour had a sudden brainwave. "I am sure Maxwell will be on the train, too, he was not going to the dance, and he can look after them . . . or do you think we ought to keep him here, too?" he asked as an afterthought.

James and his uncle tried to see what was the best arrangement. If they got Captain Maxwell as well and made a big foray it would be obvious that they had been warned, but it seemed madness to turn down help. Surely they could think of a way around it.

Finally they decided to let the girls go alone in the train; Balfour was to collect his friend, go back to the post office in Galway and send off wires to Lady Richardson and someone to meet Valerie. "Then ring up this number," James hastily scribbled on a bit of paper and gave it to Balfour. "Ask for Richard Nesbitt. Tell him I want him to come to Aunt Lucia's at once and bring something with him. He may not be in, but it's a chance and he's the only one near enough to get here in time. Don't say anything else; it's not safe."

"But supposing he gets shot by the Fenians coming here— shouldn't we warn him somehow?" remonstrated Mrs. Hamilton.

"He won't. He'll have to come down the Clifden Road and you'll be on that with Paddy and Uncle Reginald so you must stop him and tell him what's happening. Now, you girls go and see what you can pack in. It will soon be getting dark and we must all be out of the house before then."

Mrs. Hamilton went up with the girls and Ellen generously gave her her only case, lying that she could easily squash her clothes into her "other" one. After all, she could replace clothes but her hostess could never replace her photographs and other treasures.

Even Valerie managed to throw out a number of things and filled up every gap she could with ornaments hastily brought to her by Ellen.

Poor Mrs. Hamilton was so dazed she could hardly make up her mind what to save, so the two girls set to and packed seven cases of mixed letters, books, flower vases, silver, jewelery, photographs, and small pictures—everything they could get in in the time.

The General also collected some things, and James brought Doyle to the door with the carriage, explaining that Miss Tristram was in great pain from her back and must be taken straight away to the Belfast train, and that Major and Mrs. Balfour would go with her to take care of her.

Doyle never raised his eyes and the only words he spoke were, "Would the mistress not come to look after the young lady, too?" When James explained that his aunt was very tired and was just going to take the dogs for their walk before going to bed, there was a look of despair in the coachman's eyes but he only touched his hat and prepared to load the cases onto the carriage.

James returned to the drawing room where everyone had collected again. Major Balfour had carried Ellen downstairs again, to augment the story of her back being hurt, and indeed it was not far from the truth. Her whole body had begun to ache furiously from the fall and her ears buzzed. Tears of desolation and fatigue pricked her eyes and she was bitterly ashamed of herself for so nearly giving way in the face of Mrs. Hamilton's wonderful control.

A strained silence filled the room, broken by the General, in awful calm, saying to James, "As soon as they are safely away, we will go for our walk with the dogs and Paddy can meet us as arranged; then we will have got all the animals out in case they mean to burn down the stables as well, like that ghastly business in Cork. You, Balfour, can think of some way of detaining Doyle in town—anything to stop him bringing back the carriage horses before the balloon goes up."

Ellen broke in. "But what about the servants? Will they escape, too?"

James reassured her darkly. "They'll be alright. They all know about it by now, I'm certain. Doyle heard it at the races, I could tell by his face. The others won't come back and Betha doesn't sleep here; she goes home as soon as she has cleared the tea."

He paused and rubbed his head as he tried to see every eventuality.

Suddenly Valerie burst out. "But this is frightful! You can't just walk away and leave this beautiful house to be burnt. There must be something we can do—there must . . . there must!"

There was a silence while everyone struggled with their feelings for Valerie's outburst expressed so exactly what was in all their minds.

Finally the General broke the silence for the second time, saying in a broken voice, "I'm afraid there is nothing we can do. These outrages have occurred before and will go on happening until the British Government makes some effort to protect its subjects. These," he said bitterly, "are the people to whom they want to give government over us, with no provision to be made for the safety of us who have spent our lives and our money here." He cleared his throat. "I think James's arrangement is the best we can do and the sooner we start, the better. It is almost sunset and if we go out after dark there is no knowing what might happen."

"I am coming back, anyway, uncle," said James, "and will hide inside the house to see if I can do anything when the trouble starts and be ready if the fire brigade does manage to get through. Where is the nearest telephone?"

"In Rossport," said his uncle, "and that's five miles, but you could take the cob out of the dogcart if Paddy gets back alright, and Balfour can have the fire brigade alerted. The rotten cowards!" he exploded. "They always choose a house that is far from help and communication. I don't imagine they expected you to be here to help us. Oh, if I could only get my hands on them!" He clenched his fists.

"If you have a gun, sir, I could use it," interrupted Major Balfour.

"Unfortunately I sent them up to Dublin to be overhauled a few weeks ago. The beggars probably knew that, too! I only have my old Colt, and I have given that to James, and my shotgun, which I shall take with me on our walk, just in case. I often do, so it won't arouse any suspicion."

"I have a little revolver," suddenly exclaimed Mrs. Hamilton, going quickly over to her writing desk. "I had almost forgotten; I used to carry it in India. My father gave it to me. He thought India was very dangerous!" She gave a bitter little laugh as she pulled open a drawer. "Here it is, and some ammunition." She pressed it into Major Balfour's hand and said almost inaudibly, "Don't be afraid to use it."

They moved out into the hall and James carried Ellen straight to the coach, saying in an earnest whisper, "Please take care of yourself and forgive me for sending you alone. I can't leave, though, dear knows, I would like to come with you. I must stay and see what we can do to help. You do understand? I'll come to see you as soon as I get back . . ." and then, as he saw the tears welling up in her eyes, he took her hand, "My dear, don't cry,

87

please. I hate you to go like this. It may be all a scare. Please God it is!" He climbed down and Valerie and her husband got in quickly. Mrs. Hamilton and the General squeezed her hand; there was nothing to be said and in a moment they drove away. Ellen's last glimpse, as they turned the bend in the drive, was of three sad figures walking back into the beautiful old house, the whole scene bathed in the peaceful evening sunshine. It was impossible to believe that they had not been dreaming. None of the occupants of the coach could say a word.

They reached Galway with twenty minutes to spare before the train left, and had plenty of time for the Major to get the suitcases loaded, carry Ellen on board, and make her as comfortable as possible. Then he said good-bye to his wife in the empty compartment next door. The presence of the little pistol in his pocket made them both very aware that there was danger and Valerie clung to him, suddenly very much afraid and not at all the hard-boiled Londoner she usually appeared. Presently he took her back to Ellen, wondering rather anxiously who was going to look after whom. Then he went off to the back of the train where he had the good fortune to find Captain Maxwell supervising the loading of his horse. He drew him aside and as coherently as possible in the time, explained the situation, punctuated by exclamations of "Good Lord!" "You don't say so!" "My God, I'd believe anything of these ba . . .!" as Balfour came to the end of his story. "Did you see what they did to me in the race? It'll give me the greatest pleasure to take a crack at them."

He gave his groom instructions to take the horse home and look after him, as he might not be 'round until the following evening; then the two soldiers walked back along the platform to wave encouragingly to the girls as the train pulled out.

The journey to Belfast seemed interminable. Every jolt of the train made Ellen ache more; she was desperately tired, physically and mentally, and the disastrous end to such a visit absorbed her thoughts completely. The senseless waste of beauty and the injustice to a couple of defenceless old people, who had obviously spent their time in kindness and consideration for others, overwhelmed her, so that she longed for the comforting presence of James as she had never done before. Now he was in danger and who knew what the outcome of the night might be. She leaned back against the padded seat, too tired even to cry, as the hours dragged by.

Valerie, on the other hand, was not too tired to cry and wept unrestrainedly for the first hour, until Ellen, in desperation, remembered the tiny flask of brandy James had given her in the drawing room just before they left and gave it to Valerie, who drank it all and promptly fell asleep, never stirring until the train pulled into Belfast shortly after midnight. Ellen would dearly have liked a "drop of the crayther" herself, but Valerie's silence was well worth the sacrifice.

Both Sir Charles and her aunt were on the platform to meet them, bewildered by the sudden change of plans and horrified by the look of Ellen, with her woebegone face, as she hobbled down from the carriage and threw herself into their arms. And what was this mountain of luggage which the porter was wheeling along to the car? Bit by bit they pieced the story together, and while Sir Charles ordered all the luggage except Valerie's to be stored in the office, Lady Richardson got both the girls into the car. They dropped Valerie with the Colonel's wife, as they thought she was in no fit state to be alone in her own little house, and Sir Charles thought it would be as well for the Colonel to know the full story in case either of his officers were to get hurt.

Soon they were driving away to Kilwater, with Lady Richardson holding Ellen's hand tightly in her own, exclaiming every now and then in horror as she told all that had happened. Arriving home, she was put straight to bed with a sleeping draught and did not stir until late on the following afternoon.

Chapter 7

Back in Galway, the grey clouds sprawled across the sky, shutting out the last rays of sun, making the little town even greyer than usual. Everything in the West has blue in it, from the deep purple-blue of the mountains to the pale silver-blue light reflected in the parchment-coloured rushes growing round the edge of every little lake. The narrow roads are pale grey-blue in the sunlight or a dark grey-blue in the rain; the water and the stones are so scantly covered with grass and moss that even the fields have a blue-grey sheen on them. On a bright day the effect is of incandescent, glorious beauty, but on an evening like this, as the two soldiers hurried through the town to the post office to send their telegrams, the effect of the blotted sky casting deep shadows on the streets was foreboding in the extreme.

Large numbers of the people were standing about in the sepulchral black clothes worn for great occasions, turning over the events of the races. From the public houses came great sounds of merriment and there was a steady murmur of talk through all the streets.

They had to force their way through quite a crowd at the post office, and while Captain Maxwell sent off the wire to Lady Richardson, Major Balfour tried the number James had given him. After endless delays, trying his impetuous nature to its limits, he got through to the house where there was further delay while the maid went away to look for Richard Nesbitt. The minutes seemed endless; outside it was getting darker and darker, and he had achieved nothing yet . . . he still had to find the fire station and then find the hotel where Doyle had been told to take the horses. At last a voice in his ear said, "Richard Nesbitt here, who wants me?"

Feeling like a fifth-rate actor in a murder play, he delivered his message. There was a startled exclamation at the other end of the line, followed by a pause and then, "Would you repeat that again, please?—Yes, yes, I'll bring something with me. Now, where are you speaking from?"

"I'm in Galway; I'm going back to Aunt Lucia's, too," said Balfour, feeling more ridiculous than ever.

"Right, no time to be lost," said the voice and hung up.

"Quick," said the Major, rejoining his friend. "Now for the fire station: James said it was up here. What if they won't go?" he exclaimed with some misgiving.

"Tell them the house *is* on fire, then they'll have to go," said Maxwell briskly, as they hurried along the street, trying not to attract too much attention to themselves. But the town was such a seething mass of excited humanity that hardly a soul noticed them hurrying past.

By contrast, the big doors of the fire station, the one warm patch of colour in the town, were fast shut and no amount of banging produced any answering sounds. Completely nonplussed, the two soldiers stared at each other.

"Try the back," called an old fellow from the other end of the road, signing them on down a side alley where they found a gate into a small yard. An old man was carrying a bucket of water into a stable and nearly spilt the whole contents when the two men appeared suddenly out of the gathering dark.

"Glory be to God! What's on now?" he quavered.

"It's a fire, man. Quick! We need the engine, it's urgent! Where is everyone?" they cried in desperation, looking 'round the deserted yard.

"Sure they're all at the races . . . Ye'll see no sight nor sound o' them 'til mornin'." The old man scratched his head. "Where d'ye say the fire is?"

"General Hamilton's, on the Rossport Road. Did you say they'd *all* gone to the races? God Almighty! What sort of a fire station is this?" fumed Balfour in despair.

91

The old man went on scratching his head with maddening deliberation before continuing in tones of helpful consideration, "Well . . . that's not to say *all* . . . there's wan or two would be at home, and there's Patrick in the station. Ye could wake him up and see what he says." So saying, he picked up his bucket and tottered into the stable.

Half a minute later the sleeping Patrick was nearly startled out of his senses by two enormous men suddenly appearing out of nowhere and shouting at him to "come on and stir yourself!"

"Get the fire engine out at once, there's a fire on!"

When he recovered his breath and his wits, his reaction was gratifyingly effective.

"Holy Virgin! The General's house and us with not a man on the place!" he exclaimed, applying his huge frame to the big doors with commendable speed. "Mick, the horses!" he yelled across the yard, as with the help of Maxwell and Balfour he wheeled the engine out.

"We'll have to help him and then we'll pick as many of them up as we can when we go through the town . . . they'll mostly be back by now."

They panted across with the harness as the old man brought out the horses, one by one, and their unaccustomed fingers fumbled with the heavy fittings.

At last Patrick pronounced them ready to go. "We're coming with you!" they shouted as they leapt onto the narrow steps and the engine shot out into the road.

"Ring the bell, and keep ringin' it 'til we see who we can get," shouted Patrick, as they ricocheted along the streets, figures leaping out of their way and hordes of little boys and dogs in hot pursuit.

"Is Jamie within?" he yelled, pulling up with a jerk, which nearly shot the other two into the gutter outside a public house. There was an answering roar from the crowd and a little man came running out, ramming his hat down on his head, and hurled himself on top of them, his breath heavy with whisky, as he climbed across and wedged himself amongst the hosepipes and ladders.

"Where is it?" shouted the crowd.

"The Ginral's" screamed Patrick, and the horses dived away into the gloom.

Never would Major Balfour and his friend forget that ride. Bouncing and swaying through the, to them, now almost solid darkness, there seemed to be no way of staying on the contraption except by sheer brute strength to hang on. Once they stopped on the outskirts of the town at a tiny cottage and picked up two brothers—huge men who came tumbling out of the half-door at the awful clamour of the bell and hauled themselves somewhere onto the back. The soldiers could not think where they found space on the already crowded engine but the pleasant tang of turf smoke that accompanied them was a great improvement on the concentrated alcohol emanating from Jamesey.

There was such an air of unreality, the clattering horses, clanging bell, creaking body work and flaring lights; there was so much noise and they were all so busy hanging on it was almost impossible to speak; but once, as they lurched 'round a corner, Maxwell could not resist muttering to his friend, "Going to look pretty silly arriving like this if there *isn't* a fire when we get there!"

"If we get there!" exclaimed Balfour, as he was thrown against a ladder. "If we go on like this we'll never get there!"

But soon the horses had to slow their pace on turning off the main road and the surface became rougher, the way more twisting. Suddenly, ahead of them, there was a wavering lightness in the sky.

"My God! There it is!" they cried as one man.

Patrick layed his whip to the horses' backs and they raced towards the light. Then, suddenly, it happened ... With a scream and a crash the horses plunged up the bank and the engine ploughed into a dark pile stretched across the road, throwing the men off in all directions.

"The bastards have blocked the road!" roared Balfour, picking himself out of the branches and tearing his clothes as he fought his way back onto the ground. "Come on! We'll have to clear it."

Maxwell and he hurled themselves at the barricade while the firemen, rising dazedly from the ditches, started to extricate the horses. The two leaders had gone over the bank and were entangled in the harness, while the wheelers leaned up against it, their sides heaving, with great drips of foam hanging from their bits, evidence of the hard journey they had come.

Working like traction engines, the two soldiers soon had one side of the road cleared and, looking 'round to signal the engine through, suddenly realised to their horror that, although restored to action, it was now lined up with the horses heads facing back the way they had come and the four firemen in the act of jumping up on it.

With one accord they flung themselves at the horses' heads. "What the devil do you think you're doing? You can't go back now!" they shouted in fury.

"We'll not go on . . . that's no ordinary fire . . . that's the Fenians' work. We can't stay here . . . we'd all be shot!" yelled Patrick. "Get on behind if ye wish to save yourselves!" and so saying, he hit the horses a great crack on their backs, so hard that they reared up and the Major and Maxwell were flung on their backs as the engine rocketed past them and vanished into the darkness.

For some moments they lay where they had fallen, wild with rage and frustration and not clear what to do next.

"Well! No use sitting here, cursing," groaned Maxwell, getting stiffly to his feet. "We'd better get on to the house. This is a nice party you brought me out on!" he commented wryly. "Which way do we go now?"

"Better get off the road and just head for the fire and pray we see these devils before they see us," rejoined Balfour. "Melville must be somewhere about and that fellow Nesbitt ought to have got here by now, too. If we can only join up with them we might be able to do something."

The two men moved off cautiously into the wood, Balfour much comforted by the feel of Mrs. Hamilton's pistol in his hand, and Maxwell armed with a stout stick, which he had pulled from the barricade.

"I suppose it's a good thing the moon's not up yet or we'd be seen, but it's darn difficult to move quietly when you don't know where you're going!" muttered Maxwell, accomplishing a complicated reverse turn with a small tree. In the black silence of the night the noise of their passage seemed as loud to them as a cavalry charge. Nothing else stirred. The whole wood seemed to be waiting, holding its breath, as they fought their way through the undergrowth. The harder they tried to choose their footing, the more dry sticks they seemed to set their feet on . . . and always the flickering light ahead grew imperceptibly yellower and brighter, and as it grew the bushes and bracken took on strange shapes, stirring with the tremor of the firelight. All at once the sounds of their passage were dulled into insignificance by the tearing crack of a rifle; once, then twice more, then silence more sinister than ever. A branch shook, there was a soft footfall on their right. The two soldiers froze. Another footfall and a stick cracked. There was a small click as Balfour cocked the little pistol.

Then, almost beside them, a voice exclaimed softly, "Thank God, it's you! What happened to the fire engine?" James appeared from behind the roots of a tree, his face covered with mud and his tie hanging down his back.

Quickly, in low whispers, they told him what had happened. He nodded. "I thought as much when you hadn't turned up by nine. I was working my way 'round to see if the road was blocked when I suddenly heard you coming through the wood." He laughed briefly. "You were making the most God-awful noise! I thought it was the entire Republican Army, and then I saw there were only two and was sure it must be you."

"Damned lucky I didn't shoot you, creeping up like that!" returned Balfour, somewhat nettled at the aspersions cast on his woodsmanship. "What do we do now?"

"We'd better get back. That was uncle's rifle we heard just now. Richard is with him but they may have run into trouble. They were in the rhododendron bushes at the bottom of the garden. If we go back down this ditch there's more shelter and less to tread on—come on!"

Finally, gaining the shelter of a dense clump of laurels on the side of the drive, they had the awful privilege of an untrammelled view of the blazing house. The incendiaries had done their work well. Flames poured out of every window, leaping and crackling, and a dense pall of smoke rose from the roof; the once white walls now rose black and stark against the flaming interior. The air was full of burning specks of wood and ash and the noise was unbelievable. A sucking roar, broken by the crashing of floor and walls.

For a moment they gazed in horror.

"Is there nothing we can do?" whispered Balfour desperately.

"Not a thing," answered James shortly. "There is a clear space 'round the entire house and one step into that and you're a dead man. These bastards have it down to a fine art!" He drew in his breath savagely. "In a moment we'll have to try to get 'round to Uncle, but we'll have to go singly and cover each other. I don't think it's a big party and I got one of them earlier but I lost track of them going to the road."

With his eyes on the flames Maxwell cursed away under his breath. "What a lot of rotten cowards they are! If only we could have got the fire engine here . . . though I doubt if even it could have done much, seeing the hold it's got."

"No," sighed James, "it was just a chance. If it had got here early it might have coped, but even so it probably would have been shot at. You can't really blame them for being afraid; anyone who stands out in front of that blazing inferno is a sitting duck."

"What happened after we left?" asked Balfour in a whisper.

"Oh," he answered, wiping the back of his hand across his face as if trying to recall something that had happened long ago. "We hung about a bit and then we called the dogs. It seemed a bit eerie just walking out and not knowing what would happen, but I think they must have taken time off for a bit. There didn't seem to be anyone about and we got my aunt safely to the road where we met Paddy and Richard, and we sent Auntie back to Richard's house in the trap with Paddy, and then we three crept back. It was absolutely quiet and I thought if I could get back inside the house I might be able to stop anyone coming in to set fire to it and Uncle and Richard could cover it from outside." He cleared his throat. "It was grim going 'round lighting the lamps to make it look as if we were all there; I felt like a traitor . . . and then I came down to the hall and waited behind the screen. For a long time nothing happened and then I smelt smoke. I was beginning to worry if I had made the wrong decision and was going to be roasted alive when I heard something knocked over in the drawing room and I crept in to see the rotten creature setting light to the curtains on the big window. I was so mad I forgot I had the Colt and just hurled myself at him; he was about half my size anyway and I laid him out with one crack on the head. But he must have used petrol for the curtains and half the room was blazing so I thought I'd better get out while I still could. There was enough light from the flames to make me a good target, so I hoisted him over my shoulders for a protection and ran for my life to the bushes." He paused for breath and continued with disgust in his voice. "Do you know, those rotten creatures would even shoot one of their own men; the bullets whistled all 'round me—if Uncle and Richard hadn't drawn their fire I don't think I would have made it. I dropped him at the end of the grass and made for where I had last heard the rifle. That was the most dangerous part of all; Uncle must have seen me before I saw him and only that Richard knocked his gun up I'd be a dead man now." He paused. "We watched for a bit, as the house gradually went up. There was no sign of any more movement. I shall never forget Uncle's face, sitting there, unable to do a thing while everything he loved burned before his eyes. I couldn't stand it any more, so I told Richard to keep near him while I went off to see if there was any sign of the fire brigade."

James rose, and holding his revolver at the ready, whispered, "They should be 'round the other side, near the rhododendrons, and there's a path going through them to the field. We'd better fan out, and for God's sake, keep quiet. Uncle is a crack shot, though I think it shook him a bit when he found out how nearly he got me!"

They reached the bushes without further incident and found the General and Nesbitt not far from where James had left them, the General still sitting with graven face watching his house burn. Even as they looked, the stone coping 'round the roof suddenly cracked and fell to the stone terrace with a noise like heavy gunfire.

Feeling that it was unbearable to sit and do nothing, James suggested that they all spread out and make a complete detour of the house, and if there was no sign of anyone around they might as well leave. Without the fire engine there was no possible way of putting out the fire, and the Fenians had probably gone already, knowing that the house was beyond help and not being too happy about the presence of other armed men in the bushes.

So they set out, James and the General keeping nearest to the house as they knew the ground and there was more likelihood of finding someone close to than far away from it. The other three spread out at twenty-foot intervals. Cautiously they crossed the path, one at a time, and disappeared into the thicket of flowering shrubs. It was grassy underfoot now, and they made no sound as they advanced slowly, covering each bush, but no shadow stirred until suddenly they were all brought up short by a long, solid yew hedge.

"Oh, damn the hedge!" the General exclaimed under his breath. "I'd forgotten all about it. The only way through is by the arch. We'll just have to get down and crawl through one at a time. This hedge is so dark that anything moving against it will show."

Slowly they all crawled through and spread out again on the other side. The air was heavy with heat and they were running into the smoke now as they skirted the back of the house. In the stable yard the smoke was lying so thickly it was scarcely possible to see where they were going, and at the top end where James was searching, he had to get down on his stomach to breathe. There could be nobody here. He was choking with fumes and ran desperately across to the outer archway where the smoke thinned out a bit and the line of the drive beyond became every moment more clear. All at once, as he ran for the gate, his foot slipped, he fell with a violent thud, knocking his head on the wall, and lay completely stunned, unable to move.

Meanwhile, the other four men, having lost sight of James in the smoke, had collected in the laurels on the other side of the drive. When he failed to appear after several minutes Balfour and Nesbitt decided to go into the yard to look for him while the General and Captain Maxwell hid outside, ready to cover them if necessary. They had barely got inside the archway when they found his body lying stretched upon the cobbles. With a gasp of dismay Richard ran to lift him and exclaimed in horror, "He's covered in blood . . . he must have been shot!"

"I never heard a shot," said Balfour. "Good Lord, where is it coming from? It's all over his back and there is a great pool of it on the ground. They must have riddled him . . . here, get his coat off!"

Without more ado they lifted him gently and pulled his coat off to reveal a perfectly clean white shirt. Gazing at each other in complete bewilderment, Bob Balfour found his tongue first. "It must be coming from his head," he said. They turned him over again gingerly and examined his head and face. Certainly, the face was very dirty and the hair had blood on it, but not much, and there was no wound to be seen anywhere. It was most extraordinary!

Hearing nothing from inside the yard and becoming very worried, the General and Major Maxwell now crept up and gazed with horror upon the blood-soaked corpse while Balfour explained the mystery of no bullet marks.

"You can't have looked properly," snapped the General, who was by now nearly exhausted. "Turn him over. You're just wasting time. Let me see." He was down on his knees with his arm under James's shoulder when the corpse suddenly opened his eyes and said, "If you'll just stop turning me over and over I'll be able to sit up in a minute . . . my head's splitting!" He put up a hand to it and brought it away quickly. "Good Lord!" He sat up. "I must have got an awful crack! It's all blood!"

"My dear James, lie down at once." Although exhausted, his uncle's voice was still authoritative. "It's not only your

99

head . . . your whole side is covered in blood. That's why we were turning you over. For goodness sake lie still and let us find out where the bullet went in."

"But I'm not wounded! I mean, I wasn't shot . . . I only fell and cracked my head!" stammered James, sitting up again and suddenly catching sight of all the blood. He stared. "That can't be my blood . . . that must be what I slipped in. My God! You must have got one of the beggars, Uncle, when you fired that time!"

"But then where's the body?" asked Maxwell practically.

"That's the point!" said Nesbitt, and they all started to search, but the smoke was so thick they soon had to give up and after a few minutes collected at the gate again, gasping for breath.

"I'm sure," said the General, "it means they have gone and taken the body with them. They wouldn't want to leave anything behind that would incriminate them and of course he may not have been dead. I thought I hit him, but I don't know where! Well, that's one who will not do this job again!" He turned to look long and bitterly at his blazing home and then, at last, taking a deep breath, he said, "Well, there's nothing we can do here. We may as well get back to your house, Nesbitt, and get some rest, for there'll be plenty to do tomorrow . . . though I don't know what we're going to do with it now." He muttered this last to himself as the five of them continued, still cautiously but together now, the circuit of the house. Even if there had been no need for silence, none of them could have spoken.

The man whom James had knocked out and left on the grass had also gone when they got to the end of the terrace.

"He probably got away himself," said James. "I don't suppose he was very badly hurt." He felt a slight sense of relief, not because of any sympathy with the raiders but because with the government in its present extraordinary state of mind they might well have laid a charge of murder on him, though they wouldn't have got far with that, with Carson the Attorney General on the defense, he thought grimly. Where, indeed, would they be without Sir Edward? It was just a tragedy that it did not seem as if he was going to be able to help the minority in the South. It was appalling to think of this kind of thing going on happening to people like his uncle and aunt.

When they reached the road after a long walk across fields, there was faithful Paddy with the trap and Nesbitt's horse, still tethered to the tree where he had left it. Paddy, the General, and the two soldiers squeezed into the trap and James got behind Nesbitt on his horse. The moon, as if to do her best to heal their sorrow, rode out from behind the clouds and bathed the countryside in unearthly beauty, as the little party set off across the stony fields.

Chapter 8

At first, when Ellen woke up from her drugged sleep, she could not account for the awful stiffness of her limbs, nor for the sense of doom hanging over her. Then she remembered; it was no bad dream and she hastily rang the bell beside her bed to find out if there had been any more news.

As soon as she saw her aunt's face she knew the house had been burnt; it had been no false alarm.

"My dear, yes . . . it is in the stop press news." Lady Richardson read out: "Irish mansion destroyed by fire last night. No loss of life is reported."

Ellen lay back in bed with all the blood drained from her face, and her aunt sat down and took her hand.

"Dearest Ellen," she said, "I know this is an awful shock. I never was at the house but I always heard it was a gem, and I know the Hamiltons were loved and admired by people of all classes. It makes one mad to think of it, but these things happen . . . it is the tragedy of Ireland—to bite the hand that feeds her. One just has to pray that they do not happen in vain; that one day England will care what happens. It makes one realise, more than ever, how right we are to fight up here to keep up the superiority of our numbers and prevent these dreadful things happening."

"They were so alone, no children to go to, and now they have nothing left. How could anyone be so low as to attack people like that?" asked Ellen indignantly, pushing back her hair.

Her aunt stroked her hand, as she said sadly, "It's all a mixture of spite and ignorance, mostly ignorance, I think. The Irish had very bad times: they are such simple people and a great many of the English families with estates in the South just sucked the money out of them when times were good but left them to starve and went back to England when the famine came. Of course, a great many people took very good care of their tenants, but, in a way, it is rather like the Civil War in America; because some people ill-treated their slaves, the whole South, and indeed the North, too, had to suffer; and yet many of those slaves were terribly well looked after, had the kindest owners, and were part of the family group. Stranger still, large numbers of those American families were of Irish extraction."

"But slavery was going on at the time of the American Civil War!" expostulated Ellen. "No one here has been starved for years. Why can't they forget about it?"

"Because they are not allowed to by the politicians," replied her aunt bitterly. "It doesn't suit them. Someone once said, 'If there were no politicians there would be no wars.' In this case, to suit their own selfish vote-catching they have revived a religious hatred that had almost died out, and in the name of religion men will commit the most frightful crimes."

"I see what you mean," said Ellen thoughtfully. "If they are in the right, they can't possibly go to hell for what they do! How can they be so blind?"

"Oh, it's easy enough if you have very little education; and they are so superstitious it makes them easy to work on."

"But surely the good ones could do something to stop it?" almost pleaded Ellen.

"That's the tragedy of their characters, they don't seem able to; every now and then a strong man rises and tries to give them a lead, but they are too scared to follow and so, often, in the end, he is shot in the back. And yet there is no one more charming than the southern Irishman. I think that is why one gets so involved and to love them so much: it is like the way a mother often takes so much more trouble over the naughty child than the good one—and so often loves it more, too," she added.

"But they are the same people up here. How is it that these things don't happen with us?" asked Ellen.

"Oh, they do! Though not so often, thank God! The Catholics are a small minority here and not so poor. We don't have many houses burnt down, but there have been lots of other so-called incidents: only last year, for instance, just before you came over, a Protestant Sunday School outing was attacked by a Roman Catholic organisation of fully grown men, in the hills on the way towards Derry, and a lot of the little children were badly hurt in the fighting. That was one of the main events that led up to the signing of the Covenant. People felt that if England insists upon taking away our protection, we must be able to protect ourselves. There have been quite a lot of murders in Belfast, too . . ." She noticed the circles under Ellen's eyes and rose to draw the curtains, reproving herself. "This is no way to make you feel better, telling you all these troubles. Now I want you to have a good hot bath and then go back to bed for the rest of the day and I will come back to sit with you and do my sewing. Charles is going to the club and will bring back any news that he hears there."

But no news came, apart from an account in the papers of the complete destruction of the house with its history and that of the Hamiltons, along with a record of the General's career and distinguished service abroad.

Two days later Sir Charles met James in the club and learnt that he had just brought Mrs. Hamilton up to stay with his mother. She was very much shaken and not able to sleep, and he did not think she would be well enough to see anyone for some time. They had thought it best to bring her away from the locality of the disaster but the General was still down there and James had promised to go straight back and help him save whatever he could from the debris of the house, make out claims for insurance and arrange for the care of the horses, etc.

He enquired very tenderly after Ellen and gave Sir Charles a graphic account of her accident, repeating his intention of coming to call and see her himself as soon as he was free. When Sir Charles suggested that he should let them know when he was back and come for dinner, he accepted with great pleasure. Later in the day, just before Sir Charles was leaving, a huge bunch of red roses was delivered, addressed to Ellen, with a card enclosed which said quite simply, when she opened it, "Your James" or was it "Yours, James"? It had obviously been written in a hurry and she could not be sure. How tantalising! The one could mean so much, the other so little. Yet in her heart she knew the quality of his feeling; the fact that he had found time to send the roses at all proved that. The significance of them being red, deep red, had probably escaped him altogether. She did not think he was the sort of man in the habit of sending flowers and therefore she was deeply pleased. She was so glad he was coming to dinner soon . . . there were so many things to hear about; certainly, a common misfortune was a great bond. She felt as if there was a small bit of his life of which she was a part, and it was an amazingly warm and glowing feeling.

A letter, written in a thick scrawly black hand, arrived a few days later, proved to be from Valerie Balfour, also enquiring after Ellen's health, and expressing horror, shock, and indignation at the confirmatory reports of the fire. She referred nostalgically to the pleasure of living in a nice safe country like England as opposed to the horrors of Ireland. She hoped they would meet at the regimental dance next month . . . if they were all still alive by then! Many exclamation marks . . . and she ended, "Lovingly, Val."

Although it was obviously intended to be a friendly, sympathetic letter, Ellen found herself strangely annoyed by it. Annoyed by Valerie's happy assumption that she must be longing to get back to England, and dismissing the anguish of a country divided against itself as a tiresome interruption in the pleasant routine of social life.

She found herself muttering about the stupidity and insensitivity of the English before she remembered that she was English herself and the realisation of this surprised her so much that she decided to go for a long walk by herself and try to sort this out.

It was a glorious day of sparkling light, with fluffy clouds and a haze of greenish gold over the bare tops of the trees. She decided to climb the hill at the back of the house where the waterfall tumbled abruptly from the open bogland down a tiny glen into the placid depths of the beechwoods planted by the first owner of the house.

Often, when she went for walks, she would come this way and sit for ages gazing into the clear brown pool below the waterfall, watching bubbles float across its mirrored depths, some to continue their gleaming way down river and others to immediate destruction against the rocks. Sometimes a dipper would poise for a moment on one of the stones, its immaculate white front reflected in the water as if to assure itself that it was really well turned out before darting off to some smart party up the Glen. Wagtails there were in abundance, grey and pied, cheeping busily as they fussed about the banks, and on a day like this there was an almost deafening outpouring of song from the woodland birds. The delicate whistle of the robins vied with the assurance of the blackbirds and thrushes, and, in the background, the seductive murmur of the pigeons.

Today Ellen felt in a mood not for the passive solitude of the pool in the Glen, but a longing for space, wide skies, and open fields, a desire to stretch her arms to the sun and tell everything that she belonged here. To do such a ridiculous thing it was necessary to get away from the controlled restraint of the trees to somewhere nobody could possibly see her.

So she climbed on up the steep sides of the Glen, pausing often to look at, and love, the play of light and shade in its depths, until she reached the top and the fields spread all around her. Poor fields up here, with hedges so thin they hardly qualified as hedges at all, and the thin grass almost completely taken over by rushes. A few clumps of blackthorn followed the line of the now tiny stream, and as Ellen appeared from behind the last wind-withered sapling, a curlew rose from the rushes with a scream of warning as it wheeled up into the air, its desolate cry accentuating the utter solitude of the land.

Ellen hugged herself with joy. This was what she loved, this wild undiscoveredness. Here on the green hills of Antrim she felt absolutely at home.

Far to the right lay the gleaming waters of Lough Neah, stretching so far that the southern banks were invisible and the blue Sperrins in the west shimmered and shrank in the haze. Beneath her and spread like a fan across the country were the rich green fields and occasional farm with its little sheltering line of beech trees. Byond the valley were low hills, sometimes blue, sometimes green as the cloud shadows blew over them, and away to the left the ground swept up with a tremendous crescendo to the sharp escarpment which overhung Belfast Lough.

Perhaps it was because her childhood had always been spent on the move that Ellen had never experienced this feeling of belonging before which gave her such joy; yet many of the places which they had lived in had been beautiful, sought after by travellers from all over the world. Here, in this sparsely populated, poorly cultivated, almost untouched country she felt utterly and completely at home. Even if she never married, this was where she wanted to live always. A rueful smile crossed her face; if she did not marry, it was going to be very hard to explain to her mother that she wanted to stay here just the same, though of course Aunt Marion would understand. This was obviously exactly what she had meant when she said that the country had entwined itself 'round her heart, and this must also be a little of what Eric Grantham felt, although it was combined for him with a passionate interest in the politics of the country.

Although Ellen only understood about them vaguely, today she felt quite certain that if this country had to fight for its freedom, she too would fight with them.

What an extraordinary thing it was, she thought, to come on this utterly peaceful place and find oneself thinking of war. What a paradox! And wasn't it perfectly true that all wars are fought to keep peace!

It was very hard to believe that there would be a war. How could people launch themselves into a conflict that would end hundreds of lives like Harry's, and, she thought shyly, James's, when there was this wonderful life to be lived in this wonderful

107

world. She lay back on the grass and allowed herself the luxury of a long happy dream before the wet grass reminded her that she had been there a very long time and she had better hurry not to keep the others waiting for lunch.

The days passed quietly but Ellen was so happy within herself she didn't mind how quiet they were. James had duly come to dinner and told them the full story of that ghastly night; in fact, despite the seriousness of the subject, he had managed to be most amusing at times, particularly when he described his fall in the yard, how he had been completely knocked out for a while and, coming to, had found himself being turned over and over in the smokey air, and for a moment thought he was a herring being kippered!

His uncle had now joined his aunt staying with them, and he said sadly that although they put up a wonderful front, they had aged beyond belief and seemed completely lost, unable to make any decision about their future.

"I find my home a very sad place at present, and, of course, we will not be able to entertain for some time, but I think if any of you had time they would love to see you and I am sure it would cheer Aunt Lucia up to see Ellen, if she would go."

Ellen eagerly agreed with this suggestion, but they had no personal conversation even when they were alone together for a few moments in the drawing room after dinner. They both felt it would be out of place to pursue their own desires in the shadow of so much misfortune for others. They had, after all, the whole summer before them, and there was a certain thrill in not rushing out to grasp too quickly the happiness which hung in the air between them.

James asked her to keep not less than three dances for him at the regimental ball. He would have liked to have asked for the whole lot, but contented himself with the hope of contriving a few more when they got to the dance.

He was terribly busy. Work had piled up in his office while he had been going back and forth to Galway helping his uncle, and the Volunteer Force was taking up a lot of his time, too. Another consignment of the urgently needed guns was whispered to be on the way to Ulster, and that gave him a great deal of extra work as he was on the committee which handled the secret dispersal of guns being smuggled in. There were still more than half the men without any, and it was generally felt that no amount of drilling could do as much for the morale of the people as the knowledge that their men had enough guns to defend themselves with.

Sir Edward Carson had just arrived over, again, on a short visit to James Craig. The urgent matters to be discussed had not allowed more than a short interval since his wife's tragic death. Sir Edward appeared at the meeting in deep mourning, but presided with his usual concentration on their problems. The English government were becoming perturbed about the quantity of guns being smuggled through to Ulster, and although it was not yet illegal to import firearms, the customs officers had been told to be much more alert and to hold for examination anything they considered suspicious.

In England the Unionists were working hard on Carson's scheme to try to force a general election on the government. Their plan to use £30,000 to provide speakers to attend all by-elections and tell the truth about the situation in Ireland was paying off well, but the government were still clinging like drowning men to the support of the southern Irish members of Parliament and were determined to drive the bill's final reading through before the autumn in order to keep their support. It was essential to step up the recruiting and drilling of the U.V.F. (Ulster Volunteer Force) in order to be ready for a crisis that might come any day. Plans were to be drawn up for an intensive campaign of speeches and reviews by Sir Edward later in the year, in all of which James was closely involved.

The main activity, socially, at this time of year was the Point-to-Points. Although the Richardsons had gone to several of them, James had not been there and Ellen found her taste for them somewhat dulled as she no longer enjoyed standing beside the jumps, thrilling to the onrush of the horses as they leapt past, yet from a distance one race looked distressingly like another.

She had not seen so much of her cousins either, as the new

governess Margaret McInnis, had now definitely got the upper hand and lessons took place both morning and afternoon.

Mr. Grantham, still a charming companion in his spare time, somehow seemed to have less of it lately, and Ellen had a shrewd suspicion that he sneaked upstairs to the schoolroom in the evenings to pass the time with Miss McInnis. She noticed in the mornings, when the family assembled for prayers in the hall, that he was watching for the little governess's arrival and the glances subsequently exchanged between them brought a delicate blush to Miss McInnis's cheeks. Ellen wondered mischievously if she was always praying on the same lines as Sir Charles, who read gruffly out of the huge old family prayer book, and was rather inclined to dwell more on the "confusion of our enemies" than on the personal welfare of the members of his household. She was obviously not the only person who noticed this charming idyll going on under their noses, for one evening Ellen and her uncle and aunt were in the drawing room, after dinner, when Sir Charles, was standing in front of the fire, coffee cup in hand, wondering where the devil he was going to hide the twenty-five rifles assigned to him out of the next shipment, his wife asked, "Charles dear, do you think it is wise of us to let Eric and Margaret McInnis continue to see so much of each other? He has absolutely no money and to marry so young and penniless a wife from a large country family, however suitable, would be like a millstone 'round his neck so far as his career is concerned."

Sir Charles came abruptly back to attention from a mental consideration of the old ice house in the thicket at the bottom of Miss McIlhenty's garden. Being a Roman Catholic, no one would ever think of looking in her grounds for smuggled guns; she would never know, and it had very easy access to the road.

"God bless my soul! Is that what's happening? I thought Eric was dying for love of Ellen here and Cynthia was going into a decline from jealousy! I must be very out of date!" He drained his cup and moved over to select a pipe from the desk in the corner. "Mind if I smoke in here tonight, my dear? You can open all the windows in the morning."

"Of course, Charles, we always do! And you always do!

But do be serious, I am sure they are in love and they are such a nice pair I should hate anything to happen that would spoil their lives."

Sir Charles came back with his pipe and a puzzled expression on his face. "But, my darlin' wife, if they are in love with each other already, what do you imagine you can do about it? 'Absence makes the heart grow fonder'—isn't that supposed to be the case, Ellen?" he asked, with a twinkle. "So if you send one of them away it will only cement their affection."

"But continuing to live under the same roof will only cement it the more!" argued his wife.

"Oh no! They might easily fight; it is one of the hardest tests of affection to see the girl at all times of the day—it is then you get to know her real character," Sir Charles said lazily, then, picking up a paper, he continued in a more serious tone. "Really, Marion, don't worry your head about them, they are blissfully happy, and let them seize what happiness they may. God knows what troubles are in store for us all next year!"

He tapped the paper. "I see this rotten government are now putting it about that Ulster intends to open her arms to the German Army in the event of England going to war with the Huns. Just because we have been driven to protect ourselves by buying guns from the only country known to be making them at present, Asquith chooses to forget that the whole cause of this trouble is that we want to remain under the king of England and they want to force us into a republic which loathes England and might easily be sympathetic to the Germans! It makes me furious!" He rattled the paper angrily . . . "It would serve them right if *we* sided with the Germans, and that is certainly what the Hun is hoping for!" He retired behind the paper again, fuming, great puffs of smoke emanating from his pipe, testifying to the state of his feelings.

"Do you really think there will be a war, Uncle Charles?" Ellen asked rather nervously, after a few minutes silence.

"There is certainly going to be a war, but whether Britain will have to come in or not is about a fifty-fifty chance." He replied without putting the paper down, and Ellen exchanged a

111

grimace with her aunt. After a while she went over to the piano and relieved her spirits by playing all the most peaceful tunes she knew, as if willing the Fates not to allow a war to be thrust on them.

She tried to fix her mind on the new primrose tulle dress she was going to wear at the Dorset's dance, but every way her thoughts strayed led to soldiers or military activities, or war, and the thought of Harry or James going away to fight and perhaps never return, filled her with such a feeling of frustration that finally she gave up playing, closed the piano, kissed her uncle and aunt "good night" and retired to bed to dream of "love and war."

Supposing James did ask her to marry him at the dance, what would she say? He was so attractive and good and dear, she knew she loved him with her mind, and she knew he would be the most sweet and loving husband imaginable; she was always completely happy in his company, and yet . . . her body was still quite numb after Desmond's kisses, as if, after reaching such heights of passion, it was now drained of the capacity to feel any but the most banal feelings. Just as a person who has been badly wounded often loses the power of sensation for a time.

She yearned to be loved . . . to warm herself in the security of his love, and yet she had been so badly burnt, she had an inner fear of committing herself to anything that she did not feel certain about.

Supposing she was to marry James and then after years of happy marriage recover those senses and fall in love with someone else? Would it not be far worse then to have married him and led him to believe in her love than to delay now? But, again, was it right to delay now, to keep him hanging on when she was not certain of her eventual feelings? She really did not know what she should do. She would have liked to have asked her aunt's advice, but that would mean telling her all about Desmond, and that she could not bear to do. It was a humiliating secret, locked up in her heart. Everyone knew she had been led up the garden path, but only she knew how completely; that she had asked him to marry her, that he had refused . . . that, she would never tell anyone. It was not fair to ask her aunt's advice if she was not prepared to give her all the information. She must fight her own battle herself.

But, then, if James was the man she would come to love, would he be prepared to wait? She couldn't ask him to . . . and supposing he didn't wait and she lost him? He was terribly sought after, a giant among his friends, admired and trusted by everyone. Why should he wait for her? And if he did not and she really loved him and lost him? She could not bear to suffer again as she had done over Desmond. She realised now that one did recover; indeed, she supposed one could get over anything in time, but the thought of it all made her feel so frightened that she felt she would rather die than go through it all again.

However, when the night of the regimental dance finally came 'round, war and worry were forgotten and love was in the ascendancy. She was in radiant spirits and flirted outrageously with a most pompous young man she was put beside at dinner. She arrived at the dance to find James already waiting for the first waltz and to make sure she had booked the dinner-dance and the last dance—another waltz, down on the programme as "Destiny," an old favourite. Ellen could not help but feel there was a plan behind his choice of dances.

Her programme was soon full and she was whirled away into a quick-step to the saucy rhythm of the "Teddy Bears' Picnic," all the rage that year.

When the time came for her waltz with James, she slipped into his arms with much the same feelings as a homing pigeon after a long flight enters its dovecote, and it was evident that James was aware of a similar feeling, for after they had circled the floor once in silence, he exclaimed in a voice of deep contentment, "How lovely it is to dance with you again! It seems a very long time since I have seen you. I was so afraid you had been really hurt at the races and it was maddening not being able to come sooner than I did to see how you were. I hope you have forgiven me?"

"But of course!" She smiled. "You had to help your uncle and aunt first, and, really, there was nothing the matter with me except for the surprise I got to find myself suddenly converted into a water jump!"

James laughed delightedly. "Well, certainly no one could say you looked anything like a water jump tonight. What a lovely dress that is! May I tell you how very beautiful you are looking?"

Ellen cast down her eyes. "Spare my blushes, please, Mr. Melville. I love compliments but I never have the faintest idea what to say in return—all the right answers sound so terribly priggish."

"Yes, I suppose they do; I never thought of that. People so seldom tell me that I look beautiful, I have had very little practice in replying," answered James sorrowfully.

Ellen chuckled appreciatively. "How too, too sad. But you can console yourself with the thought that to be beautiful is really no particular credit to the beauty. She—or he—just happens to have been made that way, whereas to be brave and resourceful is very much to the credit of the person who is so. By all accounts you were both after we left you so ignominiously in Galway!"

"Oh good gracious! I did nothing, and even that was to no avail. You can't fight people who only stab you in the back and take advantage of the old and unprotected." James deprecated, but he was obviously very pleased with Ellen's tribute, and although they did not talk much, giving themselves up to the pleasure of dancing, each was conscious of a deep, pervading sense of contentment.

When they were cosily ensconced at a corner table in the supper room, the talk reverted to more personal things and James anxiously tried to think of a good way to ask her to marry him. About a dozen different topics came under discussion and with each he was within an ace of saying the fatal words, and then the fearful thought intruded, *Suppose she says no?* He got cold feet and let the moment pass. He had never made a proposal before, nor even wanted to, and it never struck him that there would be any difficulty. It wasn't until this moment that he realised how great would be his loss if Ellen did say no and how much she had grown into his life and his plans for the future. Could he really expect a girl who had been used to the gay social whirl of London to give it all up and settle down in this province? True he could give her as lovely a home as any to be found in England, he was well-off and reasonably popular, but his whole life was bound up in Ulster and was it fair to expect her to adopt it, too? All these thoughts rushed through his mind as they talked . . . she looked so radiantly lovely and was so gay and sympathetic . . . come along James, 'faint heart never won fair lady!' . . . be brave! He opened his mouth to speak . . . and a gay voice broke in behind him.

"Oh, there you are! Together again! We have been looking for you everywhere . . . just look whom I have found, Ellen! He's been dying to see you again!"

Turning sharply 'round, James beheld Valerie in the very latest style of dress, in lavender chiffon, and close behind her a supercilious looking Hussar in all the glory of regimental braid and chainmail. He flashed a look at Ellen and saw that all the colour had ebbed out of her face as the Hussar bowed mockingly deep to her.

James rose as Valerie introduced him.

"Just fancy," she chattered on, "Captain Campion has been attached to our regiment temporarily. Isn't it marvellous? He has only just arrived and I told him there was someone here who would be delighted to see him!" She threw a roguish look at Ellen. "I thought it might compensate him for being exiled to this savage country. I have been telling him all about our experiences in Galway, Mr. Melville. Are you going to have supper? Oh, good! Then we can join you," she said, utterly oblivious of their stricken faces, and proceeded to sit down and ply James with questions about the fire in a most untactful way.

Ellen could have murdered her, and Desmond, summing up the situation in one glance, decided that it was just the sort to produce a really entertaining evening, and proceeded to pay great attention to Ellen, just as if they had parted on the best of terms, and forcing her into a *Toi et Moi* conversation, which gave the impression of the greatest friendliness despite Ellen's monosyllabic answers and desperate efforts to get James and Valerie back into the talk.

She could feel James's hurt eyes on her as Desmond leant over to take her programme from under her bag and she said, loudly and coldly, that all her dances were booked up. But Valerie was talking on and on in her high drawl, and all that James saw was the proprietary way Desmond behaved and the meaningful glance as he said to Ellen, "What? Not even a dance for me?" and he wished with all his might that he had not dallied so long over his proposal and could have been in a position, by now, to send this insufferable bounder to his rights. As it was, he wasn't at all sure now how he stood. Perhaps Ellen liked being eaten up like that! She did not look particularly happy, but maybe that was just embarrassment in front of him. That damnable Valerie seemed to think that there was something between them.

Oh, damn, damn, damn! Why did I delay so long, and why did this odious prattling female have to come along at this moment! thought he, miserably. There was Ellen's partner coming along to claim her for the next dance and he must go to search out that silly little Connolly girl.

They all stood up as Ellen passed, and she laid her hand fleetingly on his arm as she said, "I shall see you for the last waltz, and thank you for a lovely supper, James," and she gave him her warmest smile in an effort to retrieve the situation, which was not lost on Desmond.

The intervening dances seemed endless, but when the last one came around there was no sign of James anywhere. Ellen stared around the ballroom with beating heart and could not see a sign of him. What could have happened? He was not the sort of man who would cut a dance without a very good reason. Or was he so foolish as to think that she liked Captain Campion and taken offence and gone home?

Oh dear! Why was she so unlucky in love? Everything always seemed to go wrong just when she thought it was going to be perfect.

"Lady in distress?" queried the hateful voice of Desmond, who appeared through the door at this moment. "Has the gallant Mr. Melville not claimed his dance? Dear me, these Irishmen have no finesse. May I offer myself instead?" With a low bow he said, "You may remember you used to enjoy dancing with me!"

"I remember I hate the sight of you!" said Ellen, with venom, and, picking up her skirt, rushed through the door before he could see the telltale tears filling her eyes. Running into the powder room, she bumped into her aunt who exclaimed in amazement, "Why, Ellen, what's wrong? I was just coming to look for you to see if you were ready to come home. Your uncle has already gone to fetch the car."

"Oh, yes! Please, let us go home quickly," said Ellen, and pulling herself together with an effort, "I am so tired, I am dropping!"

"Get your cloak then, dear, and we'll go at once. I have said good-bye to the Colonel and his wife and that will do for you, so we can go out by the short way and not have to queue up," said Lady Richardson, guessing that there was a good deal more to Ellen's tears than mere tiredness.

A few minutes after they had left, James stepped quickly into the ballroom, looking for Ellen, and stopped with a puzzled expression when he could not see her.

Desmond, still smarting from Ellen's last words, saw him and decided to give the pot a stir. He strolled over and enquired, "Looking for Miss Tristram, Mr. Melville? I'm afraid she's given you the go-by, gone home some time ago. Fickle creatures, girls, aren't they?" He strolled away, leaving James cut to the heart by Ellen's apparent lack of concern for him and furious with himself for caring so much. He had thought that it was just because he was late she had given the dance to someone else, but now it seemed that she had left some time ago.

James was far too straight himself to expect another man to tell a lie, especially for no apparent reason.

What a rotten evening it had turned out, after all! First that odious fellow turning up at supper, and then that foolish woman fainting on the stairs and having to be carried out just when his dance with Ellen was due—though she evidently hadn't waited for it anyway.

Well, he had had enough. It was time he went home too. Maybe there was a reason. Girls often didn't know their own minds though he hadn't thought Ellen was that type.

"You idiot!" he told himself as he walked away to the park where he had left his car. "You just thought Ellen was perfect because you are in love with her, and now you are making excuses because she cares so little for you that she will cut your dance and go home without a second thought!"

So Ellen and James went their ways, wrapped in gloom, each grievously hurt by the others supposed lack of consideration. Whereas Desmond retired very happily to his quarters, feeling that there was going to be plenty of fun over here after all. That little Tristram girl had always intrigued him with her challenging ways and it would be fun to see if he could not win her back again while he was attached to this dreary regiment. He did not believe all these stories about guns and fighting. A little show of strength by the British Army and these Ulster Johnnies would pretty quickly draw in their horns. He should get back to his own regiment before the real war began.

Meanwhile he would get what fun he could out of the situation here, and some jolly good hunting in the South, too, if he was still here in the winter.

"What a pretty, pretty girl Ellen is," he mused as he put off his light, "and that bold-faced Valerie Balfour is amusing, too. Yes, Desmond my boy, I think you have landed on your feet again!"

At Kilwater Ellen lay awake, staring at the dim lines of daisies on her wallpaper and wondered what on earth she could do. "I can't stay here and meet him at all the parties, and I can't tell Aunt Marion why I dislike him so: she would be horrified at me letting myself be kissed in the garden just like a chorus girl. Yet if I go away, I won't see James and then it will never come right. Oh dear, I was so happy this morning and now everything is wrong and then there'll be a war and they will all go away and be killed . . .!"

So her thoughts ran on until she finally fell asleep and dreamed of endless files of soldiers marching through the garden while she watched the house burning and none of them would stop to help her put out the flames.

Next morning she wondered if she had not dreamed the whole thing. It seemed so much part of her nightmare sleep, and now the sun was shining and she could hear the cuckoo calling from one of the trees in the park. Surely things could not be so very wrong on such a lovely day as this? It really wasn't surprising the meet of the Foxhounds at Mount Stewart had to be cancelled last week. She could see the corn well up already in the fields beyond the sunk fence, and it was as warm as midsummer already. She must go out for a good long ride and get all these troubles out of her head. Maybe Desmond would be sent away again soon and Harry was always wanting her to go down to see his beloved regiment, so that would be a good line of escape, if only it wasn't for James!

And this is where we came in, she thought as she got up and began to dress, not having arrived at any solution.

Chapter 9

At the end of April Ellen received a long letter from a friend, now on her honeymoon in the south of France. She wrote blissfully of their happiness and hoped that Ellen would soon be married, too. She said a little bird had told her that Captain Campion had applied for an exchange to join the Dorsets in order to follow Ellen to Ireland and she expected to hear news soon from that quarter.

Ellen was very much annoyed at this, though it was flattering to think that such a construction had been put on Campion's movements. But how she wished she hadn't made such a cake of herself over him in the past. It was fairly catching up with her now. She was amazed to read, at the end of the letter, of the narrow escape her friend had had when leaving the train at Ostend. It seemed that just after they had left the station, their carriage had blown up! Fortunately everyone was out of it, and after a search another carriage was found to have a basket of gunpowder and petrol in it and leaflets from the suffragettes scattered all around. "It's really frightful," she wrote, "the damage they are doing. They have even started burning down houses now and leaving their horrid pamphlets around, as if they were proud of their work!"

Ellen was surprised to think she hadn't even noticed anything about this in the papers. It made her realise a little that the English, in the thick of these and other troubles, were not entirely to blame for their lack of interest in the Ulster situation, and how completely engrossed she herself had become in it.

Harry came up to spend a long weekend with them that happily coincided with the Newtownards' spring steeplechases on the third of May. The glorious weather was still holding and they all set off very happily without the usual paraphernalia of umbrellas and mackintoshes. Harry was inordinately pleased when Sir Charles yielded to his entreaties and allowed him to drive his beautiful new car the last half of the journey, from Belfast to Newtownards. This necessitated Ellen and her aunt squeezing into the dicky, to the detriment of their new suits, so as to give Sir Charles full scope if Harry turned out not so good a driver as he thought he was. At first they were very much alarmed at this result of Sir Charles's bonhomie: they clung to the sides and their hats and held their breath, but after a few tricky hills and narrow turns had been negotiated without accident, they were able to relax and before they came to the last long switchback into the town Sir Charles pronounced Harry quite safe and allowed the ladies to arrive at the races in style, on the front seat with Harry, while he folded his arms and pretended to be a footman at the back. Ellen wondered, as they bowled easily along, if driving was so easy that Harry could manage like this, could she not also learn? True, Harry had had lessons from a friend in the army, but wouldn't it be fun for her to learn secretly and then surprise them all one day by sweeping up to the front door in the car when they were assembling to go out somewhere!

She was greatly taken with the idea and resolved to see if she could not persuade Neill to give her lessons on the old car when no one was looking.

The race meeting was great fun. Held on a large, flat piece of land at the top of Strangford Lough, Ellen would have been quite happy just feasting her eyes on the shining, island-studded water without ever bothering about the races. However, she soon found that she needed to have her wits about her.

They had not been more than half-an-hour in the enclosure when Valerie swept up on the arm of Desmond Campion and said he had been pestering her for an introduction to Lady Richardson, and as he had known Ellen so well in England, might they watch the next race with them?

121

Lady Richardson was somewhat surprised at the suddenness of this effusion and could not help noticing Ellen's look of embarrassment. She wondered what was behind all this—could it perhaps be the key to the odd finish at the Dorset's ball? But as Desmond was laying himself out to be utterly charming, and was, indeed, being very amusing, she was perfectly happy for them to join her party, much to Ellen's apprehension.

In his short stay Desmond had already acquired a remarkably accurate knowledge of the betting and horses, and while they were all engrossed in marking their cards he moved over beside Ellen and pointed out possible winners for her to mark down. As Neill had already, at her request, given her a list and it was not the same, Ellen was very happy to be able to disagree with him and was soon drawn into an unwilling argument about their respective merits.

At which moment, James climbed up the stand beside them, and seeing who it was she was apparently immersed in conversation with, looked somewhat put out and moved over to talk to Harry about how feeling was running in the South.

"Do you soldiers get much mixed up in these outrages? These cases of cattle being driven off from Protestant farms and killed or damaged? That's all in your area, isn't it?" he asked.

"No, not really. It's the job of the constabulary—but we do sometimes help tidy up. It's a crazy situation! Officially we are on the side of the outrages as they are doing them in the name of the government, but they can hardly expect us to stand by and have shots being fired broadcast into people's houses, no matter what side they are on. It's pretty tricky sometimes; they go 'round digging graves and putting up notices threatening Protestant landowners! Not very friendly . . . but I expect it will blow over," said Harry cheerfully. "What really gets me down is that fox Birrell pretending all this is one huge joke of the pleasure-loving Irish!"

"How I agree with you!" exclaimed James in heartfelt tones, "and to hear him telling a man like James Craig—the straightest man who ever walked—that he doesn't believe a word he says . . . doesn't believe facts which he knows to be true—what sort of a secretary-general for Ireland is that? It makes one's blood boil. Any mention of Ireland has been safe for a laugh in Parilament for a long time, but I think the time is soon coming when they'll find that 'he who laughs last, laughs longest'!"

"Mmmm, I'm afraid it might," said Harry thoughtfully.

"Even the troops are beginning to notice that the Nationalists, whom we are supposed to be protecting, are the most unfriendly and spend their time writing rude articles about us in the press, whereas the Unionists, whom we are to keep down, have opened their homes to us and do everything they can to make us enjoy ourselves. Private Johnny Bull is no fool, and he is beginning to put two-and-two together. In the meantime we try to pretend we are one big, happy family . . . and, incidentally, we do manage to have a grand time. It's a wonderful country!" His eyes sparkled with enjoyment and James asked, in amusement, "You don't find you have to work too hard?"

Harry grinned back, "Oh, Lord, no! We have a grand time! Nobody seems to do any work down there. We hunt three days a week and race the other three. People are frightfully hospitable and there are dozens of parties. I'm making the most of it for we hear there are to be some tremendous manoeuvres in the autumn when Sir Douglas Haig arrives. He's a devil for work and there'll be no fun then. Can't afford to lag behind Germany and all that!" He laughed easily.

James said, seriously, "No, I gather their latest army manoeuvres have given us seriously to think!"

"Yes, I know, all those zeppelins! The Prince of Wales actually saw one flying when he was over at Friedrichshaven last month. But I still can't see them declaring war on their relations."

"Let's hope not," said James. "I may have to go over for the Vintage in the autumn, to the Rhine area. It will be very interesting to see what is going on!"

He noticed that Ellen was still talking to Campion and leant impatiently across to ask Lady Richardson, "Who is that fellow talking to Ellen all this time?"

She looked at her niece and made a tiny shrug: "I wish I knew," she said sympathetically. "I shall have to find out about him. He seems to have known her very well and yet I have never heard her mention him until he turned up today."

She bowed and waved a greeting to a tall and beautifully dressed lady who had paused in front of the stand and was waving up at them.

Ellen was much struck by her appearance and was on the point of asking her aunt who she was, when Campion supplied the answer in his inimitable way. "That is the future Lady Londonderry. Rumour has it that she has snakes tattooed all the way up her legs!"

"You would know that!" exclaimed Ellen, half amused and half disgusted.

"Have I shocked you?" he asked in surprise. "I am sorry. I forgot what a long time you have been away. You used not to be quite so easily shocked before you retreated to the provinces," he mocked her.

"I am not shocked, nor did I 'retreat to the provinces,' as you put it," rejoined Ellen rashly. "I came to live with my aunt when my parents had to go overseas."

"Indeed! You would be surprised to know how many people in London seem to think you retreated!" he said, with a malicious gleam in his eye. "In fact, I even heard it mentioned that it was on account of your having broken some poor soldier's heart, though others said it was because of some scoundrel whose attentions were becoming unpleasantly marked!"

"Well, you may tell your friends that I will thank them to mind their own business," declared Ellen with feeling. Really, it was too much to have him laughing at all the unhappiness he had caused her, and yet it *was* rather funny when put like this!

He beamed at her. "Of course I will . . . they will be so interested to know how quickly you have found new . . . er . . . 'interests' over here!" He glanced significantly at James and Ellen was furious to find her face going a rich shade of beetroot. It was too much!

"What a pity you can't find yourself some 'new interests,' as you call them, over here and leave me alone!"

He was delighted. "Oh, but I don't want to leave you alone!

I am very happy with my old friends . . . that is one of the nicest facets of my character. I am only so sorry I can't say the same for you!" he teased.

Ellen turned her back on him. She could not help laughing at his effrontery; it was that which had first attracted her towards him, and now that he could no longer hurt her, he was very amusing. How she wished she had always been able to treat him so dispassionately instead of making such a fool of herself! She was feeling thoroughly piqued with James for cutting her dance the last time they met, and there he was, talking away animatedly to her aunt as though she herself did not exist. Perhaps it would do him no harm to see that someone else admired her! She was in no danger of succumbing to Campion's charms again, but from the safety of her aunt's circle she could allow herself to be amused. She marvelled that eight short months could have effected so complete a cure, and was filled with a sense of elation as she moved over to join her uncle on the pretext of asking him if the very striking man with Lady Londonderry was her husband.

"Yes, indeed, he is," Sir Charles told her with enthusiasm. "Fine fellow, isn't he? In every way—a great leader and a great friend of Sir Edward Carson's, who stays with them at Mountstewart for some part of nearly all his visits to Ulster. Indeed, I think the only time he ever rests is on his short stays with them!"

As James and Lady Richardson joined them now, Sir Charles observed, "We are just talking of your idol, James!"

"Sir Edward?" exclaimed James, laughing as he bowed to Ellen. "My idol, certainly, but also a bit of a slave driver, I'm afraid. He has just mapped out a plan of campaign that is going to keep my nose to the grindstone for the rest of the year!" he said ruefully.

"How do you mean?" asked Campion, who had followed Ellen.

"Oh, you'll see soon enough when the plan is put into action. At present it is not for publication," said James lightly.

Slightly nettled at being turned off like this, Campion expostulated, "Surely you can't imagine that drilling a crowd of

125

peasants is going to coerce the government? I am amazed that a man of such undoubted talent as Carson should waste his time like this!"

There was a moment of silence and then James said quietly, "It is no waste of time. These men are deadly serious and they are no crowd of peasants. They are the cream of the country, steady and determined men who mean to fight for their rights."

"Oh come!" sneered Campion, easing a small cheroot out of his case and offering it 'round. "They can't possibly stand up to the British Army; and I understand the government are quite prepared to reinforce our garrisons if need be."

"Well! I think that's the limit!" chimed in Ellen hotly. "How dare they order you to suppress people like . . . well, all our friends are Volunteers . . . James is one himself!" she exclaimed eagerly, and then, realising from the look in Desmond's eye that he would probably find no objection to suppressing James, she added, "and Uncle Charles is one, too, and that means that Aunt Marion and I would stand with him. Do you imagine you are going to suppress us?" She was so excited in her defence of the Volunteers that she completely missed the look of ardent admiration on James's face as she leapt to his defence, and it quickly became more guarded as Campion, tapping his cheroot on his case, drawled provocatively, "My dearest Ellen, one doesn't attempt to suppress women; one takes them captive and then converts them to one's own point of view by whatever means one chooses!" He looked at Ellen thoughtfully. "Rather an enjoyable procedure, I should think. The British Army is much too much aware of its limitations to try to suppress someone like you!"

Seeing the light of battle in Ellen's eye, Lady Richardson interposed hastily, "Let us hope this remains only a laughing matter, Captain Campion," and then added, with her lovely smile, "I have only one complaint about Ulster's Defence and that is that it tends to oust all other topics of conversation. I came here to watch the racing," she said with gentle emphasis.

"We stand rebuked," murmured James. "May I make amends by taking Ellen down to see the horses before the next race?"

He offered Ellen his arm, which she took in silence, not being quite sure what to say after the inconclusive manner of their last parting, and being still very frustrated at not being able to finish her battle with Desmond.

But James was not at all deterred by her silence and when they reached the paddock he turned his back firmly on the horses they had come to see and observed, in a calm voice, "I must tell you how much I admired you for standing up to your friend Campion in our defence just now. I can almost find it in my heart to forgive you for cutting my dance the last time we met!"

As she looked up indignantly to meet his direct gaze, her heart gave a huge bump and she felt decidedly flustered but stuck to her guns. "You can't put me in the wrong like that and then say pretty things to cover up your attack. It wasn't my fault, I waited as long as I could and when you didn't come and Aunt Marion wanted to go home, I couldn't very well stay longer, could I?"

"That wasn't what I heard," he answered, regarding her searchingly. "Your friend, Captain Campion, told me you had gone home before the dance began and I thought the least you might have done would have been to tell me—your partner!"

It was too much to be reproached for something she hadn't done. "Oh! And I suppose you believe him and not me?" she exclaimed in haste. "Why do men always club together? You hardly know him and yet you take his word against mine!"

"Ah, Ellen, please don't get angry with me . . . you can hardly blame me for believing him! He seems to be such an old friend of yours . . ." He paused to let the implications sink in, and Ellen felt the tiresome colour rushing into her cheeks again as she sought to disclaim friendship with Desmond. "Just because I knew him well in the past doesn't mean that we . . . that he . . . that . . . that he knows everything I do!" she stammered as she searched for the right words, aware that she was not giving at all the right impression and somehow still seemed to have been put in the wrong, and here was James magnanimously suggesting that they "Say no more about it . . . just don't ever stand me up again, please. I am too good a friend of yours to be treated like that," he finished firmly. "Now here are the horses going out and we barely looked at them!"

He turned to lean on the rails and made comments as the horses filed past them, effectively cutting off the remonstrance Ellen was about to make. As she followed him to make a small bet on a handsome bay with four white stockings, she realised that he had never told her where he had been when he was late for her dance. She was dying to ask him, only the seething crowd around the bookies made it quite impossible to follow any sort of conversation, then they were joined by Harry on the way back to the stand and the opportunity was lost.

All the blame had been put on her and she had been so busy defending herself that she had never asked him why he had been late. It was quite clear that Desmond, typically, had been making trouble, but why had James not told her? Was he just cleverly putting her in the wrong to cover up his own fault? She was sure he wouldn't do a thing like that—there must be some good reason, but, all the same, once the idea had entered her head it was hard to get rid of it altogether.

James stayed with their party for the rest of the meeting but there were no further opportunities for private talk. Ellen was feeling a bit sore with him and accordingly hid her feelings by affecting great gaiety with the others which delighted them all and did much to restore her self-respect. Harry was also in very good spirits. He had had the fortune to fall in with the youngest Miss Taggaret who was as pleased to see him as he was to see her. She was looking particularly bewitching in a periwinkle blue wool suit exactly matching the colour of her eyes and Harry wondered how it was that he had failed to remember how brilliantly blue and sweet they were. He now proceeded to make up for lost time by bringing her to join the group around Lady Richardson. The party had increased considerably and were split into two circles. The younger ones were chaffing each other about the races and forthcoming social events, particularly the rumoured visit in June of the First Battle Squadron to Bangor

Bay. It was years since a full-scale visit had been made to Belfast by the fleet, and although to the older people there was a current of unease about the timing and the intentions behind the visit, to most of the younger ones it spelt nothing but gaiety and entertainment. Dances, luncheons, yacht races, and expeditions to all the local beauty spots were discussed, a slight piquancy being added to the conversation by the presence of so many army officers, who, although much appreciated by the ladies, naturally could not compete with the glamour of a fleet of battle-ships arriving on a "once-in-a-lifetime" occasion. Ellen particularly looked forward to this visit as she not only knew a number of the officers but had a very warm corner for the navy in her heart. Was she not a naval daughter? The navy was part of her life.

Nothing could ever quite compare with the magnificence of the battle fleet. No land-bound party could conjure up a fraction of the thrill of travelling by picket boat under the charge of a fantastically young and gilded midshipman across romantically smooth or frighteningly rough seas to a great forbidding grey battleship, to find that the inside of the monster was a mass of gaily coloured bunting and shining silver and brass, with immaculate sailors and white-coated stewards hurrying about with all the trappings for a gala evening. As Ellen enthusiastically described all this to the Miss Taggarts she was pleasantly aware of Desmond's lack of enthusiasm for the turn the conversation had taken. Harry remained quite unperturbed as he would not be in the North when all this was going on and was used to these eulogies coming from a naval family, but he could not forbear to interject slyly, "Don't forget the night of that party in Malta when the storm got up suddenly and it was too rough to take the visitors home! It wasn't such a glamorous evening then and you didn't look particularly glamorous when I found you . . . alright, I won't go on!" He laughed at her. "No, give me a good regimental occasion any time, where you can depend on the floor staying firmly under your feet!"

"Strangely enough, I always got the impression that you enjoyed a good house dance, too, Ellen," chipped in Desmond.

"Most regimental bands leave a good deal to be desired musically no matter how colourful they are and I have yet to find that the naval ones are any better."

"Oh, I think a dance depends on who you are with," softly whispered the youngest Miss Taggart and then turned a rosy pink as she received a quelling glance from her elder sister. Ellen eyes flew impulsively to James's face but he was immersed in politics with her uncle and had obviously not heard the comment. She was uncomfortably aware, however, of Desmond's quizzical gaze noting the direction of her look and wished she had not given herself away so.

Fortunately, at this moment when she was at a loss to keep the conversational ball rolling, Valerie Balfour announced that, "The bookies are now paying out," and she would be most grateful to anyone who would collect her winnings for her.

"I have made quite a lot of money today," she told them happily. "You must admit the betting is a good deal easier to understand at this meeting than at the last one we were at together, Ellen, mustn't you?" and she proceeded to tell Desmond all about the meeting in Galway, to his evident amusement. Ellen felt it was rather bad taste to make such a joke out of it with James within earshot, even if he did affect not to hear. She wished he wouldn't be so aloof. He obviously had no intention of competing with Desmond and she felt somehow she had been relegated to the "children's" circle and could not very well desert to the "grown-ups" without attracting attention. Desmond stuck to her side all afternoon, no matter what she did.

She was relieved when Valerie took Desmond's arm and said, "Come on, Desmond! I would never have suggested joining Ellen if I had thought you would remain glued to her side all afternoon! You came here to look after me while Bob is taken up with his race, remember? Well! Now that it is over I think you ought to take me back to him in case he is worried at my long absence!" She laughed ironically, "I never realised when I married him that I had married his horse as well! What a blessing Blue Stocking doesn't dance or I should really be left in the cold!" she said ruefully as they said their good-byes.

Soon it was time for them all to leave. The sun was sinking rapidly behind Scrabo Monument on top of the hill behind them and with it all the warmth died out of the air and long shadows crept across the race course. The hazardous business of getting the car out of the parking ground and along the narrow road without frightening too many horses had to be attended to, and as Ellen watched her uncle dexterously handling the machine, she renewed her determination to persuade Neill to teach her how to drive. What fun it would be to see all their faces when they found out! She must lose no time in starting lessons.

Neill, of course, was like putty in her hands. He objected strongly at first, as it obviously offended his sense of dignity to think of a young lady in charge of a dangerous piece of machinery like a motor car, but he was not proof against her wheedling, and so for the next few weeks, whenever Ellen was quite sure that none of the family would be at home, she used to slip out to the yard and blarney Neill into giving her a lesson on the big Argylle. It would have been hard to say which of them was the more nervous: Ellen was so afraid of doing something that could damage her uncle's precious car, and Neill was so afraid of being discovered.

Of course it wasn't possible for a beginner to learn to change the gears without a remarkable grinding noise on a number of occasions. When this happened, Ellen almost had to hold Neill down by force to stop him climbing down and hiding in the bushes until he was sure no one was coming. As a result of this lamentable nervousness they were never able to go very far afield for fear of discovery, but this had the advantage that Ellen became extremely skilled at turning and reversing in the narrow drives and stableyard. On the one occasion when she did persuade Neill to take a chance and accompany her outside the demesne, she had the thrill of letting the big car really travel along the road and was going at the glorious speed of thirty miles an hour when he got into such a panic for fear they would have an accident and be "lifted" by the police that she took pity on him and turned for home much sooner than she had originally intended.

131

Driving the Argylle, perched high on the blue leather seats, gave her a tremendous sense of exhilaration and did much to take her mind off the sense of deflation that had overtaken her relationship with James. She had only seen him twice since the races and although he was certainly still attentive, there was a considerable reserve in his manner, whereas Desmond turned up at everything and left no stone unturned to make it appear that he and she were very close. If only James would compete, it would be so much easier to show him that she much preferred him to Desmond. But he just remained courteous, charming, and observant, in the background. It was quite maddening!

However, today her mind was fully taken up with the thrill of driving. In consideration of Neill's deplorable state of nerves she pulled the car into one of the long narrow roads leading back straight across the valley to Kilwater. It was a shame to have to go back so soon on such a lovely evening. Sir Charles had gone over to England for the Doncaster races and, for once, Aunt Marion had gone with him. She hated the journey and usually stayed behind, but on this occasion it was so long since she had gone with him that her conscience pricked her and they planned to stay some time and do a round of visits to friends as well. The children were all out at a tennis party, under the charge of the old groom in the dog-cart, so there was no real danger of discovery, and it did seem at last as if she had mastered the intricacies of the gear box. She hadn't made one bad change, yet, today.

Her original plan had been to drive the complete circle of the hills, this would have taken about two hours and given her ample opportunity to enjoy the gorgeous views but with Neill in such an unhappy frame of mind it wouldn't be fair to stay out any longer. She was bowling along a side road at top speed, with him clinging on beside her, when she became aware of a figure about a hundred yards ahead, on the edge of the road, holding a bicycle and urgently waving her to slow down.

Her first thought was to pretend she hadn't seen him and sweep past looking in the opposite direction. It was not very likely that the car would be recognised so far from home. Then the voice of doom spoke up beside her—Neill's—in accents thick with unspoken, "I told you so's" and "We should never had done it's."

"It's Mr. Grantham, miss! Ye'd better stop."

"Good gracious, so it is!" exclaimed Ellen in surprise, and she couldn't restrain a very saucy smile as she brought the Argylle to a dashing halt beside him. His face was an absolute study as he recognised the driver.

"Good afternoon, Eric! Is there anything I can do for you? You seem a little anxious, or do you wave at all the girls?" she asked cheekily.

"Well, I'm . . ." he recollected himself and grinned "I thought it was the Kilwater car when it first came into sight, and then I saw it was a lady driver and knew it couldn't be! With Sir Charles and Lady Richardson away I didn't think Neill would take his lady friends out for a drive." He shot a wicked look at Neill, who grinned sheepishly. "It just shows how wrong one can be!" he concluded innocently. "Imagine him having this frivolous side to his character! However, I am delighted to see you . . . for I have buckled the wheel of my bicycle a mile back, and if I had had to walk all the way home from here I would have been terribly late for Michael's Latin hour."

He proceeded to pick up his bike and made as if to get into the car, but was stopped by a wave of the hand from Ellen.

"Pray do not be in such a hurry, Mr. Grantham," she said very grandly. "Neill and I have by no means decided yet if we shall take you home! What do you think, Neill?" Then, not waiting for his answer, she continued, "We can only take you up if you absolutely promise . . . swear on your honour as a . . . as a . . ." she sought for inspiration, her face all screwed up—"I know! On your honour as an Ulster Volunteer! That you will never convey to Uncle Charles by thought, word, or deed that I have been using his car . . . or to anyone for that matter . . . it might get back to him. Will you promise that?" She looked at him earnestly. "It was entirely my idea and I don't want Neill to get into trouble."

"Oh, I'll certainly promise . . . though you realise that this is blackmail! On one condition—that you tell me all about it and . . ." he paused, giving her a measuring look. "I think I won't say any more until I'm safely in the car . . . I don't want to have to walk home!"

She laughed. "Alright, can you put the bike in the dicky?" Neill strapped it on and then rather doubtfully squeezed in beside it while Eric climbed up beside Ellen. "I promise I'll go very carefully, Neill, with you behind me," called Ellen over her shoulder as she let in the clutch and they moved off.

"And how long has this been going on?" asked Eric from the safety of his seat in the car.

She threw him a look of reproach. "You promised . . ."

"Yes, I know . . . I won't tell anyone, I'm just asking a civil question and . . ."

"Hoping for a civil answer!" concluded Ellen, laughing. "Well it was when Harry drove us to Newtownards races the other day . . . I couldn't see why I couldn't do it, if he could! And you never know when it might come in useful. I might be the only one who could dash for the doctor or something like that. If I got really good at it I might become a lady chauffeur and earn my living!" she finished brightly.

"I hardly think that is likely to become necessary," said Eric dryly, "though you seem to have a very dashing style of driving."

"Thank you," she bowed. "This is the first time I have really felt *au fait* with it, and now I suppose I had better not do it again, as pride comes before a fall and it would be terrible if I damaged the car. I do pay Neill to replace the petrol, but I suppose now I have learnt it would be silly to go on. I just want to be able to give everyone a big surprise one day!"

They drove along in silence for a while, Ellen concentrating on her performance with the car, when it occurred to her to ask the tutor where he had been coming from when she overtook him.

He looked very sheepish, as he admitted that he had taken Miss McInnis to Belfast to see Sir Edward Carson's departure for the Larne Steamer by train from the Midland Station before putting her on her own train to Armagh for the half-term week-end that she was spending at her home.

"Oh!" said Ellen with interest. "Was it a very special departure? I didn't know."

"Well, Margaret had never seen him and you know what ardent Unionists her family all are." Ellen noticed how the governess's Christian name had slipped out quite naturally and was much intrigued, but Grantham went on without noticing. "I don't think it was meant to be anything very special . . . no organisation or anything . . . just that the people do worship the ground he treads on and it turned out to be the most tremendous reception he has ever had. It was absolutely thrilling to be there!" He paused reminiscently.

"Go on: do tell me what happened!" urged Ellen, turning up the last road below the drive gates.

"Oh, there was the most enormous crowd. Everyone seemed to have got the same idea as me, and then all the dockers were coming out of work and they brought detonators and put them on the railway. At first the train could hardly pull out for the crowd round it, cheering and screaming. He had to make a speech and then everyone wanted to shake hands with him. Finally Dawson Bates and the Duke, who were with him, made it clear that he must go or they would miss the boat, and then it was bedlam! The whistle blowing and the detonators going off and the shouting . . . you never heard anything like it! At first I wasn't a bit sure that it was all for love! It sounded awfully like gunfire! But he was as calm as anything, and of course it was all terrific fun. These people are so dour and hard-headed one doesn't expect them to get into such a state of excitemnet, but there was nothing dour about them today! My goodness, you should have heard them!"

"Wasn't Margaret frightened? I would have been. I think crowds are terrifying when they are excited!"

A curious grin came over Eric's face as he answered, "You know, the funny thing was I thought she'd be frightened, too . . . she's such a little thing . . . but it must be in the blood! I'd got her up on a porter's trolley, loaded with boxes, so that

135

she could get a good view . . . and there she was, dancing up and down, shouting and waving with the best of them and I was the one who was scared! Everyone was pushing all around me and I was trying to hold onto her in case she fell off! And then they pushed the trolley over my bicycle wheel—that's what buckled it! However, they were all terribly friendly and, in the end, when Sir Edward had gone and the crowd thinned out a bit, a very decent fellow with a gig gave us a lift to the other station where we put Margaret on the train and then he brought me and the bike halfway home!"

"And I brought you the other half," said Ellen, turning in at the gates. "You certainly fall on your feet. I don't believe that anything has happened in Ulster since you arrived that you haven't managed to be in the middle of!"

He laughed happily, "Well, I hope it continues like that, for it looks as if a great deal more was going to happen soon and I'd hate to be out of it! My only worry is that if Michael continues as well as he is doing at the moment, he will pass into his school next term and then I'll be out of a job and it may not be easy to get another one over here."

"Gosh, I hadn't thought of that!" exclaimed Ellen. "It would mean leaving the Volunteers, too. How awful!" She thought to herself, *What about Miss McInnis? I wonder if Uncle Charles has thought about all this. His love life seems to be just as complicated as mine! I wonder if I could help at all about the job?*

She drove into the garage, switched off the engine, shook Neill warmly by the hand, and thanked him a thousand times for being so patient and brave in teaching her. "I never dared to thank you properly before!" she laughed. "I was so afraid it would provoke the gods into making me break the car up or something awful, but now I think I've learnt enough and I'll be good and not ask you to take me out any more. I don't want to ruin your reputation forever!" she said mischievously. "What would Mrs. Neill say?"

"Och, away wi' you!" mumbled Neill, all embarrassed. "But I'll not say I'm not glad ye have the sense to stop before there's trouble. I wouldn't like to meet Sir Charles if anything happened to his car!"

Ellen suddenly felt very much aware of the risk she had been taking and felt rather ashamed of putting him in such an awkward position, but covered up her feelings by clasping her hands to her chest and saying impishly, "Och! I do hope we can trust Mr. Grantham not to say anything, otherwise every creak and squeak in the car for months will be my fault. It will be, of course, my fault as far as Neill is concerned, anyway. I realise that . . . but I have learned not to be afraid of him! It's Uncle Charles I'm worried about . . . I've got to live with him!"

"Poor little orphan Annie!" said Eric unsympathetically. "I promise I won't tell. I won't even tell Michael, who would give his ears to learn, too!"

Ellen and Neill looked so horrified as they burst out with one voice, "Not Michael . . . certainly not Michael!" visualising themselves being blackmailed into teaching him to drive in such tones of alarm and consternation that Grantham burst out laughing.

"Alright! Not even poor misjudged Michael!" and they all shook hands as if they had done a deal in fat cattle, before going their several ways.

Chapter 10

When Sir Charles and Lady Richardson got back from Doncaster, Lady Richardson decided that she must do something for Ellen, even if it meant going against her firm policy of noninterference. She had noticed the withdrawal of James and that this new Captain Campion seemed to be insinuating himself into their company all the time, also the corresponding depression in Ellen's spirits.

She also realised that if James was foolish enough not to realise that Ellen much preferred his company to Campion's and left her alone, then she was bound to have to talk to someone, and that someone was sure to be the smooth and determined captain. She couldn't stand around alone waiting for James to seek her out; not that there was any danger at all of her being left alone—there were always dozens of young men eager to be with her, but this Campion had a very good way of riding them off; nothing you could really put a finger on but he was more sophisticated and less scrupulous, and, of course, he made a great deal out of their previous acquaintance.

Lady Richardson would very much have liked to know just what that had consisted of, but Ellen had offered no confidences so all she knew was that Harry had been very cool when introduced to him and had immediately pulled Ellen aside and asked, "Is that the fellow I heard so much about last year? What's he doing up here?" But as he had chosen to ask this almost within earshot of everyone else, Ellen's reply had been inaudible and no more was said, leaving Lady Richardson to draw her own conclusions.

She decided to give a dinner party on Derby Day, June 5th, and the young people could dance afterwards in the drawing room with the carpet rolled up. Sir Charles always got very excited about the Derby, and if he did indeed succeed in backing the winner, it would be a very fitting way of celebrating. On the other hand, if he was on the loser, it would cheer him up.

While he drove into the club to have lunch and be near at hand to hear the results, Ellen helped her aunt to do the flowers, and spent a very happy afternoon arranging a bank of pink and white peonies against a background of copper-beech leaves. She was very pleased with the effect against the eggshell walls of the drawing room and was full of happy anticipation about the dinner party.

Harry had returned to the Curragh after the meeting at Newtownards, but the Miss Taggarts were coming and the adjutant and subaltern from the Dorsets, stationed at Hollywood Barracks on the other side of Belfast, also the amusing land agent with the stammer, Miss O'Neill and her brother, Lord and Lady Templeton, and two of their daughters, and a Lieutenant John Montgomery, who was doing temporary aide de camp to the naval officer in charge at Belfast, who was very busy arranging for the visit of the battle fleet in two days' time. In addition there were three older couples of her aunt's age group, and, best of all, James. It would be the first time she would have met him without the embarrassment of Desmond being there, since the Dorset's ball, and she was both happy and nervous.

She went up early to change so as to be sure of looking her best and did not hear her uncle coming in or the result of the race.

She was absorbed in her own thoughts and took much longer than usual dressing. She chose a white chiffon dress with a draped skirt and softly folded bodice partially concealing the low cut of the front. Studying her reflection critically in the mirror, she decided that the cut was perhaps a bit too low for the country and broke off a couple of carnations from the vase on her dressing table and tucked them into the dip between her breasts. Desmond's wandering gaze, in the past, had made her much more conscious of the cut of her clothes and she was particularly anxious not to appear too smart and "Londony" tonight. Yes, the shell pink of the flowers was a decided improvement against the whiteness of her skin; she really did look very nice, and giving a little twirl 'round with pleasure, she caught her foot in the hem of the dress; there was a loud rending noise and the silk lining pulled down and trailed across the floor. Muttering under her breath, she burrowed in a drawer for a needle and thread. It was maddening to have this happen and make her late. She had meant to be down first to help her aunt, and now she thought she could hear people arriving already. Yes . . . She hopped across the room to look out of the window, two carriages had pulled up outside the door, and another—no, it was a car, probably James's—coming up the drive.

"Damn the hem! They'll think I am being coy, not being down to meet him . . . there, that will have to do!" She bit off the thread and hurried downstairs.

She stood for a moment in the doorway, suddenly feeling unaccustomedly shy. The introductions were over and everyone was engaged in conversation, surely more animated that usual? She wondered what could have happend. James was in the bay window listening to her uncle who was waving a decant of sherry about in one hand and an empty glass in the other, looking as if he would dash them together at any moment as he talked. James looked up suddenly, as if he sensed Ellen's arrival, and raising his eyebrows in a look of comical alarm, beckoned her over to join them.

She smiled back, delighted at his friendliness, and edged her way around, pausing briefly to shake hands with some of the other guests on the way. Undoubtedly they all had something very interesting to talk about, she had never seen a party so animated at this early stage.

"I'm dying to know what's happened!" she exclaimed, as she reached her uncle. "Why are you waving that decanter about so dangerously? Surely it will make the sherry all bubbly!"

"Yes, I have been getting very worried about it, too!" said

James. "That's why I enlisted your help. I thought Sir Charles might listen better to you!"

"Uncle, do put it down and tell me is it the race? Did Anmer win? Did you make a lot of money? Is that why you are being so careless with the family heirlooms?" she asked.

"Good heavens! Haven't you heard?" exclaimed Sir Charles. "It's been the most disastrous race in history! You never heard anything like it! All the horses were in a bunch, Anmer going very well in the middle, coming 'round Tattenham Corner . . ." he raised the decanter, then, catching Ellen's eye he set it down on a small table near him and resumed. "Then suddenly he fell. There was the most frightful mix-up, and only by the grace of God the whole lot didn't come down. Some fool woman had jumped out and tried to seize his bridle, knocking him down and the next horse on top of him."

"Was he hurt? What an awful thing!" she asked, horrified.

"Anmer wasn't hurt—at least, he got up alright—but the jockey was, and I'm glad to say the woman is seriously ill!" Sir Charles replied with venom. "Get James to tell you about it. I must go and do host." He picked up the decanter again, winked at Ellen, and walked off.

"Why on earth did she do it?" asked Ellen in bewilderment. "No wonder Uncle Charles was so het up! Was she trying to commit suicide? Surely it would have been a popular win, the King's horse?"

James looked down at her in some amusement. "I can see you are not up with the times, Ellen," he smiled. "It was a suffragette stunt. Throw yourself under the king's horse in the Derby and you can't fail to be noticed!" Then, looking at the amazement on her face, he asked, "Don't you have any burning hot feelings about 'women's rights'? I am sure you should!"

"Well, certainly not to the extent of knocking down some poor unfortunate horse that has nothing to do with them, just because it belongs to the King!" she declared with feeling.

His eyes twinkled, but he said seriously, "The jockey, of course, is of no importance! It doesn't matter about him getting

141

hurt! But seriously, leaving our dumb friends out of it, do you not feel that women have a very hard time? Should they not be equal to men?"

"Oh goodness, no!" she exclaimed. "I'd hate all the things men have to do, like making machines and counting money and all that. I can't do sums at all!"

"But forgetting about sums, would you not like to have the vote?" he asked with interest.

Ellen sighed. "Oh, dear! I never know what to think about these things. Surely one ought to vote the same way as one's husband anyway, so why worry?"

"Oh, not necessarily!" he exclaimed. "Supposing your husband thought that no woman should ever be allowed to own or drive a car, or something like that . . . would you let him vote for you if such a bill came up?"

Ellen shot him a suspicious glance, but decided he couldn't possibly know anything about the car-driving efforts. It must be just a chance example. A lot of men, including Neill, were obviously not in favour of women drivers. So she said, "No, I would not . . . but that would hardly be worth knocking a horse down for!"

"But then, supposing it was something you did feel strongly about, like the government of the country—this Home Rule Bill, for example. If you felt very strongly about staying in the empire and your husband wanted the country to break away—what would you do then?" he asked curiously.

"Why . . . I wouldn't dream of marrying a man who could think like that!" she answered simply. "I think it's awfully important to have the same basic ideals!"

"I couldn't agree with you more!" he laughed delightedly. "But you still haven't answered the question!" As she looked at him doubtfully, he suggested, "Imagine I am doing a survey for a newspaper: 'Now, Miss Tristram, I should like to know your opinion: should women have the vote?' " He held an imaginary piece of paper and pencil in his hand and looked at her expectantly.

She broke into laughter, exclaiming pathetically, "Oh dear,

it's not fair to have to think so hard before dinner . . . well, I suppose I am in favour really . . . I always think it is frightfully unfair the way a woman's money belongs to her husband the minute they are married, no matter how dishonest he is, but as I haven't got any, I never worried about it much. I suppose if she should be able to control her fortune, she should also be able to share in controlling the country, though I can't think of anything I would rather not have to do . . . and I must say I think the suffragettes are going the wrong way about getting it," she concluded.

"You mean you think there is a certain lack of grace and charm about their methods?" smiled James, in question.

Ellen gave a gurgle of appreciation, and Lieutenant Montgomery, who had joined them to see what was being so earnestly discussed in the window, ventured to comment "I think that is the understatement of the year"—and then went on, "You know, this woman who threw herself at the horse is the same one who hid herself in a hot-air shaft in the House of Commons earlier this year and pounced out on some poor unfortunate Scottish minister as he was passing and beat him up."

"Good heavens! What on earth for?" asked Ellen in astonishment.

"She thought he was Lloyd George, apparently . . . same long hair and everything. I gather the poor man nearly had a heart attack!"

"Well, I don't suppose she got his sympathy after that!" said Ellen, with feeling.

"I feel sure you would have managed things better than that, Ellen." James gave her a warm look.

"I could hardly manage worse . . . could I?" she asked, her eyes sparkling michievously. "I am quite sure, for instance, that Uncle Charles will never support women having the vote if they go on jumping in front of the horses he has backed—and he is one of the most chivalrous of men, can't bear to see ladies in distress or anything like that."

A general move towards the dining room ended the conversation, and when they followed the others in they found everyone in a certain amount of doubt about where they were to sit, Eric having been put in charge of Lady Richardson's seating plan. However, they soon discovered that he was using it upsidedown, having thought that "M" stood for Marion, instead of "Me" for Sir Charles; and then there was a great deal of chaffing: Sir Charles suggesting that Eric was fiddling the seats to his own advantage, and Ellen seriously alarmed the young Land Agent by telling him, "It is all a terrrible mistake and there is no room for you after all!" "Sh . . . sh . . . sh . . . shall I just slide quietly away?" he asked with a worried look, and then, seeing her mouth tremble, he added more boldly, "or may I just sit at your f . . . f . . . feet where I already am, metaph . . . ph . . . ph . . . phorically speaking?"

"Oh, the Blarney!" exclaimed Ellen, "I can hardly turn you out after that pretty speech. But look, order is coming out of chaos, Aunt Marion has a place for you after all!"

Eventually they were all seated, and when Sir Charles had said Grace, James turned to Ellen, fanning himself rapidly with his napkin, and murmured: "That was very worrying . . . for an awful moment I thought my place was going to be at the other side of the table and I find Miss Neill most alarming . . . she knows so much about everything!"

"Whereas I am so foolish that I flatter your ego?" enquired Ellen archly.

Helping himself calmly to salmon mousse, James observed: "If you talk like that you will frighten me."

Not at all squashed, Ellen continued to tease, "Do I understand, then, that it is the doormat type you admire?"

He studied her carefully for a moment and then replied, "I wouldn't have said 'doormat' was the type precisely, but I think you know what I admire."

Ellen went pink all over with pleasure and she laughed into his eyes: "Oh, the suffragettes should get you to teach them soft speaking, James, then they'd get whatever they wanted!"

He smiled but said rather seriously, "Unfortunately one doesn't always get what one wants as easily as that. Sometimes there are outside influences!"

Ellen wasn't very sure whether he meant the double entendre and was referring to Desmond and herself, or whether he was still thinking about the suffragettes, so she thought it was better to generalise and suggested rather diffidently, "Daddy always says if you want something badly enough, you may be sure to get it." She waited rather nervously for his reaction.

But, Ulsterman, thy name is Caution! Although secretly delighted at Ellen's response, he had no intention of committing himself further at the moment, and after looking at her rather searchingly, he contented himself saying, with his sweet smile, "I am sure he is right . . . if his career is anything to judge by. Your aunt was telling me how brilliant he is," and added wickedly "on the other hand, Captain Braithwaite has been wanting very badly to talk to you for some time and he is not getting what he wants at all!" He nodded in the direction of the man on Ellen's other side who had, indeed, made several bids to draw her attention, without success.

She turned around, with a feeling of regret at having to leave a conversation that had such possibilities for one which was purely dutiful and explained, "We have been getting very deeply immersed in women's rights' and how to get them."

She noticed, while she talked, that almost everybody at the table was discussing some aspect of suffragism, and this was so unusual a topic for an Ulster dinner table that when her uncle started to tell, for the second time, what he would do about the next woman who ruined a race, she broke in and said "But, Uncle Charles, you must admit she has succeeded by the mere fact that we are all talking about her . . . and I have hardly ever heard the subject of suffragettes mentioned over here before! Much less whether we should be given the vote or not!"

There was a general murmur of acknowledgment and Sir Charles exclaimed, "Well, I hope they don't start that game over here! I have the highest possible regard for women and I should hate to have to change it." He smiled across the table at his wife, who said comfortingly, "I don't think you need worry, dear. We have too much else to think about these days for there to be divisions amongst us."

Conversation then turned back to politics amongst the elder group, while the young people teased the soldiers about how their noses were going to be put out of joint the next week by the Navy—greatly to the enjoyment of Lieutenant Montgomery, who was used to being sadly in the minority amongst the large numbers of military stationed in and around Belfast.

"Of course, we in the Navy are used to being feted wherever we go . . ." he said airily, in response to a rather querulous comment from the adjutant that no one had arranged a series of picnics and yacht races when he arrived in Ulster.

"Perhaps it was wintertime?" suggested the youngest Miss Taggart, who did not like to see anyone's feelings being hurt, and earned a grateful look from him.

"You can't say we have actually suffered from neglect, though, can you?" chipped in the subaltern rashly. "I, for one, am having the time of my life!"

"Right!" said Braithwaite quickly. "You may have the privilege tomorrow of helping me to arrange how to run my battalion while all my officers are entertaining His Majesty's Navy."

"Oh, Lord! Sorry I spoke!" groaned the subaltern, burying his head in his hands in despair.

But he got no sympathy from John Montgomery, who roared with laughter. "That's what comes of dodging all the work up till now. Had you been like me, conscientious and hardworking over the last few weeks, your efforts would now be behind you and you could contemplate the week's festivities with a clear mind." He tucked his thumbs into the lapels of his coat and waggled his fingers ostentatiously.

"Just before your brain clears completely, John," observed James dryly, "May I put in a claim for a civilian versus military tennis match, a two-day event at the Downshire Club? I think the soldiers could lend you a few ladies if none of the naval wives have come over, and we can present quite a strong team here." He turned to Ellen. "I understand you are very good. I hope I can count you on my side?"

"Oh, yes! I'd love to play," she answered enthusiastically.

146

"I haven't played any tennis since I came here . . . I'm afraid I'll be awfully out of practice."

Just then it was time for the ladies to leave the dining room, and much pleasant speculation passed amongst the girls about the week ahead of them before they were joined by the men.

Lady Richardson had had the carpet rolled up, and immediately he saw the floor clear for dancing, Henry Chichester-Grieves, the agent, sat down on the piano stool and began a tremendously dashing waltz that soon drew the entire party onto the floor, pretty dresses swirling under the soft light from the wall-sconces.

As the dance dashed to its end, with a great display of fingerwork, Ellen and James paused, laughing and breathless, beside the piano.

"For Heaven's sake, Henry," exclaimed James, "could you not play it any slower than that? We were nearly killed trying to keep up with you!"

In answer, Henry rose and bowed deeply, stuttering "If you d . . . d . . . don't like my music, y . . . y . . . y . . . you play the piano and I'll d . . d . . . d . . . dance with Miss Tristram!" and without further ado took her in his arms and pointed his foot ready to begin, as at a dancing class for children, saying to her, "Only fair that I should have a reward after all that work."

"Oh, very well," said James, sitting down, laughing, "see if you can dance this!" and with three great chords he led straight into a most spirited version of the Quick Step. Not willing to admit defeat, Henry gave a great leap and set off with rapid stealth in a remarkably good burlesque which took Ellen all her time to keep up with, but it was greeted with shrieks of joy and applause by the rest of the party.

When they stopped for breath, Lady Richardson intervened, walking over to the piano and saying, "Now I shall play while you dance . . . I can't have my two best dancers either permanently off the floor or else making it quite impossible for anyone else to dance. Go on, away with you!" She waved her hands at James and for the rest of the evening she and Mrs. Young took it in turns to play until at last it was time to go home.

No one was more sorry to see the end than Ellen. She had danced a great deal, which she loved; James had sought her out as often as he could without actually being rude to the others, and without Desmond there to cast his shadow on the fun, she had spent an evening of unalloyed happiness and parted from James with many assurances of how much they were looking forward to the tennis match on Tuesday.

"Well, dear, was that a nice party?" asked her aunt as the door closed on the last visitor, and she set to plumping up the cushions on the sofa and fished her bag out from behind them.

"Oh, Aunt Marion, it was lovely!" exclaimed Ellen, putting her arms round her neck and kissing her warmly. "Thank you so much. I haven't enjoyed myself so much for simply ages!"

"And well you might," thought Lady Richardson, "seeing you danced half the night with James!" After she and Sir Charles had reached their room and were preparing to go to bed, she observed in a satisfied tone to her husband, "I think that has got things running much more smoothly, don't you, darling?"

"What sort of things, my dear?" he asked sleepily, taking off his dressing gown and throwing it in a heap on the end of the bed.

"Oh, come, Charles! You know exactly what I mean." She tossed her hair impatiently back and started to plait it. "Ellen and James, of course."

"Well, I never could see what you were worrying about . . . women are always in such a hurry about these things. You must give the man a chance to make up his mind!"

"You didn't take such a long time to make up your mind, did you, Mr. Cool and Calm?" she observed, sitting down on the side of the bed.

"Might have been better if I had," he murmured teasingly, and slid a hand over her long shiny brown hair. She caught and kissed it, and then continued, holding it, "While we are on the subject . . . what can we do about our other young lovebirds?"

"Good Heavens! I want to get to sleep—it's after two o'clock! What's wrong with them"

"Well, darling, you know Michael will be going to school

in the autumn and we can't afford to keep Eric here just to make love to Margaret McInnis! Much as I like them both! If he doesn't get another job, he will never be able to afford to marry her. I'd hate to be the means of breaking up their sweet young dream."

"Ah, Marion," he pressed her hand, "hurry up and get into bed. You women think you are the only ones who know about love, but it is we men who are the practical ones. I was talking to Templeton and he is very much in need of some help in the office and would be delighted to take Eric on. I said he could stay on here with us. He's leading my bicycle corps and I couldn't really do without him the way things are going at present. He's a very good lad."

"And you are a very good husband!" she hugged him warmly. "I might have known you would have the situation under control. I only hope we will be able to help the children, when the time comes, with their problems. Please God, all this may not lead to war ... I want them to grow up strong and free and have all the wonderful times we had."

He put out the light and held her in his arms. "Don't worry, darling, we are all doing our best ... and I can't believe this pigheaded fool of a prime minister won't realise he is beaten and leave us in peace. He can't imagine we have drilled and are arming sixty thousand men for amusement ... no matter how Birrel tries to laugh about it."

"Oh!" she shuddered, "I feel like a goose walking over my grave when I hear all this talk of guns! I know we have to have them, but please God they may never be used!"

"Amen to that!" he echoed. "But we are still desperately short of them to make any effective opposition. I don't think more than ten percent of our men have got guns, let alone the ammunition for them, despite all the smuggling that is going on."

"Well, let's not talk about it or I shan't sleep at all tonight," she said resolutely. "Let's talk about the party: it really was a great success, wasn't it?" she said happily, and talked on about it for a while until a long sighing breath assured her that her husband was fast asleep beside her.

149

"How is it," she asked herself sadly, "that if I talk about something nice he always goes to sleep? And yet he would have talked all night about those beastly guns! Ah well!" She yawned. "It was a lovely party and it made Ellen happy, anyway." Then she also fell asleep.

Chapter 11

Two days later the whole family rode up to the top of the Knockagh Hill, overlooking Belfast Lough, to watch the first battle squadron as it steamed into Bangor Bay under the command of Sir Stanley Colville in H.M.S. *Collingwood*.

The whole expanse of northeastern Ireland was spread out below them while they stood, like a Red Indian scouting party, statue-like against the skyline.

The horses seemed to get as much pleasure from the beauty of the scene as their riders; they gazed with pricked ears into the distance, showing none of their customary fidgetiness. Even Alice's pony, which normally had only thoughts for its "inner man," seemed to be temporarily transported to thoughts on a higher plane, its sharp little ears cocked and a wisp of grass hanging from its mouth which it had forgotten to chew.

The fields were brilliantly green and the Lough, far below them, as deeply blue. The opposite line of rounded hills was slightly misted by the haze of smoke from the city, but even the haze couldn't hide the shining silver waters of Strangford in the distance.

Against this sparkling and colourful backcloth the grey ships were even more solid and purposeful and seemed strangely out of place. Their long lines spelt speed and efficiency, as they steamed broadside on into the Lough. As they dropped anchor, one by one, and swung with the tide, they were transformed into squat, impregnable fortresses, and Sir Charles commented to his wife, "When you see them like that, hull on, it makes you realise that this is not just a courtesy visit, doesn't it?"

"Funny thing is . . ." interposed Ellen, gathering up her reins as though waking from a trance, "I always thought there was no more wonderful sight in the world than the battle fleet. I loved it so much that it used to make me weep, and yet when I see it here in this setting I feel it looks almost sinister." She smiled apologetically, "Mummy and daddy would be horrified to hear me, wouldn't they?" she said ruefully.

"They certainly would," laughed her aunt. "But don't get too partisan in your feelings . . . remember we are all relying on your connections to get us on board this week!"

"Yes, indeed," agreed Michael, edging his pony up beside Ellen. "For once you have my full approval to flirt as much as you like, as long as you get me asked on board!"

"Thank you so much, Michael, it is nice to have your approval," said Ellen in a kindly voice. "But I read in the papers that there are to be conducted tours for schoolchildren . . . so I feel you will be able to achieve your heart's desire without my assistance!" This rejoinder was greeted with cries of joy and delight from his unkind sisters.

"You bought that one, Michael!" exclaimed his father. "I am delighted to see how well Ellen is 'able' for you. Practice, I suppose, makes perfect! My goodness, look how late it is. We shall have to get home pretty smartly if we are to be in time for lunch." He urged his horse into a canter along the grass verge, putting an end to what promised to be an energetic discussion.

Six battleships, two cruisers, and a host of smaller craft lying anchored in the Lough created an atmosphere of excitement that could be felt rippling through the country.

Invitations flowed between the hospitable Irish people and the ships, and an absolute whirl of entertainment went on. The sun shone on with undimmed splendour all week, so that even the simplest picnic party had an aura of brilliance, and the Grand Banquet at the city hall arranged by the Lord Mayor reached a pinnacle of glamour never touched before. Vast crowds turned out to see the ladies arriving in their jewelled dresses, and when the naval officers arrived in gleaming gold braid, with their cloaks flying back to reveal white satin linings, a spontaneous roar of approval burst from the ranks of onlookers.

Parties were in the air and everyone, no matter what their political opinions were, was anxous to make the visit an outstanding occasion.

Michael need not have worried about receiving an invitation to see over the ships. Not only did Ellen's cousin in the *Temeraire* invite them all for tea in the wardroom, but passed the enthusiastic Michael on to his friends in other ships so that by the end of the visit Michael was probably one of the only people who could boast of having been on board each ship in the flotilla.

To Alice and Cynthia it was one of the highlights of their lives, though they were quite happy to confine their attentions to the *Temeraire,* not feeling able to go a second time through the awesome experience of boarding ship.

Ellen and her aunt were secretly highly amused to see so vivid a portrayal on the children's faces of all the mixed feelings which they were too well schooled to show themselves. "It is no wonder that the navy is always surrounded in mystery and might," Lady Richardson remarked to Ellen, as they took their seats in the piquet boat. "One starts off at a disadvantage from the moment one's foot leaves terra firma; even if one doesn't feel sick on the way out one's hat is almost bound to blow off before one arrives," she smiled reminiscently, "and then one is expected to step gracefully onto a heaving platform, the size of a tea tray, and climb a steep flight of steps, holding a long dress up and a large hat on . . ."

"Oh, yes," laughed Ellen, "but I think the worst bit of all is when you arrive at the top and are faced by a whole row of saluting officers and hundreds of grinning sailors peering 'round every corner. I never know whether to shake hands or bow, or salute back or walk straight past . . . and I get so confused I'm inclined to miss the top step and arrive on hands and knees instead!"

"Oh, don't" implored her aunt, "you bring it all back so vividly, and your mother was always so cross with me for letting her down. I really think it was her ability to come aboard gracefully that won your father's heart!"

"Well, in that case I am not likely to follow in her footsteps and marry into the navy!" exclaimed Ellen, gathering her skirt firmly in her hands as the boat drew alongside, and Lady Richardson, despite what she had said, stepped onto the platform with unimpaired grace and dignity.

Not so her daughters! Alice was so busy throwing wreathed smiles at the midshipman in charge of the piquet boat that Cynthia, giving her a sisterly prod in the back, made her miss her footing and but for the prompt action of the seaman at the foot of the gangway might have fallen into the sea.

With sublime disregard their mother ascended the ladder, followed by the cross and dishevelled Alice and the blushing Cynthia. Ellen and Michael brought up the rear just in time to see the girls turn bright crimson as the line of officers again clicked to attention in their honour. Alice was enchanted but Cynthia looked about to throw herself over the side and was only able to scamper past in the shelter of Ellen's arm with downcast eyes.

However, once they got down to the wardroom and saw the magnificent tea spread out before them, and the warmth and friendliness of their hosts, they completely forgot their shyness and talked so much that the grown-ups could hardly make themselves heard.

Ellen's cousin, Mervyn Hawke, was one of the members of the visiting tennis team in the match organised by James at the Downshire Club. He was very put out to find Ellen playing for the opposing team, and when they all foregathered on the first day at the clubhouse, he remonstrated, laughingly, with James about it. "Absolutely dishonest!" he accused. "Ellen is a daughter of the fleet and has no right to appear in your team!"

"Oh, no," disagreed James, smiling not at Mervyn but at Ellen, "we look upon Ellen as very much one of us. After all the work I have put in with her over the past nine months I should be more than chagrined if she were to revert to the enemy!"

"Never mind, Mervyn," said Ellen. "As host team we shall have to make a point of letting you win to show our good manners, won't we, James?"

"You must have changed more than your allegiance," exclaimed Mervyn in amazement, "if you intend to let anyone take a point off you without a struggle, Ellen! I can see that we 'simple sailors' are up against some most experienced gamesmanship; I shall go and warn my team. The honour of the British combined military strength is at stake!"

"Don't believe a word he says," answered James with more than a little truth. "These 'simple fellows' have been handpicked to show us poor natives who is master here! We are going to need all our ingenuity and determination to show them we can hold our own."

They all laughed, and Ellen suggested to James that they should go and study the list of players to work out a system.

The combatants were all gathered 'round the board outside the clubhouse on which the teams and order of play were displayed, and much badinage was going on over the introductions and accounts of each person's prowess at the game.

As Ellen ran her eye down the list, she felt an unpleasant shock run through her when she came across Desmond Campion's name. How stupid! She should have known he was bound to be playing for the service side . . . but somehow life had been so pleasant lately without him appearing at any of the parties, she had almost forgotten his existence: now she felt there would be a cloud over the proceedings. He never did anything just for the fun of it: he would play to win only, and it would infect everyone and spoil the carefree atmosphere of the match. She felt now that it was terribly important that James should be a better player than Desmond. Suddenly she was desperately anxious to prove to herself as well as to Desmond that James was the better man. She knew inside herself that he was in every way a better, nicer, finer man, and yet she wanted to be convinced, still, by some deed of arms. Although she realised all this and that Desmond was no good, still the knowledge of his extraordinary ability in every field of sport, his wit and intelligence, and above all her fear of the strength of the feelings that he had awakened in her in the past, made her afraid of his power again. So she longed for a show of strength from James to convince herself finally that he was, indeed, a strong enough character to hold this love which she now freely admitted to herself she had for him. A much more mature and spiritual love which she dimly perceived would, when grown, show her previous feelings for Desmond as the innocent physical infatuation for experience which they had been, none the less painful for their adolescence and still a force of which she was unsure and nervous.

Had she but known it, it was this underlying lack of confidence which endeared her to James. Her beauty and vivacity were enough to attract any man at first, but it was the hint of uncertainty, the basic insecurity and need for friendship despite so many obvious gifts, that intrigued him and awoke in him a desire to "have and hold and to cherish" this particular girl.

While they were still talking, young men in immaculate white flannels and striped blazers, some with straw boaters tipped over their eyes, swinging their raquets as they leant against the pavilion and talking to their partners, Desmond walked rapidly around the side of the building.

Mervyn looked up from the boxes of balls that he was sorting. "Ah, the captain of our fate at last! I was beginning to think you must have had an accident and we would have to carry on without our 'Pro.' "

Desmond replied with a touch of sarcasm, "Sorry if I kept you waiting, but we soldiers sometimes have work to do . . . they seemed to have kept the whole paper work of the army for me today. A lot of Tom Fool schemes being thought up by some Johnny at the war office! I won't be a moment." He vanished into the pavilion to change, reappearing a few moments later very spruce and fit looking, with two racquets tucked under his arm, which immediately called forth a howl of derisive comment. He was, however, quite unruffled and, catching sight of Ellen, strolled over and enquired, "Am I to have the privilege of playing with you again, today?"

She could not resist a somewhat saucy smile as she replied, "No, actually I am on the other side now—against you!" She looked up at him.

"Are you, by Jove!" he exclaimed, giving her a hard look, and she had a feeling he was more annoyed than he showed. "Well . . . we shall have to see what sort of a beating we can hand out to little girls who change sides! I hope I've got a good partner . . ." he turned away to look at the board as he made his parting shot "this time!" and raised his eyebrows significantly.

Ellen could not refrain from laughing though he had definitely won that round. It was clear that he also remembered the time they first played together and was not pleased at the change in her allegiance. Evidently he could forget her but did not, himself, care to be forgotten!

In fact she had not, never could, forget him; but now that the process of disenchantment had set in she found herself noticing that he always stood too close when he talked to her, and she had to move away. In the past she had thought "how masterful!" Now she felt it was just bad manners and disliked it. She used to admire the assurance with which he assumed that he had a natural right to the best partner and the best place at everything; now it struck her as selfish and rude. Yet he was still very attractive and although it was balm to her spirits to be able to annoy him, he could still make her feel both nervous and upset.

It was very pleasing to note that he was scheduled to play with the General's daughter, who was a very fair, square, young lady, quite impervious to his wit and determined on the attention due to the General's daughter from one of his officers.

Ellen couldn't help thinking how clever Mervyn had been in his arrangement of partners: no doubt, he had organising ability and would go far in the navy. She felt quite cheered up and, contrary to her forebodings, the day passed exceedingly pleasantly.

James maintained his high position in her esteem by proving to play an extremely steady if not dramatic game. In one match against a very inferior pair, they had an absolute walkover; in the other two matches against couples of very much the same standard as themselves, he wore them down by sheer determination not to give in, keeping the game open until he saw his chance and then placing the ball so neatly into the one unreachable position that Ellen was positively jubilant.

If they were to meet Desmond and the General's daughter tomorrow, she felt they would have a very fair chance of winning and would certainly not be wiped off the court.

In the meantime what bliss it was sitting in the shady pavilion in a big basket chair with fat pink cushions, watching James expertly filling two bowls with early strawberries and cream and sugar before settling himself in another chair by her side.

"I can see now why Mervyn Hawke was so upset at not having you on his team," he remarked contentedly. "You do play a delightful game of tennis; I was even luckier than I realised in securing you as my partner."

Ellen was conscious of a warm sensation of happiness flowing through her body and gave him a glowing smile. "I do love tennis," she sighed, "and it is nice to have a partner who doesn't poach—that always put me off completely."

"Then I shall never, never poach!" he exclaimed with a twinkle in his eyes belying the solemn utterance. "For that is the one thing I most certainly don't want to do!"

"Oh dear, I wonder how much he means by that?" thought Ellen, as she smiled and said cautiously, "I don't think you are in any great danger . . . of putting me off! . . . I mean . . ." with a sudden access of boldness, "I think you are a very careful person . . . I can't imagine you ever doing anything rash!"

He looked at her in surprise. "That makes me sound very dull indeed!" he exclaimed.

"Oh no, not dull!" she interrupted, and hurried on to explain. "But I do notice that you don't leave things to chance. You always prepare the ground very well before you make any move . . . I think that's probably why your plans always work out. Mine seldom do. I rush into everything!" she concluded sadly.

He balanced the bowl of strawberries on his knee and pressed the tips of his fingers together as he thought about this. "I wish I was half as sure as you that my plans will always work out. I have some plans at the moment that I am not at all confident about."

He gave her his quick, clear look, and she felt the blood pound in her throat. *What does he mean? Is it me? Or is it something to do with his everlasting Volunteers?* She was almost sure it was herself and her throat was quite dry as she tried to think how to answer. His eyes held hers and she felt he must understand how she felt. The moment was full of significance . . . and then a crowd of laughing, chattering tennis players came up the steps and the spell was broken. With an extraordinary feeling of suspension, they responded to the raillery of the new arrivals.

"Yes . . . we hurried through our game . . . so that we could finish all the strawberries. We were so afraid you might get there first . . ." James, as host, had to do the honours of the tea table, and by the time everyone was satisfied there was no further opportunity to talk alone; but it had been arranged that James would drive her home and stay to supper, so she felt a delightful tingle of anticipation as she collected up her things and retired to the changing room to get ready.

A quarter of an hour later, poised and glowing, she stood on the top step of the verandah, looking 'round for him to take her home. Everyone was busy saying good-bye to everyone else, the air was full of happy promises of "revenge" tomorrow and plans to give people lifts, but of James there was no sign!

Probably he is busy making arrangements about tomorrow's play, she thought, and continued to stand happily surveying the scene. Gradually the party thinned out, various people asked her how she was getting home and would she like a lift. "No, thank you. It's alright. James is taking me, he'll be coming in a moment." She waved them away. *What a long time James is, he must be a very slow changer!* she thought.

Then Desmond wandered up, an expression of concern on his face.

"Don't tell me you have been let down again, Ellen?"

he asked in affected dismay. "May I offer you a lift back in my car since James seems to have gone home without you?"

Ellen felt all the blood drain from her face. It couldn't be true. James would never do a thing like that! He could barely have had time to change . . . she had not been so very long in the dressing room herself.

She managed to say casually, "Oh, no! He's coming back, I'm sure. Don't bother about me, please."

But Desmond had every intention of bothering. With his usual gift for timing his arrival, he had gone into the men's changing room just in time to see James hurrying out with Henry Chichester-Grieves, deep in conversation, and with a very worried look on his face. He had watched them vanish 'round the side of the pavilion and heard the sound of a car starting up before continuing inside rather thoughtfully. His day had not gone particularly well. Admittedly they had won all their three matches, but the General's daughter bored him to tears and she had stuck to him like a burr, so that he had had no opportunity to amuse himself elsewhere. Furthermore, he had been piqued more than he would like to admit by Ellen's defection. So when he finished washing and changing, and emerged to find her alone on the step, the temptation was more than he could resist to make a little capital out of the situation for himself.

"I hate to disillusion you," he said untruthfully, "but I don't think he will be coming back. He went off with Henry Grieves and they took their things with them." He allowed a moment to let this sink in and then added, "It seems to be a habit of his to walk out on his dates—but it is my good fortune to be in a position to profit by his carelessness! I really think you had better let me take you home."

She was too upset to be able to think clearly. She could not believe James had walked out on her when they had been so happy together all day, but then she remembered how he had left her standing without a partner at the regimental dance and had never given any reason why. She pushed the thought out of her mind: there must be a reason. Anyway, there was nothing else for it now, she would have to go home with Desmond for all the others had gone and she couldn't stay here alone. Just supposing he didn't come back and she was stuck here all night—she would look pretty silly then! She felt unbearably depressed but was determined not to let Desmond know just how much she minded. It was the last straw to have it happen in front of him a second time. She picked up her racquet and followed him to the car in silence.

He produced a dust coat and helped her into it, saying solicitously, "I hope you won't find this car too cold. This model is built for speed rather than comfort."

He wrapped a rug 'round her knees and she could not help thinking ungratefully how typical of him it was to carry a spare lady's dust coat in his car. If she had not been so depressed she might have been nervous about setting off on a long drive with the last man on earth she wanted to be alone with, but she felt quite numb and merely asked conversationally, "What did you do with the General's daughter?"

"Her mother picked her up early. They are dining out and she had to change," he answered equally briefly, and gave his full attention to weaving the car amongst the many home-going carts and equipages on the road leading out of Belfast.

There was a long silence while Ellen racked her brains to think of an explanation of James's disappearance and could think of none that could preclude him from sending her some sort of message.

She didn't entirely believe Desmond's story, but as James had not appeared, what else could she think? Perhaps there would be a telegram waiting for her when she got home. This thought brightened her up considerably and she began quite to enjoy the drive. If only she had not been "at war" with Desmond it would have been fun to have revealed her ability to drive! It was a superb car, long and silver grey, like a huge fish with great bulging brass eyes.

Like everything else that he did, Desmond drove with a finesse and concentration which she could not help but admire. Having succeeded in his intention of driving Ellen back, he made the most of his advantage by exerting himself, once they were

161

out in the country, to talk amusingly and charmingly, and she had quite relaxed when, only two miles from Kilwater, the car gave an expiring groan and the engine died out. They were on a country road with straggly hedges along each side and not a soul in sight. Ellen's heart sank. Could he have made it do that on purpose? Desmond wouldn't have any scruples about doing a thing like that! She watched apprehensively as he climbed out of his door without speaking, unbuckled the bonnet and spent some time looking inside.

She couldn't see what he was doing . . . it might be just pretence, and the stillness which precedes the onset of dusk did nothing to allay her fears. What a fool she had been to come with him! After a few minutes he came 'round to her side of the car, still without speaking, opened the door and put his arm across her knees. Immediately she stiffened and half rose in her seat, whereas he gave a crack of laughter. "Don't be so silly, Ellen! I'm not going to kiss you now! I only want to get the toolcase out."

He pulled a flat box from under the dashboard and retired again.

She could have died of mortification. She cursed herself for coming, but there was nothing else she could have done. She cursed him for not hesitating to embarrass her and recall that hateful night, and she would even have cursed James for letting her into a situation like this, only that she still couldn't believe it was his fault.

When Desmond eventually shut down the bonnet and fastened up the strap she could not look at him, but stared stonily into the hedge as he reseated himself and pressed the starter. The silver car burst into shattering life and she silently thanked God for it, though, she thought confusedly, it was really Desmond's engineering ability she had to thank!

"Many men would consider that an opportunity wasted," he observed dryly, as they drove on, "but I believe there is a time and a place for everything. We don't want your aunt getting in a fuss about you, do we?"

Ellen did not deign to answer, but looked steadily ahead,

wrapped in unhappy memories. So deep in thought was she that the car had pulled up at the front door of Kilwater and Desmond was alighting before she shook off her abstraction. She was determined not to ask him in for the dinner that was to have been James's but he followed her into the house, ostensibly to reclaim his dust coat and carry in her tennis things, despite the fact that she almost threw the coat at him when she took it off.

However, once inside, he lost no time in explaining to Lady Richardson, very amusingly, that James had absconded with Henry Chichester-Grieves and it had fallen to his lot to rescue the Lady in distress! In common politeness her aunt could not fail to ask him to stay on to dinner after the long drive. She was quite aware that this did not please Ellen and was not pleased herself. She had been looking forward to seing James, and now all the good work she had done with her little dance seemed to have gone for nought, but it would have gone against her native good nature to send anyone away back so far without something to eat.

Ellen was noticeably silent during the meal, but Desmond exerted all his charm on her uncle and aunt and even Ellen found herself laughing at some of his witicisms. When he finally left, she could see that Lady Richardson was a good deal better impressed with him than she had been before. She longed to tell her it was all part of his game, that he was just making use of them, but she couldn't tell that without explaining how she knew, and she was too proud to confide in anyone. If she had made a fool of herself (and she had), then she would suffer the humiliation alone and not shift the burden in easy confidences.

On the way up to bed she asked if there had been any message from James. "No, dear, nothing at all," said her aunt, adding kindly and hopefully, "but don't worry, I am sure there is some perfectly simple explanation and he will tell you all about it at the tennis tomorrow. He wouldn't leave you in the lurch like that without a very good reason. He is a most dependable person."

But next morning there was still no message and Ellen was very loath to go to the tennis match when there was a doubt if she would even have a partner; and if he was there, it seemed doubtful if they would be on speaking terms. Furthermore, she was determined not to have to see Desmond again; it would be unbearable to have his sardonic eye watching her discomfiture.

In the end Lady Richardson drove down to the post office and made a telephone call to Mrs. Melville, only to find that she was unable to speak on the telephone, being confined to her bedroom with one of her worst attacks of arthritis. Upon enquiry, the maid said that Mr. James had not been back last night, she thought he might be away some days but she knew nothing further.

Completely baffled, Lady Richardson then sent a telegram to Mervyn to regret Ellen's inability to play tennis but assuring him that they would all be with him for the ball on the flagship the next night.

Ellen was a little comforted to think that whatever it was that had happened must have been of considerable importance to keep him away for several days, but she still couldn't understand why he had not found time to send her some sort of message, and found it much harder to forgive him this lapse.

She spent a miserable day, helping the children to pick (very appropriately) gooseberries for jam and found it impossible to fix her mind on any subject other than James. The following day—the last but one of the Naval visit—Sir Charles, looking very glum, showed his wife a copy of the *News-letter* that he had been reading in his study after breakfast. He pointed to a heading "Discovery of Huge Quantity of Arms for Ulster in a London Suburb." This was followed by a short account of how the London police had received a tip-off about a disused warehouse which had led to the discovery of the guns, largely Italian in make, and undoubtedly in transit to Ulster.

Lady Richardson read it slowly before she looked up and met his eyes anxiously. "Those are the ones Fred Crawford was so confident of getting for our men, I suppose?" she asked.

"Yes. But not only that—look here . . ." he pointed to a paragraph further down the page where it proclaimed, "Dublin Sensation: furniture van found loaded with five hundred rifles and ammunition in County Cavan," and again "It is believed that these arms were manufactured for Ulster."

"It is a frightful loss. Hundreds of pounds' worth that we can ill afford," he said heavily, and then more hopefully, "but if it awakens England at last to the fact that we mean to fight for our freedom, it will at least not have been in vain."

But when, next day, the papers carried an even larger head-line—"Four Thousand Rifles for Ulster Seized in Hammersmith Stable"—followed by the news that the second reading of the Home Rule Bill had been passed by a government majority of ninety-eight, they were cast into a state almost of despondency.

These consignments of arms were to have brought such confidence to the Volunteers, who for so long had practised and drilled with dummy rifles. To think that their discovery, not to mention the seriousness of the situation, had not dimmed even for a moment Mr. Birrel's flippancy in the House of Parliament on the Irish question was depressing in the extreme.

It was not possible, though, to remain in low spirits at the ball in the *Collingwood*.

Promptly at nine o'clock they embarked in the piquet boat from Carrickfergus, and the sight of its gleaming brass, the gallant midshipman in his romantic boat cloak standing at the wheel, the sailors with their blancoed webbing and all the ac-coutrements of a ceremonial occasion, made them forget tem-porarily that they had a care in the world. The six battleships were a magnificent sight, "dressed overall," flags flying, and lights shining. Lanterns were hung all along the decks and big awnings had been erected to shelter the dancers from any possible cold winds. This, combined with the sound of music coming across the sparkling water, made it impossible to believe that their hosts had been sent here in readiness to impose the will of an un-sympathetic government upon them, and that at least half the guests present were actively employed, in their spare time, in preparing, if need be, to fight their hosts.

Ellen had not really expected to enjoy the evening at all, as she was deeply hurt by the continued absence of any message from James, whom she had looked forward so much to dancing with tonight. She had a new dress for the occasion—white lace over a soft blue silk slip—and she had almost decided against wearing it lest she "christen" it with an unsuccessful evening. Then she had thought it was just possible that James would be there . . . and so she wore it after all, and although he did not appear, the dress was obviously a big success with the Navy. She danced every dance until her feet ached and the stars began to fade in the sky.

Her Cousin Mervyn looked after her assiduously and saw that she was never without an introduction. He did not ask awkward questions about what had happened to James and herself to prevent them playing in the tournament, but said that he was sure his team would never have succeeded in winning if she and James had been there. They had clearly had a very happy day's play and Ellen felt more than a little angry at having been obliged to miss it.

However, she soon cheered up when, towards the end of the evening, Desmond, whom she had not noticed there earlier, came up and tried to break into her circle. She was inspired to say, "Oh, no! This is a naval occasion! I am only dancing with the Navy tonight!" to the evident delight of Mervyn and the considerable annoyance of Desmond, who was not at all pleased to find the girl who used to hang on his every move now prepared to flout him publicly. There was nothing he could say in reply, and whereas in the past he could have reduced her quickly to confusion by holding her too close to him as they danced, or just not asking her to dance again for several weeks until she was longing for him, he realised now that she had somehow achieved immunity, and the knowledge made her appear doubly attractive to him. Ellen also was surprised and delighted to find how easily she could turn away and remain mistress of the situation. It was, of course, the result of having all her interest now centred on James, which was a depressing thought in one sense as he now seemed to be turning out as fickle as Desmond had been.

At least Desmond no longer had the power to hurt her. It was very comforting to her damaged ego to have him so obviously admiring again even if she despised him, and she couldn't believe that it would be very long before James appeared with some good reason and deep apologies. She would be very forgiving, and he would, of course, be so relieved that everything would be wonderful again.

At the end of the week, however, when no word had come from him, she began to have serious doubts.

What job in connection with the Volunteers, as Aunt Marion seemed to think, could possibly keep him away so long? And make it impossible for him to write and explain? She had been so sure not only that he loved her, but that he was steadfast and true, not a flirt like Desmond. Surely she could not have been wrong again? Surely she could not have been such a fool as to have fallen in love twice with men who were no good—just amusing themselves?

It was a humiliating thought and she did not care to share it with her aunt, so she kept up a reasonably cheerful front, but all the time, inside, her mind was turning over and over the same old questions and answers.

And then she heard that he was back.

Sir Charles had met him at the club and he had asked after Ellen, and what the result of the tennis match had been. She felt as if a colossal load of anxiety had been lifted off her shoulders, and she was dying to see him and hear his reason and tell him it did not matter now . . . but the next thing she heard was that he had gone away again. This time it was on a business trip connected with his wine business.

It was really *too* much, she told the daisies on her wallpaper at night. Never, never, never again would she let herself fall in love. But how could she stop herself?

Was it just that she was an appallingly bad judge of men? Or was there something about herself that made them feel that they could treat her so cheaply? Something about her that appealed only to philanderers? What a horrible thought . . . she put it from her. No, it couldn't be that because she had received plenty of proposals from honest and estimable boys, and even charming people like Markham had obviously cared for her. It must be her own fault that she had this crazy penchant for the faithless type of man.

Anyway, this was the last time; she would not be led up the garden path again. There would be no ugly scene, she would just play their own game and be charming and evasive and keep her feelings under lock and key.

But it was one thing to plan, another to act.

By the time she met James, on his return from the Rhine Country, there was nothing cool or evasive or even charming about Ellen's behaviour.

Chapter 12

They had been asked to a garden fete at Lord Templeton's house, held nominally to raise funds for the Ulster Volunteers but in actual fact it was to try to cover the awful financial loss incurred by the confiscation of so many rifles in the last few weeks.

Captain Crawford of the U.V.F. who was in charge of finding and importing the guns, had cleverly noticed that the government order to confiscate had referred only to "rifles and ammunition," and had therefore despatched James post haste to see the agent in Hamburg and suggest that he indent for the return of the unmentioned bayonets and fittings. This he had achieved, but the loss of money still ran into several thousands of pounds. To have lost so much money and still be largely unarmed was an appalling blow to the people of Ulster, and something vital would have to be done if the situation was to be saved.

It meant not only the loss of arms, but also that the route by which they had been successfully smuggled for some months had been discovered and therefore had to be abandoned and another one found, particularly if they were to save the other consignments which were on their way. It was in order to halt these and deflect them temporarily from landing that James had gone off so precipitately from the tennis match.

By responding so promptly to Crawford's urgent message to catch the collier which was bringing them, and intercept the incoming consignments of rifles, he had had to walk out on Ellen and had since been deeply involved in plans which were so secret that he could not even tell her where he had gone. True, he had made Miss O'Neill promise to give Ellen a lift home, so Ellen would not have been left standing, and he had sent a letter back by messenger, asking her to understand that only the most urgent business could make him leave her like that, but he could not tell her more, and he had been so desperately busy ever since, coming and going with messages for Captain Crawford in their efforts to deflect and detain the other loads en route to the depot at Hammersmith that he had had no chance to follow up his letter and make sure that she understood.

If he had known that Miss O'Neill duly offered the lift to Ellen as she stood on the steps of the pavilion but stupidly neglected to say that James had asked her to, nor why (she was too clever to bother about trivialities and thought the whole tennis match was rather a waste of time) and that Ellen, in her happy conviction that James was still inside the clubhouse, changing, had thanked her very much and said that she was already fixed up. . . .

If he had known that in addition to this, the letter he had written was still lying, forgotten, in the coat pocket of the captain of the collier plying between Glasgow and Belfast, he would not have sought out Ellen with such happy anticipation on that lovely Saturday afternoon.

He arrived rather late and immediately set out to search through the crowded gardens for her; but such is the price of popularity that it was fully an hour before he managed to discover even Sir Charles. Everyone he knew seemed to be there and to want to talk to him. They had all rallied 'round to help the funds and knowing that he was closely involved with the cause of it all, everyone wanted to speak to him. Without being downright rude he could not get away. When he eventually ran Sir Charles to ground in the rifle range, he said he had not seen Ellen since they arrived, but suggested that she must have "done" the stalls by now and was probably doing a more extensive tour of the garden.

James was feeling tired and ruffled by so many interruptions and the need to force his way through the crowds in the heat. It was a relief to get away into the cool woodland garden and his heart leapt when he saw Ellen in the distance, sitting on a rustic seat fanning herself with a bunch of chestnut leaves, apparently lost in thought. He was a little taken aback by her lack of enthusiasm when he rapidly approached, exclaiming with relief, "I have been searching for you all afternoon!"

And even more so, when she coolly responded, "Oh! you should not have bothered to do that," withdrawing her hand gently from his.

"What do you mean by that?" he asked, all his eagerness disappearing along with his smile.

Her heart beat wildly and her mouth felt quite dry, but she forced herself to reply lightly, "Oh, I mean . . . there are lots of other people here, why bother about me?"

Much bewildered, he exclaimed, "You know perfectly well why I 'bother' about you, as you so charmingly put it . . ." but she interrupted hotly before he could finish—

"Oh, yes! I know! I am an amusing companion when it happens to suit you, but two can play at that game and at this moment I don't feel at all amusing. I'm used to people with better manners than you have and I am *not* in the habit of being left in the lurch for everyone to see!"—and that's a lie, she thought miserably, but her wonded pride made her rush stupidly one— "So please go back to your friends and don't bother about me."

She rose as if to dismiss him, but he didn't move out of her way and she found herself looking up at him from uncomfortably close range. He looked very angry indeed. His usually blue eyes had turned completely grey and stony, and the expression in them sent a little flicker of fear running through her veins.

"Will you kindly explain yourself?" he asked icily.

Somehow, when she tried to say something about his cutting her dance and missing the tennis, it all sounded so petty she could not bring herself to speak. *He always succeeds in making me feel in the wrong!* she thought unhappily and sought refuge in saying, disdainfully, "Oh, well! If you can't even remember, there's no point in my telling you . . . it must be too trivial. Perhaps it is just as well that we do things differently in England!"

She could have kicked herself the moment the silly words were out. It was a stupid and cheap thing to say, and not true either. She loved Ulster and its people and their ways, no matter what James did. She was so upset that her knees trembled and she had to bite her lips to keep from crying.

James also was in the grip of very strong emotions. He was cut to the heart by her behaviour and yet the pathetic silliness of it made him love her all the more.

He made another try.

"If it is the tennis match that you are so upset about, I can explain . . ." but she cut him short.

"Oh please don't bother . . . I quite understand," and she made as if to pass him.

Suddenly his temper boiled up. He had a very strong temper which he very seldom allowed to get out of control, but this was too much! His emotions were too much involved and he was tired and strained. His eyes were like stones and his voice snapped like a whip as he declared, "I would give a lot to have the right to turn you up and beat you for being such a silly, stupid, rude little girl," and it seemed as if he was having difficulty in keeping his hands at his sides as he spoke.

Now Ellen was really frightened; she realised she had gone much too far . . . but she also had a temper and she was too proud to draw back. Raging at him for making her behave like this, she almost shouted back, "Well, you haven't . . . and you never will!" and picking up her skirts, the tears pouring down her face, she rushed away from him into the wood before he could have the pleasure of seeing that he had made her cry.

James stood like a statue, watching her run away, his face a study of conflicting emotions. His anger evaporated as quickly as it had come and every instinct urged him to go after her and catch her in his arms and smother her with kisses and tell her how terribly he loved her. But his brain, working clearly and coldly, held him back. If he did that and she demanded an explanation which he could not give, they would not be any better off. She was evidently not satisfied with his having written, and more than that he was not at liberty to say.

172

A cold hand laid itself upon his heart; suppose she did not love him after all! He had been so certain that she did, but there were things which he could not understand. This fellow Campion, for instance—there certainly was something between them; he really knew so little about her still and he could not ask more. Could she have failed completely to understand about the tennis match—after he had written—if she really cared about him? And at the dance—surely it was she who had left him standing? Could it be that she was just a spoilt beauty, after all?

His mind was in a turmoil and he felt too uttlerly depressed for words, but he couldn't go on standing here—someone might come along and he was in no mood for conversation. He pulled himself together and strode rapidly off to the place where he had left his car, taking considerable trouble to avoid any part of the grounds where he might run into people he knew, and drove slowly home. What a damnable end to the day!

Ellen was in no better state. She knew she had behaved like a fool and was thoroughly ashamed of herself. The fact that in her temper she had said the exact opposite of everything she really felt stared her in the face like an accusing judge.

She had accused him of having no manners, and yet whatever had happened she knew this was not true. He was the kindest and most courteous man she knew . . . far better than she could ever hope to be herself. She had implied that people over here were inferior to those in England . . . she blushed at the mere recollection of such stupidity. She had refused to listen to his explanation of the tennis match incident . . . and then, maddest and most untrue of all, she had ended up by saying in effect that she never could, never would, marry him. This was the one thing above all else that she wanted to do, and the sole reason for this argument at all.

If she had been a dog, she would have lifted up her voice and howled, but being merely a girl in love she did the next best thing and threw herself down on the grass in her good silk dress, and sobbed as if (and indeed she thought it had) her heart would break. After half an hour of this she felt a great deal better but looked a great deal worse, and she had no idea how long she had been crying or whether the Richardsons would have gone home without her. She thought she had better try to make herself look a little more respectable before she went to look for them.

Her fresh, creamy dress had two or three good green smears of grass on the front, half the pins had come out of her hair and she must have been using her gloves to dry her eyes for they were crumpled up into a tiny, sodden heap. She had no way of knowing what her face looked like but every reason to suppose that it was pink and gummy-eyed. So she pinned up her hair and tilted her hat as far forward as possible without making it look as if she was drunk as well as disorderly, then, summoning as much composure as she could muster, she returned to the main lawn.

There she soon found her aunt amongst a thinning crowd, talking to Lady Templeton and discussing the financial success of the afternoon. She looked at Ellen with slightly raised eyebrows but made no comment on her appearance until they were on their way home in the dog-cart.

"Poor Ellen! You look very woebegone! What happened? I don't know how Bridget will get the stains off that dress, and it is such a pretty one."

"I fell down," answered Ellen, aware that it sounded a very lame reason. "I was looking at some ferns in the wood and I tripped over a stone."

Her aunt felt like saying, "And I suppose you cried for half-an-hour because your dress was dirty!" but she restrained herself, remembering the ups and downs of her own girlhood and merely asked casually, "Did James find you? He was looking for you everywhere."

Ellen coloured vividly and seemed to be searching for an answer before finally saying, in a very small voice, "We had a fight."

"With sticks and mud?" exclaimed her aunt, with an irre-sistible smile, and was rewarded by an answering, watery gleam from Ellen.

"No, it was after that I fell down . . ." and then with a sudden burst of confidence, "I was terribly stupid and I said a

174

lot of things I didn't mean, and now I'd give anything to unsay them, and I can't." She stifled a sob and looked blankly into the distance.

Lady Richardson took her hand and gave it an affectionate squeeze. "Oh, darling, I am so sorry for you! But I am sure it will come right in the end; remember the course of true love never does run straight. I don't think it will seem anything like as bad when you have slept on it."

Privately she couldn't imagine how two such nice people, so obviously in love with each other, could possibly be blind to each other's feelings or find anything to fight about. Love seems so simple when you are happily married, and yet she could remember sobbing herself to sleep on occasions before she had become engaged to Charles though for the life of her now she could not remember what the reasons had been for her sorrow. Although she was so sympathetic to them, she could not refrain from laughing a little as she recounted what she knew to her husband later that evening. "And, really, if I had not known them both so well I should have had the deepest misgivings! Ellen appears all covered with grass stains, her hat on crooked, face blotched with tears, and says she 'fell' in the wood! Later on she admits she had a fight with James. Her mother would be horrified if she knew. Do you imagine we shall have to go through all this with Alice and Cynthia?"

"Probably far, far worse!" chuckled Sir Charles comfortably.

"I don't know that I could bear it." His wife sighed. "It seems such a terrible waste of time and youth and beauty. Do you think I should give another little party . . . to the Opera House or something? and ask James? Would that help, do you think?"

"No, my dear, I should just leave well (or rather 'unwell') alone this time. We don't know what it's all about, and if they really are in love, it will sort itself out before long."

But when a month had passed without any developments, Lady Richardson began to wonder if it would sort itself out.

It was the most glorious summer they had had for years.

There were picnics, seabathing parties, endless tennis parties and dinners and no shortage of men with so many military stationed in Ireland.

Ellen was as much in demand as ever despite her depression. Campion seemed to be very much in evidence and Henry Chichester-Grieves made no bones about his devotion to her. James hardly appeared at all, though Sir Charles saw him frequently at the club and they all saw him walking with his Orange Lodge in the Twelfth of July parades which they went to watch from a graveyard on the Lisburn Road. This seemed a very macabre choice of situation to Ellen, when she was told where they were going, but on arrival it proved to be an excellent one. The actual tombstones were all at the back of the church and the part where they were to sit was a grassy slope descending to the top of the wall bordering the Lisburn Road along which the Lodges were to parade.

When they arrived at ten-thirty in the morning they found several friends there already and a considerable crowd lining both sides of the road below them. This would be the first public appearance Sir Edward Carson would have made for some time although he had been working tirelessly for their cause all summer and for the last two weeks had been inspecting a different battalion of the U.V.F. every day.

The people of Ulster knew of and appreciated his tremendous efforts to convince the British government that the Protestants could not accept Home Rule. They knew that when he was over here he worked like ten men to rally their enthusiasm, advise and enlist sympathy; and that when he could not be in Ulster he was working as hard as ever to awaken the people of England to the way their countrymen in Ireland were being coerced. No matter how much he was abused by Redmond, the leader of the Nationalists, or jeered at by Birrel, the Secretary of State for Ireland, he remained steady, determined, wise, with the immense experience of his legal practice behind him.

Today was the opportunity for the man in the street to do something for him. When he came in sight at the head of the procession in his carriage, dressed in mourning for his wife, an

Orange Lily stuck in his buttonhole, the crowd went quite mad. They cheered, they sang, they ran along beside his carriage, throwing their hats in the air, and Ellen felt tears rising to her eyes and a lump in her throat at the sight of such enthusiastic devotion.

The procession of Lodges also made a lasting impression on her. At the signing of the Covenant, on the day she had arrived in Ulster, there had only been the one, closely guarded, banner which had been carried before King William at the Battle of the Boyne on the Twelfth of July so long ago, but today every Lodge had its banner and she was endlessly fascinated by their themes.

Sometimes an angel with a fiery sword defended the open Bible, sometimes a well-known Orangeman, but most often King William on a mettlesome white horse, paused in the fording of the Boyne River to give a reassuring wave to posterity. The next favourite seemed to be Queen Victoria presenting the Bible to the "blacks." There were one or two which had to be explained to her, such as a river surprisingly full of naked women and children seeming to have a rather chilly bathe, but, according to Uncle Charles, having been driven into the water to drown by the troops of King James.

All these pictures were painted on huge six-foot squares of cloth with bright Orange silk trimmings and much gold adornment. The two poles supporting the banners were often topped with a clump of sweet william and orange lilies, and in some cases a man carrying an unsheathed sword walked in front of the banner.

Ellen was fascinated by the procession and so impressed by the stern, determined bearing of the men that she did not notice the number of James's Lodge appearing but suddenly found herself looking at him without him noticing her. Her heart beat in slow hammer strokes and she was overwhelmed with pride for him. He looked so steady and straight, walking along at the front of his Lodge. She could not imagine any of her friends in England having sufficient conviction for a cause to parade down the main street of a capital city before the rest of their friends.

Suddenly he caught sight of Lady Richardson and his charming smile leapt across his face as he raised his hat to her. Was it imagination, or did his eyes search the crowd with eagerness, for a moment, before the marching column swept him out of sight?

"Anyway, what is the good?" she thought dejectedly, "he couldn't really want to see me or he would have made some effort before now."

"But how can you expect him to approach you after what you said to him?" argued her conscience.

"He should have known I didn't mean it," she answered illogically, "it was his fault in the first place."

"Why don't you write to say you are sorry?" urged the voice again, and indeed she was sorely tempted. Only the bitter memory of how Desmond had snubbed her when she tried to overcome the impasse with him held her back. Men could and did hurt you if you loved them, and she could not bear to go through the chagrin of offering her love only to be snubbed again.

Half of her was convinced of his answering love, but the other half said, "That's just how you felt with Desmond, surely you can't be such a fool again!" And then she remembered how James had never apologised or explained about the dance, and again how he had not come to see her for a whole week after the fire in Galway despite her having been hurt and his evident concern—but then she had to admit he must have had a great deal else to do, and he did send her flowers.

So the argument continued in her head. Her conscience said she was in the wrong and should apologise but her once-hurt ego said, "No, don't risk being hurt again," until she was sick and tired of thinking about it and it was a relief to talk to anyone else to escape her thoughts.

Since Parliament had come down for the summer vacation the papers were much less occupied with the Home Rule Bill and had turned their attention to the scandal of the Marconi Case, which seemed to go on forever, and there was what came to be known as the "Romantic Will Case," in which Lady Sackville was accused of influencing unduly the late Sir John

Murray-Scott to the very considerable neglect of his relatives. Cynthia was quite fascinated by this and read the latest claims and counterclaims with avidity.

Ellen and her aunt were more aware of the gathering war clouds in the Balkans and the tales of horror from that battlefront and the possibility of war spreading nearer home.

Lady Richardson dreaded it with the horror of how it might affect her family, but to Ellen it seemed as if the sands of time were running out and still she could not bring herself to make the first move.

James was no happier than Ellen. He had been deeply hurt by her lack of understanding and was thoroughly ashamed of losing his temper. He was kept terribly busy by the intensive round of parades being held in every corner of the province, organised and addressed by Sir Edward, and had hardly any time to analyse his thoughts. But he did know that this girl, without any doubt, meant more to him than anything else except his country, and even there he was not sure of the order of priority. Her lovely face was always before his eyes, and he was sure he must have a lump of lead inside him, so heavy was his heart. Their alienation had proved to him, finally, that she was the only one for him, and it was only the fear of a rebuff that held him back from approaching her once more. It was better to live in this hell of indecision, with a faint hope, than to know the worst and have no hope at all.

Harry paid a brief visit for the autumn race meeting at Newtownards on September the third, and the county horse show. He seemed to have grown up a lot since Ellen last saw him, or maybe it was because she herself was more grave. He could not stay more than three nights as the whole British Army was due to start manoeuvres extending the length and breadth of Ireland on the following week. Even Desmond, protesting mightily, was going to have to take part in them as he was still attached to the Dorsets and they, together with Norfolks, the Cheshires from Derry, and the Royal Field Artillery from Dundalk, had all been ordered South to base themselves on Banagher.

"I thought the wretched place only existed in funny songs!"

wailed Valerie Balfour. "But now they are all going to be away for weeks!" when she met Ellen at a lunch party held shortly after the troops had gone.

"Well, for my part, it is rather a relief to get away from Derry," chipped in one of the visiting Cheshire wives. "Things don't seem to be nearly so strained down here. Ever since that man was shot by the Nationalists, watching the 'Black Men' parade in August, we have felt as if we were living on a volcano! We have to protect the Nationalists, but I must confess my sympathies are entirely with the other side!"

"Hush!" exclaimed a friend, "that is almost treason! Let us think of something else to talk about."

Strangely enough, at that very moment their husbands were feeling very much the same sympathies.

The Sixth Division had divided itself into two armies, and the two were locked in most complicated combat. The Brown Army was operating from Thurles, near Limerick, against the White Army in Kildare. The weather had broken after the wonderful summer, exactly as the manoeuvres began, and to the unaccustomed soldiers there did not seem to be any part of southern Ireland that was not bog. They were also disheartened by the unfriendliness of the peasants whom they had always been led to believe were an open-hearted, smiling and hospitable people. Not so on manoeuvre! They found themselves being watched with ill-concealed suspicion almost amounting to hostility. There were no offers to dry the soldiers sodden coats in the cottages, no strong, friendly brews of tea. Far from offering a brotherly welcome, the locals had a most disturbing way of melting into thin air whenever the soldiers arrived in a village.

"Pretty funny sort of friendship this, if you ask me," said Desmond, setting his empty glass down with a snap on the dirty table in a gloomy little village bar, while the rain poured down outside. The place was almost deserted, and the dark brown paint had peeled off the walls to show the rubble underneath in numerous patches. The few customers had either melted away out of the door or withdrawn into a silent group in the far corner. "If you ask me, the only good thing about this country is the whiskey, and I'd as soon switch to Scotch as fight to keep this stuff on the market!" observed his friend.

"H'm," agreed Desmond, shrugging on his coat. "The whiskey and the hunting, but you can get them both in England for half the trouble and ten times the comfort!"

"Do you feel you've learnt anything from this party?" enquired a depressed looking young subaltern.

"Yes," responded Desmond tartly, "one, how to walk with webbed feet, and, two, not to get mixed up in other people's squabbles in future. If we don't get a proper war next year, I shall resign my commission and retire."

Harry, manoeuvring with the White Army, was not much happier. There had been little opportunity to use cavalry in the close country and bogland and he had spent most of his time carrying despatches until he had been captured by a skirmishing group of Norfolks.

While he was kicking his heels in "prison" he could not help reflecting how charming everyone was while the army was not on duty. What fun they had had all summer! But how different was the attitude of the peasants once uniform was donned! He supposed that to them all armies were usurpers and it did not make much difference to the native Irish what section of the population the army was supposed to be supporting. He was particularly irritated to read in one of the local papers a reference to the Yorkshire and Befordshire Regiment who were stationed with him at the Curragh as "crouching in rain-sodden tents, these pitiable little men could be caught on flypaper."

It made him furious and he cut the piece out of the paper to show to his colonel at the end of the manoeuvres.

Meanwhile in the North, Sir Edward continued his inexhaustible recruiting campaign. He aimed to put one hundred thousand men in the field and arm them, he declared. This was perhaps a little valedictory as another consignment of rifles had just been discovered by customs men on a steamer at Dundalk and duly confiscated. But if Sir Edward said they would be armed, the people of Ulster believed him, and at last it began to look as if the people of England were beginning to believe him, too.

They could hardly help it! Lord Londonderry had published names and plans for a provisional government in Ulster in the event of hostilities. Sir Edward and Captain Craig had launched an indemnity fund with a target of one million pounds to insure against accident or loss of life on U.V.F. duty and had got halfway to this target in ten days!

Five thousand Englishmen had volunteered to Lord Willoughby de Broke to join the U.V.F. No wonder the London press had begun to take a grave view of the situation in Ulster!

The only pleasant thing there seemed to be in the papers was the preparation for and account of the wedding of Prince Arthur of Connaught and the Duchess of Fife. It was the one bright spot in the gathering storm, and yet, apart from the news, life seemed to go on very much as usual. The sun shone again and parties continued to be planned and carried out. Work had to be done just the same, the harvest brought in, the linen mills and shipbuilding carried on as if their future was settled and clear.

Chapter 13

At the end of September Ellen went down to stay with friends of Harry's near the Curragh. She had not seen him in his uniform since he had first joined the regiment and looked forward very much to seeing this side of his life. Also it was a tremendous relief to get away from a circle in which she was always hoping to meet James and always being disappointed.

Here at least she knew she would not meet him anywhere and so she was able to enjoy the parties without one-half of her mind continually being on the jump if anyone who looked or spoke like James came near. She still longed to be with him, and every nice thing that happened to her, her first thought was "how lovely, I must tell James!" only to be cast down when she remembered the impasse in their relationship.

Equally, if she felt sad or lonely, she longed for his sympathetic understanding. It was an extraordinary thing but she loved him more every day and yet she had not seen him for weeks and was in no way shaken in her resolve not to take the initiative in any friendly overtures.

The knowledge that dozens of people must have noticed the termination of her friendship with him made it something of an ordeal for her at the northern parties. Down here no one knew anything about her except that she was Harry's sister, and the sense of freedom which this brought did her as much good as a tonic.

The atmosphere in Kildare did not seem so very different

from the North as the majority of the landowners were Protestant and just as much concerned as the Ulster people about the effect of the Home Rule Bill. The only difference was that they were no longer so sure of the outcome. They were still giving concerts and variety entertainments for the Carson Defence Fund, as they called it, but everything was done at a much slower pace and with half the conviction, due partly to being a religious minority and partly to their much more lackadaisical temperament.

The life was singularly pleasant, and Ellen's host and hostess, a Colonel and Mrs. Fox, with a grown-up son and daughter, could not have made her feel more at home. Their house was one of the rambling and spacious houses so plentiful in the South and so rare in the North, well settled into the ground, with beautifully planted old trees in the small park; it gave a general impression of enchantment when the sun shone and decay when the sky was overcast. There seemed to be at least three horses for every member of the family and a continual coming and going of gay young people.

They would assemble for a delicious breakfast each day at nine-thirty, and each person seemed to have their individual taste catered for with deep interest by the cook, a slip of a girl with huge eyes, who often came to the door of the dining room to see if her sister, the parlourmaid, was giving the right egg to the right person. No help-yourself, take-it-or-leave-it side table here! It appeared that soft or hard centres could make or mar the day!

Then, after a leisurely meal and a long discussion as to who should ride which horse, they would all gallop off to the huge plain known as the Curragh where half the countryside and most of the soldiers would be found exercising their horses. Racing and jumping competitions would be organised and a certain amount of horse-coping went on, on the side, and then as often as not there would be an impromptu lunch in the officers' mess before they all dispersed again.

Once or twice a week there were rough shooting parties in the Wicklow Hills, and Ellen was entranced by the beauty of the scenery.

In the North the mountains were wild and grand, with sombre mixtures of purple and every conceivable grey, blue-grey, green-grey, brown-grey and silver, contrasting with the odd patches of dead grass, parchment yellow or blackened burnt heather, all beneath magnificent banks of silver-edged clouds or cloaked in mist.

These Southern hills were less grand and more pretty, smaller and lower, they were patchworked in brilliant colours of much lighter shades and all the little loughs seemed light silvery blue—not the slate grey of the North. Indeed the only really dark colour here was the sudden black cut of a turf bog.

Ellen was fascinated by the turf. She adored the smell of it, the blue-opal smoke which drifted from the turf fires in the tiny cottages, and the orderly stacks of rich turf bricks at intervals all across the bogs.

When she sat on the top of the hills after driving up with the picnic lunches, and before the men arrived, she would try to see how many donkeys she could count working in the bog below. At first there would seem to be none, so good a camouflage were their little grey bodies, and then a movement, the stamp of a silver hoof, and like a magic picture a tiny grey shape would become visible, standing with its panniers waiting to be filled, or picking its way across the bog to wander all alone along the track towards its home.

No wonder the people believed in fairies here! The way objects came and went in the translucent light was enough to bewilder the most prosaic person.

Commenting on this to Harry one day she was surprised to find what a thoughtful reply he gave and realised with a little shock that even brothers grow up sometime! He had always been her lighthearted and charming companion but quite clearly, as well as the gay and pleasant regimental life, he had found time to observe and consider the people around him.

"That's exactly the key to these people!" he exclaimed eagerly, in answer. "I don't know if it can be the effect of the light or the weather, but they themselves come and go . . . I mean, one day they feel tremendously strongly about something

—and they are so quick, they understand a point in half the time we do—but the next day it is as if the light had changed and they forget all about it and see something else!"

"Perhaps that is why they are so frightfully attractive," suggested Ellen.

"Attractive! Yes, to play with . . . but maddening to work with!" he said. "You think you have got something all fixed up and you make your plans accordingly, and then you find they have thought up something else and forgotten to tell you . . . all with the best will in the world! The thing that baffles me is that they all understand each other. You never find any of the locals being left in the lurch . . . they seem to have a kind of magic insight and all know what the others will do. It makes me feel it doesn't matter what either lot of politicians do, the Irish people will just go on in their own fantasy world regardless of government."

"You sound a bit depressed! Don't you really like being here? Or is it a case of *cherchez la femme?*" she asked with interest.

His easy laughter answered the last half of her question. "Oh, the girls! They're lovely and they're fun, but I think it would drive me mad to fall in love with one of them! No . . . I'm not depressed, but sometimes I feel we are living on borrowed time. Everyone drifts along so happily, talking about serious things sometimes, but no one actually does anything much. I want to be active!" He struck his hands together. "The whole of Europe is boiling like a volcano and we amuse ourselves and play at soldiers while the politicians exchange countries for votes and history slides past us!"

Ellen was very impressed at these deep thoughts from her young brother. "Goodness, you are serious, Harry! I didn't know you felt so strongly. I feel a bit like that, too, only I don't want there to be a war or anything like that. And you can't say that nobody in the North is doing anything much." She was thinking of James particularly, who seemed always to be "doing something"—especially lately—and, in a lesser way, her uncle, and Eric . . . indeed, nearly everyone she knew.

186

He laughed shortly. "Yes. They are all working like mad . . . and the ironic thing is the politicians don't take any notice of them either, so perhaps the South is right after all to butterfly their lives away and to hell with any government! Who knows?" He shrugged his shoulders and, falling into tune with the rest of the party, called out, "Hey, you Goths! Spare a bit of food for cultured people like us who can delay a moment to admire the scenery!" A brown-faced young man tossed him over a leg of chicken. "Here you are, Harry! I'll go shares with you. Poor Bobby here has to eat the whole pie . . . for it may be his last square meal!"

"Good heavens! Can't Barbara cook?" asked another soldier in astonishment.

"He doesn't know! Didn't dare to ask her before he proposed and now he is afraid of finding out she can't! There's no escape, now, is there Bobby?"

Bobby Peterson grinned. He was getting married on the following Saturday to the daughter of one of the oldest families in the South, with whom he had been hopelessly in love from the moment he first set eyes upon her. But as he was the only child of a rich and autocratic widow he had had his share of troubles in getting the consent of first one and then the other. It had been a common sight all summer to see him, having gained the hand of the dashing Barbara Selincourt, running his hand over his brow as he worried how he would bring his mother to approve his choice. For if she did not, she could, and would, cancel his allowance and then he would have to leave his expensive cavalry regiment. If that were to happen, would his sophisticated bride care to be the wife of a mere infantryman? Still more worrying, would her parents allow it?

To his enormous relief, his mother had thoroughly approved his choice, and the wedding was to be the social event of the regiment's autumn activities.

Although Ellen had not met Bobby or his bride before, she had entered so much into the life of the Curragh since she came South that she had easily been persuaded to stay on to see them married.

Saturday, contrary to the usual run of wedding days, could hardly have been said to dawn at all . . . so dark and wet it was. It was the first real winter's day, with torrents of rain and a wild wind lashing the last of the leaves off the sodden trees. Even the villagers, who normally would have turned out in their hundreds to see the daughter of the big house married and all her grand friends arriving, were daunted by the weather and contented themselves with peering from their windows as the carriages passed, or standing in dripping huddles under the yew trees in the churchyard.

Ellen and the Foxes arrived early and were fortunate to be given seats halfway up the aisle from where they had a splendid view of all their friends coming in, straightening their hats and collars after their dash through the downpour to the church.

Harry and his brother officers, looking magnificent in their Lancer full-dress uniforms, scarlet and gold braid brightening up the pews, already colourful with wedding hats, spurs clinking as they escorted people up the aisle and showed them to their seats.

There was a wave of whispered comments as Bobby Peterson slipped into a front seat with his best man, followed by what seemed a very long wait, during which he gazed anxiously and often over his shoulder towards the porch door and the organist exhausted his variations on the theme of the first hymn but did not dare to depart from it in case the bride should arrive and catch him unawares.

Then, suddenly, the doors opened from the main entrance and in walked Barbara Selincourt, looking supremely calm and elegant, not a hair out of place, her veil floating out crisply over her exquisite satin dress. Six bridesmaids followed in white pleated organdie dresses, carrying posies of late roses. Ellen was so busy wondering how on earth they managed to look so completely unruffled after coming through such a storm that she never noticed some late arrival being ushered into the seat on her right. It was only as she put out her hand to pick up the hymn sheet that she felt it touch something firm and warm, and looked up with a gasp of amazement to find James, immaculately clad in black mourning coat and folded grey silk cravat, regarding her somewhat whimsically as her hand rested on his which firmly grasped the front of the pew.

He bowed politely and affected not to notice how hastily she withdrew her hand from his and how fierily she blushed as he turned his attention to the wedding service. As the clear voice of the clergyman asked the fateful question, "Wilt thou, Robert, take this woman to be thy wedded wife, to have and to hold, to love and to cherish?" Ellen felt a tremor run through the man standing so close, which communicated itself to her so that she felt her knees turn to water and an almost uncontrollable impulse to lean against him for support. She could think of nothing in this world that she wanted more than to be "loved and cherished" by James, and the physical effort of remaining standing on her own feet made her feel quite faint. She had never really noticed before the significance of the words of the marriage service, and to have to listen to it now, standing, almost touching the man she loved but had so foolishly alienated, was a tremendous test of her self-control.

James was is no better state. He had arrived so late that he had had no time to choose a seat but had hurried down the side aisle at the same time as the bride went down the centre, and slipped into the first space he found. He had thought fleetingly, *What a pretty hat!* before it suddenly dawned on him who the owner was.

He was on the point of searching for a different seat to save embarrassment when she laid her hand on his, and he knew a moment of pure joy before he realised that she had not even noticed he was there.

He was so saddened by the thought of her nearness and of the barrier between them that he hardly heard the service at all, despite the appearance of keen attention which he put on. The bride and bridegroom, ring duly encircling her finger, walked solemnly up to the altar and sank to their knees for the blessing, but no more gratefully than Ellen and James sank to theirs, thankful at last to hide their faces and their feelings in their hands while they strove to regain their poise. Then, the blessing over, the happy couple disappeared with parents and attendants into the vestry, leaving Ellen and James in speechless proximity, acutely conscious of what had happened the last time they met.

Both racked their brains to think of some neutral comment to make. Anything to do with the wedding was unbearably poignant.

Finally James broke the silence in a rather strained voice. "I didn't know this was where you were. I missed you up in the North," he said, simply.

Ellen's heart leapt. "Did you really miss me?" she wondered as she introduced Colonel and Mrs. Fox to him, explaining, "I have been down here for a month . . . but I never expected to see you at this wedding; which of them is it whom you know?"

"Oh!" He smiled at her lack of appreciation of Irish relationships. "This is a very small world! I have known the Selincourts all my life. I think I probably dandled Barbara on my knee when she was in the nursery! I couldn't have missed her wedding, though I can't stay for the reception, unfortunately. I have a job to do in Dublin that won't wait!"

Ellen felt her heart sink again at this. She had so hoped that he was staying on and would be at the party that night. What could he be doing that took up so much of his time? Or was it just all an excuse to avoid too much of her company? Just as Desmond had done when he realised that she cared for him. She was so disheartened that she did not hear his muttered, "Don't stay away too long!" as they crowded out of the church and prepared to dash through the rain to the waiting carriages. She would have been greatly comforted if she had known how bitterly James was regretting his promise to Captain Craig to go and discuss a way of conveying the consignment of rifles, at present stuck in Dublin by this everlasting dock strike, up to Belfast without exciting suspicion.

Barbara Selincourt's wedding had provided an admirable cover for him to come South to meet the captain of a collier who was prepared to tranship the crates from the Italian ship they were now lying in outside Dublin and carry them up to a pre-arranged point on the Ulster coast. If he had had any inkling that Ellen would be at the wedding he could so easily have deferred the meeting for a few hours but although he had missed her from the Ulster scene, he had been too proud and too busy to ask where she was. It was doubly unfortunate, he thought, as he changed out of his wedding finery in the train, that he had to leave so early, as the unexpectedness of this encounter had done much to overcome the awkwardness of their first meeting after their quarrel at the Fete, and he thought he had detected a considerable softening in her manner which encouraged him to think that perhaps she had not meant all she had said on that occasion!

He was rather shocked to think how much less it meant to him to arrange the safe disposal of five hundred rifles than to have a few moments alone with the girl he loved. However, Captain Craig had entrusted him with this mission, and there was no doubt that the need for guns was quite desperate at present, with Mr. Asquith threatening to use the Royal Irish Constabulary as well as the regular army to "put down" the Ulster Volunteer Force. Though, of course, this threat would hardly work out as half the members of the Constabulary were in fullest sympathy with the Volunteers. There was a very strong move afoot in Parliament to have the importation of any kind of firearm into Ireland made illegal, which would make things considerably more difficult. He left the train and took an old cab down to the docks where he was moved to compassion for the near-starvation state into which the dockers had fallen since the beginning of their now five-month-old strike. He felt that anyone as well fed and dressed as himself must surely excite a lot of notice and was greatly relieved when he eventually met up with the collier Captain and found him to be a very well nourished individual who nevertheless appeared to provoke very little interest from his fellowmen.

Two hours and six bottles of Guinness later, they had evolved a foolproof plan that the Captain was as eager to put into action as a small boy.

His ship and the Italian were to rendezvous in a quiet bay in the early hours of the morning and transfer the rifles to the collier, after which he was to make his way up the coast, avoiding the shipping as much as possible, and land the crates into a convoy of fishing boats off Ardglass, who would, in turn, dispose of them at intervals along the coast for collection. If by any chance the customs officers got suspicious, the guns were already packed in waterproof bags inside the crates and could be slung overboard with a marker and collected again at their convenience.

James now had to take the earliest train North to make arrangements for the reception at that end. All these had to be done personally to be sure of secrecy, and no sooner had he reported those plans to the U.V.F. headquarters than a fresh batch of problems arose, so that it was with the utmost difficulty he managed to put in half the normal number of hours necessary in his own business, even working far into the night.

He was by no means the only man to find his private life completely taken over by the urgency of the situation. Henry Chichester-Grieves and dozens of other close friends were responsible for the disposal and storage of guns and ammunition, and for the assembly and manufacture of cartridges under Captain Fred Crawford's imaginative leadership. They were all out several nights a week drilling and lecturing the Volunteers; much time was taken up in carrying messages from one place to another which could not be entrusted to the post or telephone; and many of them had to make the journey to England to keep informed the various champions of their cause over there or to receive further orders from Sir Edward. Even the British Army was beginning to lose some of its free time. After the King finally signed the proclamation on December the sixth, prohibiting the "Importation of Military Arms and Ammunition into Ireland," an order was given to double the guards on all the military ammunition dumps from Carrickfergus to Enniskillen, to prevent the Volunteers seeking supplies "already imported."

As the army was still considerably under strength in the North of Ireland, this entailed a continuous "watch and watch" by the garrisons, and loud was the sound of their lamentations. Moreover, so confused were the orders to the customs officers about the smuggling of arms that more than one sportive army officer found himself being held and questioned for hours on end about cartridges found in his personal luggage. After all, most of the officers of the U.V.F. went on shooting parties to Scotland, too, and it was a point of honour to bring back as many arms with them as possible.

The North of Ireland Football Club met on December the twentieth and decided to cancel all future matches in order to enable their members to devote their time to drilling in the U.V.F. and announced their decision quite openly in the papers. Altogether there were very few entertainments in the winter months that were not affected and dampened by the increasing tempo of the political crisis.

To Ellen back from Kildare, it seemed that all the nicest men had gradually vanished from the social scene, leaving only the drones and butterflies to carry on. She said as much to her aunt one night, as they were on their way home from a party. "It's extraordinary how all the nicest men seem to be completely occupied with the U.V.F. and even the nicest soldiers seem to be the ones on guard duty! The one bad penny who turns up at everything seems to be Desmond Campion!"

"Oh, I thought you liked him!" exclaimed Lady Richardson, much intrigued, and Ellen found herself explaining without any embarrassment, "Well, I suppose . . . I liked him a lot once . . . and then I hated him. I think I used to be rather afraid of him! Isn't it odd how one changes without realising it?"

"I'm very glad to hear it!" said her aunt, terribly pleased at last to be taken into Ellen's confidence. "I did not think he was really your sort, but he was so emphatic about being such an old friend of yours that I didn't want to say anything . . . and, of course, he is a very amusing asset to a party—he does everything so well and his manners to older people are very good."

"Oh, yes, he's much too smart to do himself out of a good party by being rude to the elders!" laughed Ellen. "I think that's why he always choosed people like Valerie who is really rather like him and thinks his rudeness is amusing, or else mugs like me who don't know how to hit back! Though I must say I am improving; he was very, very annoyed with me tonight," she reflected with pleasure.

Lady Richardson gave a delighted chuckle at the victorious expression on her niece's face. "Do tell us what happened!" she entreated.

"Oh well, you know how he is always so sure one will do what he wants? He never bothers to book up dances beforehand, he just reckons all the girls are falling over themselves to dance with him, that he only has to ask and they will promptly throw over whatever partner they had previously promised? I was such a fool . . . my whole evening used to be ruined if he didn't ask me—and he knew it. Well, tonight when he came along at about midnight and asked me to dance—just as if Mervyn wasn't there at all—I clasped my hands to my breast and rolled my eyes at him and exclaimed, all of a quaver, 'Oh this is the moment I have been waiting for all evening!' He was frightfully nonplussed."

"What horrible creatures girls are!" exclaimed Sir Charles, sticking up for his fellowmen, though secretly highly amused. "You have probably completely undermined his confidence and he will never be the same again."

"Well, that could only be an improvement," replied Ellen cheerfully. "When I think of all the times in the past that he has undermined my confidence!"

"You think it has improved your character?" asked her uncle innocently. "Were you not always so sweet and guileless as you are now?"

She flashed him a look. "I don't believe you approve of the master species being teased, but believe me he is well able to look after himself."

She would have been very surprised to realise just how much less sure of himself Desmond had become of late. He found himself a little out of his element in this unsophisticated corner of the kingdom. His smooth manner, which won him such popularity in London, although gaining him access to all the right houses here, was regarded with a hint of suspicion. People were unfailingly friendly on the surface but they were not really his kind. Besides he was in a very curious position in the military sense, having been sent to Ireland to guard against a revolt—only to find all the most responsible men more or less openly drilling for such a revolt and his own sympathies in an increasingly mixed state.

He had always looked on the army as a very straightforward affair and he was not accustomed to having second thoughts about it. He had half a mind to apply for a return to his own regiment. Only two things held him back.

One was the fear of looking cowardly by applying for an exchange just when trouble seemed to be boiling up, and the other was the Tristram girl. He had become extraordinarily fond of her lately, she seemed to have acquired so much more spice since he knew her in London. He had always thought her quite lovely to look at, but then she had been so inexperienced and tiresome, making all that fuss about a kiss. It was so stupid when she was really dying to be kissed. She'd been in such a state because he hadn't asked her to marry him but, dash it all, he couldn't marry every girl he kissed! He laughed a bit wryly to himself as he pulled off his boots. The funny thing was, he still wanted to kiss her . . . terribly much. She seemed much more entrancing over here than she had in London. Maybe it was just because there was so much competition? But somehow he didn't think so. She really was the sort of girl any man would be glad to marry now, and, if he wasn't mistaken, there were two or three here who would be only too glad if she would have them.

He wondered what she felt about him now. A year ago she was very willing, but he wasn't so sure now. It was rather intriguing! He must make a bit more effort to win her back again! It shouldn't be too difficult. She was madly in love with him a year ago and he had not changed much in the interval.

The next time they met was at a concert held by Lady Annesley at Castlewellan, to raise funds for the Volunteers (as usual!). He couldn't help thinking how ridiculous it was for him as an officer of the British Army to be giving his money for a ticket to help the "enemy." On the other hand, one of the attractions of the evening was "Songs by Miss Ellen Tristram," and he could not stay away.

He was standing just inside the doorway into the big drawing room when she went to stand beside the piano and he thought she had never looked so beautiful. Her hair was dressed in a big soft circle 'round her head and threaded with pearls. The cobwebby lace of her dress fell softly against her body and the tall lamp beside the piano cast dramatic shadows on her eyes and cheekbones and into the soft dip beneath her chin. The first song she chose was "The Lass With the Delicate Air," and as her voice lilted lightly up and down over the last bars of the music, he reflected how admirably the song suited her. She followed this with "On Wings of Song," and then, in response to rapturous cries of "encore," she chose "Juanita," the Spanish love song she had sung to James so long ago in Galway and which was now and forever inextricably associated with him in her mind. She hadn't wanted to sing it tonight, but the accompanist had a rather narrow selection of songs she could play and had been terribly anxious to include this one, so Ellen had given in.

In a way it was one of the few things she could do for the Volunteers and therefore rather unfair to cavil at something the organisers asked her to do. *Anyway*, she thought, *there is no sign of him tonight so it won't be so bad. I couldn't bear to sing it if he was here.* Nevertheless, as she sang the melting appeal, "be my one true love," she could feel a lump coming in her throat and the pathos in her voice was deeply moving. More than one listener felt a prickle behind their eyes and Desmond was overwhelmed by the novel conviction that this was the one girl in the world for him. As soon as she had finished he would try his luck . . . he only wished he was as sure of her feelings as he now was of his own.

Coming to the last line of the song, with its soaring entreaty again, Ellen was so filled with memories that she had a moment of uncertainty about getting the top note and hastily shifted her gaze, to relieve the intensity of her mood, from the middle distance to the back of the room, and was suddenly thrilled to see James leaning against the doorjamb, arms folded across his chest, and a completely unguarded expression of enchantment on his face as he watched her. Before she could help herself, a smile of joy lit her eyes and her top note rang out, pure and certain, all the more poignant for the slight hesitation preceding it. Desmond, standing just inside the door, was as unaware of James standing behind him, as James was of Desmond, so concentrated was their attention on the singer; each took the smile from Ellen as directed to himself as an acknowledgment of his own feelings and started to make his way across the crowded room.

Desmond was at her side before the applause had quite died down, and taking both her hands in his, squeezed them, exclaiming in a tone of such sincerity that she was momentarily startled into taking her attention off James, who had been delayed by Lady Annesley, and giving it fully to Desmond, "My dear! That was superb! Why did you never sing like that before? You are far too good to be wasted in the provinces! Will you come and let me get you some supper—while I suggest to you where I really think your talent should be directed?"

Ellen didn't in the least want to go and have supper with him. She had never felt less hungry . . . she was sure that James had read the message in her eyes and she was certain he was going to come and speak to her. But with her attention momentarily diverted by Desmond's unexpected enthusiasm, she had lost sight of him. Now, looking 'round anxiously for an excuse to refuse Desmond's invitation, she could not see James anywhere at all.

He had, indeed, been thrilled by her singing and started off impetuously to tell her how wonderful she was when his hostess, pushing back her chair as she rose, completely blocked his way.

"Oh, James! How nice of you to come. I do feel flattered as I know how tremendously busy you are at present. I do hope you are enjoying the concert?" She chattered, and then observing his anxious eye on Ellen, she laughed, "But I am sure you must be . . . the little Tristram girl has the most exquisite voice, has she not? So unusual to have both looks and talent together . . . and in the back of beyond like this! I was delighted when she consented to sing—I knew it would bring the young men, and if you get the young men you get the girls and their parents, and then the evening is a big success and makes lots of money for the Cause!" She laughed again.

Ordinarily James liked her very much but tonight he could

have murdered her. As he tried to edge past, he saw Campion taking hold of Ellen's hands and pressing them warmly, in the manner of one extraprivileged.

He saw the surprise and warmth in Ellen's expression and the horrid thought struck him that perhaps her lovely singing and smile had not been for him at all but for Campion, who was standing just in front of him. This thought so appalled him that he stood quite still, trying to reason with himself, and as he stood, he saw Ellen glance quickly 'round—probably for her aunt—and then walk off towards the supper room with her hand resting on Desmond's arm as he bent confidentially over her.

How long he stood watching the door they had vanished through James could not have told; he was only conscious of his leaden heart. Funny . . . he felt as though it had completely stopped beating, and yet he could hear it! Suddenly he realised it was his hostess tapping his lapel with her fan. "James, James! I don't believe you have listened to a word I have been saying to you!"

At the startled look of unhappiness in his eyes as he tried to respond to her raillery, she felt a twinge of remorse and exclaimed "Well . . . I must go and talk to some of my other guests and not monopolise one of the most popular ones! I am sure you want to talk to some of the others." Giving him a charming smile, she walked away to thank Lady Londonderry for coming such a long, long way to support her concert.

James turned quickly on his heel and left the house. He couldn't bear to remain there for everyone to read his feelings. What a conceited fool he had been to think she would ever look at him! He could hardly have expected a London girl, least of all a stunner like Ellen Tristram, to fall for a provincial like himself. Obviously she must have been secretly engaged to Campion all the time; probably she was just waiting for her parents' return before announcing the engagement. Naturally she must have been bored over here. He could hardly blame her for having tried to take an interest in their local goings-on to try to pass the time . . . and yet . . . and yet . . . he could have sworn she had not been merely passing the time . . . if she had been, would she have minded so much about the tennis match? He had written to explain, but she didn't seem to have understood. How stupid he was! Of course she was angry at being let down—she had been the toast of London where these things don't happen. Of course she was angry and had obviously decided he was not worth bothering about. But what else could he have done? He had to get the message to Crawford. Certainly these times were well named "Troubled." Well . . . now he could throw himself into the gun-running with a clear mind. He had only one thing to concentrate on . . . he tried to comfort himself as he drove rapidly home through the cold, wet night.

Desmond, meanwhile, had steered a somewhat distrait Ellen into the supper room, pressed a plate of aspic and salad into one hand and a glass of champagne into the other, and, lifting his own glass, exclaimed, "To the most talented and beautiful girl I know!"

She smiled ironically. "I never knew you were such a patron of the arts, Desmond! What has happened so suddenly to arouse this enthusiasm?"

While she sipped her drink, her eyes searched the room for any sign of James, and she was only partially aware of Campion's skilled attentions. She was not in the least bit hungry and followed him around the laden buffet tables simply in order to look for James. She couldn't believe he could have disappeared again; she ought really to be grateful to Desmond for being always at hand to save her from being obviously abandoned! Strange to think that it was little more than a year since she would have given her soul to be the object of the attentions to which she was now so indifferent.

Having found a tray and loaded their plates and glasses onto it, he now guided her into what had to be the smoking room, with shabby, plush chairs and a crackling wood fire. In the distance a violin had struck up and she supposed the second half of the concert must have begun. She felt suddenly terribly tired and sank gratefully into one of the armchairs while Desmond hovered attentively 'round with a little table for her to put her plate on.

"Honestly, Desmond! I'm not at all hungry," she protested. "I just feel frightfully tired. I suppose it's because I was so nervous earlier on."

"I can't believe you were in the least bit nervous—your performance was every bit as finished as a professional." He pulled up a prie-dieu beside her: "I think this is a rather appropriate seat for me to take," he remarked, "for I want to ask you when do you intend to return to a setting more suited to your talents? How much longer"—he smiled as she raised her eyebrows in a look of comical dismay—"do I have to continue on foreign service to be near my love?"

"Oh come, Desmond!" she exclaimed somewhat impatiently, "don't be ridiculous! You can hardly call this 'foreign service!'"

"No? All right . . ." he agreed comfortably. "But I am staying over here to be near my love!"

Ellen began to wish she had not settled down so far from the rest of the guests; plainly Desmond was in a very queer mood. She cast about in her mind for some way of turning the conversation.

"I didn't know you had brought any of your horses over with you," she answered hopefully.

He roared with laughter. "What a sweet girl you are! Fond as I am of horses, I station them near me rather than myself near them, and *none* of them is called My Love. I think you are being rather dense," he said meaningly.

Ellen moved restlessly. "Oh, Desmond, do talk sense."

"I am talking sense. Why shouldn't I be in love with you?" he asked, leaning forward and taking her hand. "No, don't pull your hand away . . ." as she drew back. "I'm asking you to marry me—the least you can do is to listen politely!"

"Oh, Desmond! It's no good . . ." she exclaimed in distress, trying desperately to pull her hand from him and at the same time to clear away the table and open a line of retreat with the other. "Please let me go . . . I tell you, it's no good . . . I . . . please . . . I don't love you . . . please, please let me go . . ."

But Desmond was thoroughly piqued. She used to love him—

he would make her love him again. It was just reserve that held her back—she didn't really know what she wanted. He had aroused her with kisses before . . . he could do it agin. So he suddenly let go her hands, and as she relaxed gratefully, looking down at them in speechless embarrassment, he took her unawares.

He drew her out of the chair so swiftly that her arms were pinioned to her sides and her head was being forced back by his eager mouth until her lips parted and he was kissing her so fiercely that she could scarcely breathe. His teeth were against her lips, bruising them and his nostrils pressed against hers so that she seemed to be suffocated by his hot breath. For a moment her traitorous body responded to his passion. Then something snapped in her head, the mists whirled away, and she was fighting like a demon, simultaneously kicking and biting so that he flinched with pain and in a moment she broke free. With all her might she struck him across the face and then staggered back, clutching the mantelpiece, horrified at what she had done. How could this man drag her so low? She must get away from him and find her aunt. But he was between her and the door.

"You little bitch!" he exclaimed, staring at her with admiration as he caressed his smarting jaw. "You damned attractive little bitch! I'm going to make you love me if it's the last thing I do."

He made a move towards her and she was suddenly filled with fear. She made a wild rush to get past him and, catching her foot on a small stool, fell forward to hit her head a violent crack on the side of the bookcase, sinking unconscious into Campion's outstretched arms at the exact moment in which Valerie Balfour sauntered past the half-open door. Not having seen Ellen's head hit the cupboard, Valerie watched with considerable interest Ellen Tristram throwing herself headlong into Desmond Campion's arms and allowing herself to be carried to the sofa and smothered with kisses.

At this even Valerie felt herself to be slightly *de trop* and passed on down the passage murmuring softly to herself, "Well,

well! Stillwaters certainly run deep. I wonder if Mr. Melville knows about this, or 'auntie,' if it comes to that!"

When Ellen failed to respond in any way to his kisses, Desmond's passion gave way to alarm and he hastily smoothed her hair and dress, felt anxiously for her pulse, and feeling extraordinarily deflated and ashamed of himself went in search of Lady Richardson.

He was lucky enough to find her almost at once, just coming out of the buffet, and whispered in her ear that Ellen was not feeling very well and wanted to go home.

"Oh dear! Where? Where is she?" exclaimed her aunt in surprise. "I thought she was on top of her form tonight!"

"Yes, she was, but she tripped over a stool and hit her head," explained Desmond, as if it was the most natural thing in the world to do, "and now she is lying down . . . in the study."

Lady Richardson gave him a searching look and hurried anxiously ahead of him into the study without speaking. To his enormous relief Ellen was now sitting up, looking very pale and ill, and leaning her head on her hand.

He was only too pleased when Lady Richardson told him, somewhat abruptly, to go and order her car. He hoped Ellen would have the sense not to tell her aunt what had happened. But he underestimated both Lady Richardson's intelligence and Ellen's changed feelings towards him.

She had been badly frightened and was disgusted with herself for having got into such a situation—as well as having a very sore head. She now not only did not love him but positively loathed him and poured out the whole unhappy story to her aunt on the long drive home.

Lady Richardson listened in commendable silence, only putting in a murmur of sympathy here and there. Finally she kissed Ellen and soothed her to sleep on her shoulder with the comforting words that, "The course of true love never did run smooth," and that she was perfectly sure that James did care and it would all come right very soon.

"I shall find some way to see that it does," she promised herself. "No matter what Charles says, this has gone on quite long enough. It is bad enough to have a war on our hands without a broken heart as well. Particularly when she and James are so obviously in love with each other and making themselves miserable about nothing. I must find some way of getting them together without interruptions."

Chapter 14

She planned to do this at some of the dances over Christmas and was not prepared for Ellen flatly refusing to go to any of them.

Ever since the Castlewellan concert Ellen had been depressed and listless, not even wanting to to go riding with the girls as she usually did, but spending ages in her room, lying on her bed with her hands clasped behind her head, counting the daisies on the wall, and generally allowing herself to give way to the miseries.

To all her aunt's entreaties to show some spirit and come out to meet people, she just said, "No, Aunt Marion, honestly, I couldn't . . . Desmond is sure to be at all the parties—he always is—and I won't meet him. I'm not going to go anywhere until I hear he has left the country."

"But, my darling child! He may be here for years! This trouble is just coming to a head and he is not in the least likely to be sent away—they are sending in reinforcements all the time," expostulated her aunt.

"Very well then, I shan't go anywhere for years," Ellen replied coldly.

Lady Richardson regarded her niece with exasperation. "How are you going to meet James, then, if you never go anywhere?" she asked.

"Oh, auntie! I don't know . . ." wailed Ellen, turning her face into her hands. "I only know I can't go out yet. You don't understand Desmond . . . he's bad . . . you can't trust him . . . he hasn't got any standard of behaviour . . . and I just feel too battered to be able to cope with him at present. Please understand, Aunt Marion, and don't ask me to go," she pleaded.

So Lady Richardson left her alone, though the dances seemed very dull without her pretty niece to chaperone. James she did not see at all, so at least Ellen was not wasting her chances. She wondered, disloyally, if he also was lying on his bed and refusing to go out and managed to get a small giggle from Ellen when she suggested as much to her.

Harry's Christmas leave was postponed and there was a general feeling of the crisis being very near at hand. With so many of the men away in the evenings drilling, the women filled the time with first-aid classes and bandaging parties, and in these Ellen did take part, although it seemed a terribly dull form of help to be giving.

The talk was all of the fantastic sums of money flowing into Sir Edward Carson's indemnity fund, and of how Lady London-derry had followed it by launching an appeal for the women, too.

In England the Duke of Bedford announced that it was a known fact that five hundred thousand men and women had now signed the Covenant, and that over a million pounds had been guaranteed to the indemnity fund to ensure financial protection to the people thus making their stand for freedom.

The most astonishing sums had been guaranteed by quite poor people. One country clergyman with seven children, five of them boys, to educate had guaranteed three thousand pounds, and when his wife remonstrated with him that this sum represented their entire capital, his reply had been, "My dear, if we are not prepared to support this Cause with everything we have got we won't win—and then we will have nothing anyway!"

This spirit was quite commonplace as the Home Rule Bill approached its third reading in the House of Commons and feeling was beginning to run very high.

The soldiers were coming in for a certain amount of abuse from the Nationalists and the army officers were continually being approached by the press about their attitude to being asked to fire on their fellow countrymen if it came to war.

The English press was particularly persistent. Few of the soldiers were rash enough to give an opinion, but all of them found the situation both trying and unsesettling.

Conversation became so serious and sometimes heated at the dinner parties that Lady Richardson began to think Ellen had been wiser than she knew in deciding to cut them.

The children were much concerned by Ellen's lack of spirits —the girls with a somewhat respectful awe for the power of love—but Michael, home for the holidays and in great excitement over the political situation, was disgusted.

He hoped the war would break out while he was at home so that he wouldn't have to go back to school, and to find his pretty cousin sunk in such a state of gloom because she was in love, at a time like this, was only one stage worse than the state of exaltation in which Mr. Grantham and Margaret McInnis were wrapped, to the exclusion of almost any interest in him. How anyone could waste time on love with affairs of war at such a pitch Michael was at a loss to understand and he was obliged to fall back on his sisters for company.

However, his wishes were answered in one way.

Two days before he was due to return to school, he began to feel very hot and uncomfortable and rather sick, and was put to bed by Lady Richardson, while the girls assured everyone that it was the natural consequence of his having been so mean about the big box of preserved fruits his godfather had sent him and which no one else had so much as tasted since it arrived. However, on the fourth day a mass of little red spots absolved him from blame on the score of greed but cast an additional despondency on the rest of the family, none of whom had had measles before, and who now envisaged months of quarantine ahead of them.

Ellen was really glad at first, as it gave her a splendid reason for not going out. Michael was not ill enough to cause any anxiety and when eventually Cynthia succumbed she also had a fairly mild attack. She was rapidly followed by the cook and two housemaids, and as Ellen and her aunt dashed about filling the gaps, cooking, dusting and organising trays and occupations for the invalids, Ellen began to feel much less depressed and took more interest in events outside.

Sir Edward Carson was over, staying with the Londonderrys, at the end of January, making splendid speeches at a number of rallies. He had spent much of the winter making speeches in England to try to awaken her people to the injustice being done in Ireland. His superb oratory coupled with the wisest legal brain in the country was having such effect that Birrel, the secretary of state for Ireland, was somewhat perturbed at the way his Liberal government was losing ground in their by-elections. He was unusually vituperative even for him, giving vent to the most appalling tirade against the Ulster leaders in the House of Parliament and doing everything possible to speed up the third reading of the bill before his party was finally forced to concede a general election. In the midst of all this arrangements for a splendid banquet to celebrate one hundred years of peace in Britain seemed singularly inappropriate!

When the Londonderrys announced that all arrangements had been made to turn Mountstewart into an emergency hospital immediately on the outbreak of civil war, Ellen suggested that her aunt should do the same with Kilwater Park, particularly as they were all in such good training for nursing at that moment!

But on the twelfth of February—the date of the opening of the debate on the final reading of the Home Rule Bill and in the midst of the most appalling gales and torrents of rain—Ellen collapsed with measles herself.

Lady Richardson thought that it was probably the result of her previous listlessness and the lack of fresh air while nursing Michael and Cynthia, but whatever the cause, Ellen's bout of measles was very serious indeed. Her temperature soared up at the most frightening speed, and the rash went into her eyes causing enormous swelling and irritation. For two days she was quite delirious, babbling away about Harry and James, crying that they were killing each other one moment, and arranging games of tennis or discussing the colours for her embroidery the next. On the second night she cried bitterly to her aunt to "tell him to go away ... please, please make him go away, he frightens me ..." and, suddenly, with a great cry of "No, no, Desmond ... no!" she sat up and threw off the bedclothes, trembling all

207

over and trying to get out of bed. Then, all at once, as her aunt held her tightly in her arms, she relaxed, her eyes cleared and drooped, and she sank peacefully into a clear, untroubled sleep. The next day her temperature was down and she lay in a state of lassitude that lasted for several days, then slowly she began to regather strength. Her eyes remained swollen and sore for a long time and she had to remain in a darkened room, her aunt and cousins taking turns to read to her and report the stirring events which were going on in the world outside.

The violent weather had temporarily halted social activities but the politicians were very busy indeed in England. The government lost three by-elections in quick succession and heavy pressure was put on them to provide an amendment to the Home Rule Bill.

Lord Roberts proclaimed that it was "unthinkable" that the British Army should be called upon to suppress Ulster. This, coming from a field marshal, carried great weight, and General Sir Arthur Paget, when he was speaking at a dinner in Dublin, assured the army that it would not be called upon to use arms against Ulster people. But there was still great anxiety, and on February the twenty-fifth Parliament debated the possibility of civil war and pressed Mr. Asquith to reveal his promised altered plan for Ireland.

The English had at last realised that Ulster meant to stand firm for her right to remain under the Crown, but the Liberal government, hanging onto power by the skin of its teeth, was determined to go on so fast with giving Ireland Home Rule that it would be too late for anyone to stop it.

While politicians, generals, field marshals, dukes, and ordinary people fought verbally and in the papers, Ellen regained her strength. Although she had grown much thinner, her colour had returned and at the end of four weeks she was well enough to go for a short ride each morning, rain or fine, so long as she rested in the afternoon.

No one else had developed any signs of measles and the family was able to return to normal activities.

Sir Charles and his wife went off to a dinner party at Lord

Templeton's house nearby and Lady Richardson was particularly pleased to find James among the guests. It was ages since she had seen him and she was determined to use the opportunity to try to heal the breach between him and Ellen.

It was a large dinner party of about twenty-two people and although James looked up and gave Lady Richardson a very warm smile as she came into the drawing room he was not immediately free to come to talk to her so she had leisure to observe him from a distance. She thought how much he had matured in the last year and how well it suited him. Those thoughtful grey eyes, that look of interested amusement as he listened would win any girl's heart. She did hope she could put an end to this ridiculous fight, although usually she was very much averse to meedling in other people's affairs. She was wondering how she was going to set about it when the butler swung open the double doors and announced dinner. Immediately James crossed to her side, saying in delighted tones, "Marion, I am in luck tonight, I am to take you in to dinner—I hope you are as pleased as I am!"

She laid her hand on his arm and said with perfect truth, "My dear James, nothing could please me more. You have become a complete stranger to us and we miss you!"

He looked at her rather earnestly for a moment, as if about to speak, but there was a general movement into the dining room and for a few moments after they sat down his attention was claimed by the lady on his left.

When he was free, he observed gently, "I don't think I am entirely to blame for not being seen, there have been several occasions lately that have not been graced by the Richardson family. I thought maybe it was this dreadful weather but then someone told me the children had all had measles."

"Oh, yes!" she exlaimed. "We have been in quarantine ever since Christmas and not able to go anywhere. It has been an absolute nightmare!"

"Did they all get it?" he asked sympathetically. "How bad were they—not really ill, I hope?"

"No, not all of them . . . Michael got it first, the day before

209

he was due to go back to school and of course he was delighted . . . though he was bored stiff by the time he finally did get away. He and Cynthia didn't have it at all badly, but it is maddening the way it always waits unitil the very end of the incubation period before the next one succumbs. Ellen was the last and she was really terribly ill."

"Ellen?" he went very pale and there was a look of unbearable sadness in his eyes as he spoke her name. "I didn't hear . . . how dreadful . . . is she alright now?" he stammered.

"Quite alright," she assured him compassionately. "A little thin and pulled down, but that will soon mend—and her eyesight does not seem to be affected at all, which is what I was really worried about."

"Her eyes?" he exclaimed in horror. "Good Lord! How terrible that would have been! I never knew she was ill. Do tell her . . . give her my . . ." he broke off, and resumed after a moment, in a calmer voice, "I suppose that is why the engagement has never been announced . . . Poor Ellen! What rotten luck!"

Now it was Lady Richardson's turn to be surprised.

"What engagement? What are you talking about? Who is engaged?" she demanded.

"Why, Ellen's engagement to Captain Campion," he replied in astonishment. "Everyone is talking about it and wondering why it has not been made official yet!"

"What absolute nonsense!" exclaimed her aunt indignantly. "She loathes the man! How on earth did that story get about—and who is 'everyone'?"

"But I got it as an absolute fact from Valerie Balfour after the concert at Castlewellan," said James, a small ray of hope beginning to dawn. "She said it was to be announced any day . . . and she had seen them—I hope you will forgive me if I quote her words—'locked in each other's arms' in the small study at Castlewellan! I am sorry to repeat such gossip to you—if gossip it is—but you are her aunt . . ."

"Yes, I am her aunt, and I am very glad you told me," declared Lady Richardson wrathfully, "for there is not a word of truth in it. I always disliked that young woman extremely, and only that you introduced her to Ellen I would have had nothing to do with her!"

"I am extremely sorry, Marion," said James humbly, but with a pronounced twinkle in his eye. He suddenly felt a surge of lightheartedness. "I promise faithfully I won't do it again!" Then, suddenly serious, he said, "I can't tell you how glad I am that you were set beside me tonight for I have been so depressed. You know how much . . . how fond I am of Ellen . . . and I could not like that man."

Lady Richardson could not resist smiling broadly as she said, "Well then, at least you and Ellen have one dislike in common. But how could such a story get about?" she persisted. "And why did you believe it?"

He was a bit taken aback at such a direct question, but knowing that it was asked in friendliness, decided to answer equally truthfully.

"Well, to tell you the truth, Ellen and I had a row some time ago. I don't honestly know very well what it was about . . . but we haven't spoken much since and she has been seeing a lot of this fellow Campion. I didn't really think she did like him much, but he seemed to have got a sort of a hold over her . . . and then I knew they had known each other in England. Valerie told me they were almost engaged then, and I didn't believe it. But lately I couldn't make it out, and then I saw them go off together at Castlewellan after she had finished singing, just as I was going to congratulate her—she did sing beautifully, didn't she?—I suppose I was annoyed, anyway I went home and the next thing Valerie told me what she had seen . . . and I believed her!" he said simply.

Having listened with deep interest, Lady Richardson explained. "What actually happened that night was that Major Campion inveigled Ellen into that little sitting room for supper . . . Ellen was very tired and didn't want to go at all but there was no one else about . . . and then he asked her to marry him and wouldn't take no for an answer. She tried to run away and tripped over a stool and was completely knocked out against the library shelves . . . not exactly a love scene!" she observed grimly, as she looked at James's furious expression. "I don't know how long she was unconscious, but I know Major Campion was a very worried man when he came to look for me. Ellen was still very dazed and had an enormous lump on the side of her head when I reached the study. I can only suppose that wretched girl saw him carrying her to the sofa and jumped to conclusions. Now I shall have to contradict this ridiculous story. Poor Ellen! It is bad enough to have been frightened and then ill without having to compete with this!"

They were so immersed in their conversation, which meant so much to both of them, that their neighbours had been completely isolated. But now the Dean, on Lady Richardson's right, intervened determinedly.

"I cannot allow you to be monopolised any longer, my dear Marion," he exclaimed. "Unless you promise to tell me the subject that interests you so much! Charles is one of my oldest friends and I will not be a party to his wife devoting her whole time to another man!"

Lady Richardson laughed and shook her head. "How nice for Charles to have a champion—but it is not he who needs one!" she said in her clear voice. "It is my niece Ellen, who has been extremely ill with measles—we have all been in quarantine—and now James tells me there is a nonsensical story going around that she is engaged to Major Campion."

She was aware that her voice was clear enough to have reached several other people and noticed with satisfaction that most of the ladies, though pretending interest in their partners' conversation, were undoubtedly straining their ears to hear what she was telling the Dean. So she continued, "It is most unfair, for there is no truth in it at all . . . she does not even like the man and will be most distressed when I tell her what has been said."

And that she thought to herself, *will start ten counter-rumours, which is quite good for one night's work. Dear James, it has certainly made his evening—he looks ten years younger!*

He did, indeed, feel as if a great burden has been taken off his shoulders though he was still far from certain how he stood.

At least now there was no definite obstacle in his way; he was free to try again if only this damned war did not boil up before he had a chance. It looked horribly as if he would have to go abroad again about these wretched guns. Seventy percent of the Volunteers still only had dummy guns, and although this was still an admirably well-kept secret, it was absolutely vital, both to the stubborn resistance of their leaders and the morale of the men, that their stand could be backed by force if they failed to make their point peaceably.

Fred Crawford never ceased to press the urgent need for guns with which to add weight to Ulster's stand for freedom, and he was even more insistent at this moment when their cause had begun to arouse so much sympathy in England that the government was sufficiently alarmed to be making a final attempt to frighten Ulster into submission by concentrating navy and army in and around her shores.

Despite all efforts, Crawford had managed to slip very few guns through the customs network since their importation had been made illegal, and now that both time and money were desperately short, he had come up with a most brilliant idea to stake all on getting one enormous shipload through rather than hundreds of isolated packages. He had worked out a most daring scheme but was having some difficulty in putting it over to his superiors. Sir Edward Carson and Captain Craig hoped to gain their point without resort to arms.

James had been enrolled as Crawford's aide if the plan ever materialised. His knowledge of the Rhine and Moselle districts and the shipping facilities for his wine business enabled him to give valuable information and also to make trips abroad without arousing suspicion. He had spent some time in Germany during the autumn with Captain Crawford, visiting ammunition firms, arranging for packing guns, discovering the routes and the timing of the barges that would have to carry them up the Rhine to the open sea.

Fred Crawford was a dynamic character to work with. His enthusiasm and vision had foreseen the ultimate need for arms more than twenty years earlier when the Liberals had first mooted the idea of Home Rule for Ireland. With an almost schoolboy spirit of adventure he had worked ceaselessly ever since to prepare Ulster for an emergency. As a result there was hardly an arms manufacturer or a shipping agent in the length and breadth of Europe whom he did not know personally.

At first James found it rather alarming to be despatched to an unknown city, such as Cardiff, and told to find a foreign captain of a foreign ship to discuss possible freights with him—all under a veil of secrecy. However, familiarity bred not contempt but a keen interest in the plans and a devoted admiration for his fanatical little leader.

It was easy to sympathise with both sides in the constant clashes between Crawford and Captain Craig. The one was so eager to get the guns before suspicion was aroused and it was too late; the other was loathe to give permission for such a dangerous mission to begin, thereby taking one step nearer to possible bloodshed.

The last thing Ulstermen wanted was to be the first to strike; it was their intention only to stand firm unless attacked. The two men were so utterly different in character and yet both so essential to the freedom of their country that it was quite painful to be present at their meetings and to see their difficulty in working together.

Only last week Crawford had delivered an ultimatum: if he was not allowed to put his plan into action forthwith he would not do it and Ulster would have to make her stand without any arms for there was no other possible way of getting them. Put like this, the committee recognised the ugency of the situation but, still loathe to take this final step alone, arranged a further meeting at which Carson himself would be present to make the final and irrevocable decision. This was to be held tomorrow and James only hoped that Sir Edward's well-known tact would be able to keep the peace between the two men.

In a way he was as keen as Fred Crawford to get on with the job, although it was not hard to visualise the appalling consequences if they were unsuccessful—the awful blow to the morale of the Volunteers who had such implicit faith in their

214

leader's promise to supply them with guns, the loss of strength for negotiating with the government and the possible resultant failure of their whole stand, not to mention the problem of whether they were laying themselves open to a trial for treason in the event of being caught redhanded.

Crawford, of course, did not contemplate nor allow anyone else contemplate defeat: it was not in his character, and finally he won the day. His plan was to be put into action immediately.

That evening Ellen was surprised and Lady Richardson delighted to see a smart trap drive up to the door, its driver alight, take a huge bunch of Malmaison carnations out, and ring the bell. Lady Richardson recognised the trap and positively purred with pleasure. She had not wanted to raise Ellen's hopes too much and had therefore contented herself with telling Ellen merely that she had heard a ridiculous rumour, at the Templeton dinner, about her being engaged to Captain Campion, that she had taken great pleasure in telling everyone that this was quite untrue and that James had been most sympathetic about Ellen's illness.

When the maid brought the carnations in and said they were for Miss Tristram, Ellen turned first pink and then white. She could hardly bring herself to open the accompanying letter in its blank envelope. If they were from Desmond, she couldn't bear it. Surely he must realise that they were absolutely finished and there was no good in trying to start again. He had never sent her flowers and she did not think it was in his nature to apologise. Could they possibly be from James? No, that would be too much! In any case, why should he suddenly send her flowers, such heavenly flowers, too, when he had not spoken to her since their fight? But then, who else could have sent them? It wasn't her birthday ... could it be that he really had thought that she was in love with Desmond ... and that now ... ? Her fingers trembled so much that she could hardly get the envelope open and when she recognised James's squiggly writing inside she sank into a chair for support before beginning to read it.

Lady Richardson had tactfully left the room, remembering how she had hated her sister hovering expectantly about, asking who her letters were from when she had been young and in love.

The letter was very short and had no beginning. It just said how terribly sorry James was not to have heard sooner about her illness, that he wished her a quick recovery and hoped soon to be able to come to see her. "Unfortunately," it went on, "I have to go abroad on some very urgent business or I would have delivered these flowers myself. I hope not to be away very long and that in the meantime they will help you to recover." Nothing given away there, but this time the signature was definitely "Your James," quite clearly and no squiggles. Ellen pressed it to her lips and hugged herself. How wonderful! She felt absolutely recovered already—only torment at the thought of not being able to see him or even write to him until he came back.

She picked up the bouquet and waltzed off to the flower room to get a vase and then up the stairs to her room where she spent a long happy hour arranging and gloating over her gorgeous flowers. Outside the rain fell softly and steadily but Ellen felt as if her room was full of sunshine and it was only with a great effort that she was able to resume normal behaviour and spend the evening with her cousins. In fact her aunt and uncle were so impressed with her good spirits that they decided it could not possibly do her any harm to come with them to the Down Hunt Steeplechase on March the thirteenth, her first outing since her illness.

It was a fine warm day after weeks of storm and a night of torrential rain. Ellen's spirits soared at the thought of possibly meeting James although she didn't think he could really be aback yet. In fact, he was not there, but everyone seemed so pleased to see her and the countryside was so sparklingly fresh after the storms that it was an extremely happy day.

The racing was first-class despite the heavy going. When Jockey Morgan piloted himself to first place on Corriemount in the first race, on Silver Dart in the second race, on Tantetantee in the third, and the crowd realised that he had a mount in each of the remaining races, a spirit of wild excitement pervaded the course.

When he napped his earlier successes by winning the fourth race on Nando, people, who had earlier decided to make a quick getaway before the mud had them all stuck fast, returned to the course to see if he could possibly win once again on Roy's Daughter. The price was so tight there was no point in backing him but everyone remained breathlessly watching his progress 'round the course. Ellen was so busy cheering him wildly as he came up the last fence, neck and neck with Domino, that she never noticed Desmond Campion, a little to one side and by himself, staring at her with a puzzled, almost wistful, look on his usually sardonic features before he shrugged his shoulders slightly and moved off towards the bookies.

Her aunt breathed a sigh of relief. She had been very much afraid he was going to come up and talk. He seemed to have no conscience and she did not want Ellen bothered any more. She turned her attention back to the race just in time to see Morgan, riding brilliantly, coax his tired horse past the post, first again. His fifth win that day! The crowd were in raptures, they cheered and cheered. So happy and excited were they that when Sir Charles had to enlist help in pushing the Argylle out of the mud, he was given so much enthusiastic support he began to fear his whole family would be tipped out.

A week later, at breakfast, he opened an official looking letter and gave a great crack of laughter. They all looked up, begging to know what was so funny.

"Just this circular from the War Office, warning me that all officers on the reserve must hold themselves in readiness to be called up for possible active service!" He laughed again.

"What does that mean, exactly?" asked Ellen, to whom official language was a closed book.

"Oh, simply that I may soon be called upon to don uniform and protect you from the Ulster Volunteer Force, who are threatening the peace in a corner of our kingdom! Do not fear, children," he exclaimed, "what harm can possibly befall you if

Uncle Charles and James and Eric and Harry and I are all fighting on both sides at once! Bah! How stupid can the government get?" and he crumpled up his napkin, threw it onto the table and marched off to his study.

This was really ridiculous and caused a lot of amusement throughout the country as more than fifty percent of the Volunteers were in the reserve. The situation was laughable. Two days later things began to look much less amusing. Rumours were circulating that a warrant was out for the arrest of Sir Edward Carson, who, undeterred, issued a statement telling all his followers to be prepared for any emergency. Despite repeated denials from the War Office that any extra troops had been sent for, large groups of soldiers were soon on the move all over Ireland, converging on Ulster.

Four warships arrived in Kingstown Harbour in the South of Ireland and were busy taking on troops.

At the Curragh the Sixteenth Lancers and the Fourth Hussars were supplied with live ammunition and all sentries were doubled.

In Belfast, for fear that the troops in Victoria Barracks should be surrounded by the Volunteers, the entire Dorset Regiment was formed up and marched to Hollywood Barracks, six miles outside the city, to join the Norfolks already stationed there. This movement naturally caused consternation among the wives and families of the regiment who could not be accommodated at Hollywood and who were either furious at being left unprotected in the midst of the enemy, so to speak, or else considered the whole situation raving mad and said they would never speak to their husbands again if they so much as contemplated firing on these kind Ulster folk!

Many of the officers sent their wives back to England, Valerie Balfour included, but the situation still remained impossibly complex. Many people swore that they had it on the highest authority that a military governor was to be set up in Belfast with the Ulster constabulary under his control.

Sir Charles asked the family not to ride or drive more than a few miles from the house until they knew what was going to happen next. The whole household hung upon any scraps of news that came their way and found they could settle to nothing.

In Dublin, the garrisoned troops, composed of West Kents, Duke of Wellington's Regiment, K.OY.L.I., East Surrey, K.S.O.B., and the Royal Irish Lancers, were ordered to emergency stations. Rumours ran wildly up and down the country that fighting had already broken out in the North. But where? Nobody knew. Warships were supposed to have shelled the coast—nobody was sure where.

When the order to issue live ammunition was made at the Curragh the effect upon the officers and men was catastrophic. Up till now, despite many anxious moments, they had managed to persuade themselves that this situation could never arise. Now it most plainly could.

Harry was sitting in the mess with his head in his hands, facing the ruin of his army career, for he neither could nor would take a step against Ulster, no matter what orders he received. Nor be prepared to stand back and see others engage in warfare against his relations and friends up there. He wondered what the penalty for disobeying orders and possibly even informing was, and had an uncomfortable suspicion that it was the firing squad.

"What the hell do they think we are, at the War Office? A collection of orphaned mercenaries with no brains and no loyalties?" he raged as one of his brother officers entered the room.

"Calm yourself, Harry boy! The general is even now trying to solve your little problems!" said his friend comfortingly. "He has called a conference of all commanding officers . . . and they have been closeted with him for an hour already." He swung himself onto the back of a chair and leant over to ring the bell.

"Have a drink, old man? I need one." He ordered two Irish whiskies from the waiter and resumed. "I met Bobby Peterson this morning—now he *is* in trouble! His regiment has been ordered to march on Dundalk and half his wife's relations live up there it seems. He wants to resign his commission but his mother is dead keen on his army career and she holds the purse strings. You know what an old battle-axe she is! Poor Bobby! He sent off two telegrams yesterday, asking what he should do and so far he has had no answer. You never saw a man in such a state!"

At this moment they were joined by one of the Fourth Hussars, his eyes popping out of his head with excitement.

"The colonel wants all the officers in here in ten minutes. He has a most urgent communication to make. Quick! Come and help me find them all."

When they were all crowded into the mess in ten minutes' time to the dot, Brigadier Gough cleared his throat and, conscious that he was addressing one of the most attentive audiences in a lifetime, explained that he had just received the following instructions from Sir Arthur Paget: "The cavalry brigade are to make certain moves of a precautionary nature . . . the government believes that these moves will be understood and no resistance offered. I feel bound to tell you that I do not share this opinion." The general glanced around at the faces clustered in front of him. "I think they might easily lead to taking active operation against members of the Ulster Volunteer Force." He paused to let his words sink in before resuming, "Sir Arthur is also of this opinion and has been in close contact with the War Office, endeavouring to obtain a concession for those officers who feel deeply upon this subject. Today we have received an ultimatum from Colonel Seely, through the help of Sir John French, that 'All officers actually domiciled in Ulster would be exempted from taking part in the operations . . . will be allowed to disappear (I am quoting his words!) until after the operations are terminated . . . when they will be allowed to rejoin their regiments at the same rank, without their career or position being affected'!"

He paused, held up his hand as a murmur of incredulity went around the room, and continued in a slightly louder tone, " 'All officers *not* domiciled in Ulster but unprepared to undertake military operations in Ulster must understand that they will be dismissed from the service and lose their pensions at once!'

"Well, there you are, gentlemen! You must let me have your decisions before one-thirty P.M., as I wish to lay a full report before Sir Arthur Paget at two P.M." With one compelling glance around the dumbfounded officers, he collected his papers and left the room.

Immediately an absolute babel of comment and discussion broke out on all sides.

"Well, I'm damned! . . ."

"That's the end of my career! . . ."

"Fortunately, I've got an uncle in business! . . ."

"How the hell are they going to know if we live in Ulster or not? Who is going to find time to rake up our genealogy on the verge of war?"

"My God! It makes me sick! I have lived in Ulster all my life, until last year when my parents died, and now I am expected to take up arms against my relations!"

Harry was one of the first to arrive at his decision . . . and only he knew what it cost him to write out his resignation. As he sat at the desk and scrawled briefly: "Sir, I desire to hand in my resignation on this twenty-first of March, 1914, Yours truly, Harry Tristram, Lieut. 16th Lancers," he saw all his military dreams go up in smoke. Many of his brother officers were extremely well off and would not have to change their way of living very much. Although Harry had high hopes from a great-aunt, they were still only hopes. She might well view this act with misgiving or go batty in her old age and leave all her money to a cats' home, and his father had very little beside his naval pay. Nor was Harry equipped for any other kind of life, as the cavalry had been his one ambition from the age of ten.

He had never imagined an order could be given that he would feel himself unable to carry out and he was heartbroken. "What are you going to do, Harry?" asked a friend, as he stood up.

"I have resigned my commission," replied Harry mechanically, as he laid the scrap of paper on the table and turned away.

"Good man, so have I!"

"And I!"

"And I!" And I!" echoed voices all around the mess, followed by a moment's silence of awe at so many resignations.

221

"By Jove! What is the general going to say about this?" exclaimed one.

"You're mad!" said a dissenter, with conviction. "It would never come to blows . . . you are throwing away your careers for nothing!"

"That's where you are wrong!" came the answer. "These Ulster Johnnies mean what they say and I for one admire them for it. I'm not going to lay a finger against them, no matter what the consequences are!"

Harry could bear no more. He retreated to his room and sat sadly running his hand up and down the shiny scabbard of his sword, which he had taken from its hook.

He had no idea how long he sat there but was woken from his reverie by a loud shout and a bang at his door.

"Hey, Harry! What do you think? The general has sent in his resignation, too! There are over a hundred and forty altogether. Can you beat it?" Tim Darnford stood in the doorway, with shining eyes, as he gabbled out the news. "They say Sir Arthur will send his resignation in as well. That will fix the War Office! They can't possibly send the brigade to war without its officers, even if the troops would go . . . and that's doubtful. They are in a shocking state!"

"I say! Do you think so? I never thought of that!" exclaimed Harry, coming slowly to his feet. "Won't they just send some other cavalry?"

"My dear boy! Where are your wits? There are no other cavalry available. The only other horse troops in Ireland are the North Irish Horse, and they are in the Ulster Volunteer Force to a man!" He roared with laughter. "Cheer up! I don't believe anything is going to happen after all. It will all fizzle out like a damp squib."

And so it did, as far as *they* were concerned.

There was a tremendous to-ing and fro-ing between Sir Arthur Paget, General Gough, and Colonel Seely at the War Office, a visit to the King at Buckingham Palace by Sir Arthur and Colonel Seely, and then an announcement was made withdrawing all officers' resignations on the twenty-third of March and reinstating them in their positions, with the King's approval. Furthermore, the government gave an assurance that no active operation would be taken against Ulster.

It was a complete climb down.

Some of the officers could hardly believe their ears.

To Harry it was like a reprieve from the death sentence. He could have stood on his head for joy.

When, on the following day, General Gough returned to the Curragh after achieving this tremendous success, he was given the most tumultuous reception. The entire camp turned out to cheer him as he announced that Curragh troops would not be asked to go to Ulster, and, if they were, they would not carry arms.

All troops having been confined to barracks before the trouble began, no inkling of the mutiny would have reached the North for several days had it not been for the prompt action of Miss Maguire, who ran the Sandes Soldiers' Home at the Curragh and who sent off a long and descriptive telegram to her relations in the North the moment she heard of the resignations.

Needless to say the news spread like wildfire throughout Ulster and great was the joy of the Volunteers, particularly those with dummy guns who had been viewing with considerable misgiving the arrival in Belfast Lough of H.M.S. *Pathfinder* and H.M.S. *Attentive*, carrying reinforcements of the King's Own Yorkshire Light Infantry from Dublin to land at Carrickfergus.

All this had an electrifying effect upon the ordinary people of Ulster, who were in such a high state of excitement that Dean Grierson preached the sermon of his life in Belfast Cathedral on the subject of self-restraint. The devout Protestants who had packed the cathedral to its doors to give thanks for the reprieve from war were enormously impressed and the theme was taken up by clergy and leaders throughout the length and breadth of the province.

By the Monday evening immediate danger of hostilities seemed to have died down.

Ellen and the Richardsons were jubilant and consumed with

curiosity to know what part Harry had played in the mutiny; they could hardly sleep at night for excitement. Every day more details leaked out of the remarkable events which had taken place.

Lord Charles Beresford revealed that the navy had received orders to concentrate on Lamlash Island preparatory to proceeding to Ireland followed by the cancellation of those orders immediately after the Curragh incident. Then General Sir John French handed in his resignation, succeeded by a rumour that the entire Army Council had followed suit.

Colonel Seely, the secretary of state for war, was called upon to withdraw, after a stormy scene in Parliament.

"Wonderful reading in the papers these days!" exclaimed Sir Charles jubilantly. Indeed, none of them could bear to wait until another day for the next event, which was "Sir John French's Resignation Refused!" The day after this, Sir John French was insisting upon it being accepted. Finally, Seely himself resigned and the prime minister, still determined not to risk going to the country, took on the secretaryship for war himself, in addition to the premiership.

By the end of the month life in the country had almost returned to normal and there was a heavy feeling of reaction after all the excitement.

Sir Charles decided that he could safely allow himself a little trip to England to take in a few race meetings which he had sorely missed all winter without any harm coming to his platoon of Volunteers. It did not look as if there was going to be much more for them to do and he could always come back if things began to warm up again.

Ellen and her cousins were thrilled to get a very long letter from Harry, giving a graphic account of the mutiny and hoping it would not be long before he saw them all.

The only person of whom there was no news at all was James.

Chapter 15

As dinner ended on the twenty-fourth of April, Ellen prepared to follow her aunt from the dining room with nothing more exciting to look forward to for the evening's entertainment than the completion of the last of the set of chair seats in petit-point. She had set herself to do these as a house gift to Lady Richardson, a small return for all the kindness and happiness she had enjoyed since her arrival. It was rather ironical that she should have finished this "thank-you" present just at this moment, for she felt she had arrived at the end of an epoch. The love and kindness and the beautiful friendly house were still hers for the sharing but the sense of purpose seemed to have gone. With the mutiny at the Curragh the immediate urgency and excitement had gone. Although the political situation remained unchanged and the guns were just as badly needed as ever, there was a strong feeling of anti-climax in the air. War clouds loomed on the horizon and it seemed as if the government would never realise that Ulster was not going to be pushed under Irish rule.

Her own affairs seemed to have come to a standstill, too. It was now seven interminable weeks since the bouquet of carnations had come from James and she had been so full of joy and hope. He had said he had a job to do abroad, but it couldn't have taken all this long, or even if it had, surely he could have sent some sort of a letter? Eric was busy with the Volunteers, too, but he had found time to get engaged to Margaret . . . true he was not as senior as James, but still . . . ! She would just finish the last chair seat and go to bed early, reading herself to sleep.

She was rather surprised then, on reaching the door which Eric was holding open for them, when he murmured under his breath, "Make an excuse to meet me in the hall," accompanied by a most significant look.

Ellen stared at him in amazement, gave a barely perceptible nod, and walked on into the drawing room. What on earth could he want? He was not at all given to conspiracy, and since his engagement to Margaret had scarcely registered Ellen's presence. Perhaps he wanted help to buy Margaret a present—but surely he could have discussed that in front of Aunt Marion.

Greatly intrigued, she picked up her embroidery, made a few stitches, and then, murmuring, "Oh, I am silly! I have left my scissors upstairs! I must go and get them," she left the room and returned to the hall, where she found Eric hopping about in a great state of excitement.

"I thought you were never coming!" he burst out. "Can you keep a secret? It's terribly important and I must have your help."

"Good gracious, yes!" she laughed. "Of course I can, only do tell me quickly before you blow up and die with it. You look to me to be in a most dangerous state!" she teased, her spirits rising to meet his.

He grinned back and beckoned her into the study, shut the door, and leaned against it. "This is really serious," he said, his thin face lit up with excitement. "You know we—the Volunteers, I mean—have been keyed up for a very special occasion, for a long time?"

She nodded.

"Well, this is it! I mean we have all been told to rally for a big parade in Larne tonight. Sir George Richardson is to inspect us—it's a sort of test exercise. My unit has gone already and I was to follow later and collect a despatch on the way . . ."

"But what has all this got to do with me? I'm not a Volunteer . . . how can I help?" interrupted Ellen, rather disappointedly.

"Listen . . . I'm just coming to it. There was a message marked 'Urgent' for your uncle this morning and he told me to open anything like that while he was away."

"Well, what did it say?"

"To instruct the motor corps to be at the rally without fail, and it was marked 'Very Important' inside. They are all to collect in units and converge on Larne for nine P.M. Neill is not back yet and there's no one to drive the Argylle. That's why I need you!" he explained hastily.

"But where is Neill? Surely he should be back by now?"

"Oh, Ellen! Surely you remember! This is the day of his brother's funeral and he asked specially if he could be away, and you know what funerals are like over here. They go on all night. There's no time to spare—I waited as long as I could for him. You're the only one left who can drive the car!"

"But I've never driven it at night! I don't even kow how to light the lamps . . . I couldn't possibly do it . . . I only learnt for fun!" she said, aghast, leaning against the mantelpiece with the firelight flickering on her face.

"Oh, Ellen! *Please try*. They need every car they can get and you drive awfully well. I'm sure you can manage if only you would. I'll come with you and there are to be Volunteers at every crossroads to help us find the way and in case we break down. You must come," he pleaded.

An impish grin lit her face and she nodded her head decisively. "You know I'd just love to do it, only it's a bit frightening and uncle is so crazy about the car—if anything happened to it—especially while he's away, it would be awful!"

"It won't!" urged Eric. "You drive beautifully. The only thing that is going to kill Sir Charles is missing this! He'll never forgive himself for going away just now! Do come, Ellen!"

She looked doubtfully at him and then said, "It *is* for the Cause, isn't it? He would forgive anything for that, I suppose." She comforted herself. "All right! I'll drive. What do we do now?"

Eric suddenly looked rather diffident. "Well . . . would you mind awfully trying to make yourself look like Neill? I . . . I mean . . . they might be rather suspicious if a girl turned up!"

"Goodness! That shouldn't be difficult. We are alike as two peas already!" she mocked. "Nothing else you want besides

227

stealing my uncle's car and turning into a man aged forty years or so? How about masks and a password? When shall we start? That is, try to start!" she corrected herself, her eyes brimming with laughter. "You know, I'm not much good at starting. Neill always did that. You'll have to wind her up!"

"Oh, yes! I'll do anything—I feel such a fool not being able to drive. We ought to start as soon as possible. How long will it take you to get ready?"

"Not more than ten minutes," she said. "Goodness! To think this was going to be such a dull evening! Meet you in the garage in ten minutes. Adios!" She danced out of the room, kissing her hand to him. She had great difficulty in quelling her excitement and behaving normally as she entered the drawing room, sank down in her chair and started sorting through her sewing basket.

"Oh, here they are after all! I am an idiot." She waved the scissors at her aunt. "I'm just putting the last stitch into the last rose, isn't it marvellous? I never thought I would finish them when I began!"

"That sounds very Irish!" observed her aunt, looking up, smilingly, from her book. "I think it is a wonderful effort and I am most impressed at your 'staying power'! I can't wait to see them on the chairs!"

"Oh! Nor can I . . . I shall make everyone look at them and admire them. I've never done such a long job before. My artistic urge is quite used up!" She snipped off the final thread and held the canvas up triumphantly. "Look! Aunt Marion, do you like it?" When her aunt had made all the right answers, she rolled it up, put away her sewing, went over to Lady Richardson and asked "Would you mind awfully if I went up to bed early? I'm rather tired, and it's not worth starting anything else this evening."

Her aunt didn't mind at all. "As a matter of fact, I am just going to write letters. It is such a wonderful opportunity to catch up with them, with Charles away from home," she said, kissing her niece goodnight.

She would have been more than a little surprised if she had seen her "tired" niece flying upstairs to change like lightning into her riding clothes, only dispensing with her side-saddle habit to put on a thick tweed coat of Michael's over her jacket and one of his caps, pulled down hard to hide her hair.

"Passable, in the dark!" she murmured, surveying her reflection in the mirror. Then she picked up her riding gloves and and opened her bedroom door very cautiously.

The corridor was empty and she ran softly along to the back staircase where she paused, listening intently. They seemed to be having a very good time in the servants' hall, judging by the shouts of laughter coming from behind the door. With beating heart she ran down the stairs, across to the back door, which, fortunately, hadn't been locked yet, and out to the garage, where Eric was waiting beside the Argylle. He had pulled back the garage doors and had the winding handle already fixed in its hole.

Ellen climbed into the driver's seat, suddenly quaking in every limb. Eric had left a torch on the seat beside her and she could just make out the controls. "Retard," "Advance," "Mixture" . . . "Retard," surely, for starting. It was such ages since she had driven. She pulled the lever and switched on the ignition, feeling the pedals with her feet.

"Now!" She called softly.

Eric took a deep breath and swung the handle as hard as he could. There was a kick like a kangaroo jumping and he staggered back against the wall, the handle dropping with a clatter to the floor. Then, silence . . . followed by Ellen's voice coming apologetically through the dark.

"I'm afraid that didn't start . . . could you try again?" She gave a nervous giggle.

There was a deep sigh as Eric groped about on the floor, found the handle, and tried again. This time Ellen managed to pick it up and Eric had barely recovered from the effort of turning the crank before he began to worry about the noise the engine was making. He jumped up into the seat beside Ellen and gasped, "For goodness sake, let's get away from here before the whole house turns out! I never heard such a racket!"

"Uncle's car runs as softly as a bird, I would have you

know," reproved Ellen. "Hold tight now . . . here we go! My movements are not quite coordinated yet, I fear." She grinned as she let in the clutch and they shot backwards out of the garage and Eric nearly dashed his teeth out on the windscreen.

"I'm terribly sorry!" giggled Ellen. "It's always like this at first, but I usually get better as I go along. Can you see anything? I think we'd better not light the lamps until we get out of the gates . . . I can just manage, and I know the bends."

"I . . . forget to . . . tell you . . ." stammered Eric, as the car went down the drive in a series of hiccoughs, "we are not to light the lamps until we get to Larne. We are meant not to be seen." He hung on with both hands as Ellen grasped the wheel and bowled through a tunnel of beech trees, peering forward over the wheel into the darkness beyond.

"Won't that make the police rather suspicious?" she asked.

"I don't think there will be any police about tonight. We have surrounded all the barracks," said Eric simply.

"You've what?" gasped Ellen. "Surely that is madness! They'll break out and then we'll all be caught. Good Lord! What's that?" as an unearthly screech at her elbow, accompanied by a black shape, made her swerve violently.

"It's alright . . . it wasn't me! Only a cock pheasant!" soothed Eric, not a little shaken himself. "It'll be much lighter on the road away from all these trees."

So it was, and as they drove Eric explained as much as he knew of the night's plans.

They were to join their unit at Ballyclare (Sir Charles's unit, rather) and proceed from there in convoy to Larne, where they would receive further orders.

"But what is it all for? Why do they want the cars so urgently? Don't tell me it's just for an exercise—I'm not so stupid as to believe that!" commented Ellen, now on better terms with the big car and able to give her mind to the conversation.

Eric smiled. "I didn't think you were so stupid . . . I suppose it's alright to tell you, now you are so much involved—though, mind you, I don't know that this *is* the reason . . . but I think it is." He cleared his throat. "You know James has been away a lot lately?" (*As if I didn't,* thought Ellen grimly.) "Well, he has been helping Captain Crawford to get a consignment of guns."

"Gosh! I'd no idea he was doing that sort of thing!" exclaimed Ellen, at once dumbfounded, ashamed of herself for having doubted him, and anxious for his safety. "Go on, for goodness sake, tell me more!"

"Well, it's not just a little lot this time . . . it's a huge quantity, a 'once-for-all' load. Twenty thousand!" He heard her gasp beside him. "Yes, and they've had the most frightful time. Everything seems to have gone wrong. James got back yesterday and I saw him at the meeting last night. He was to have come with Captain Crawford in the ship with the guns and ammunition but instead of that it got lost halfway home and he was sent on a wild-goose chase all over the country, until he got a wire from Crawford saying everything was alright and to go home independently. He was frightfully fed up. No one knew where the ship had got to, only that the Danish officials got suspicious of the *Fanny* (that's what she was called) when she was being loaded up at the mouth of the Kiel Canal and took her papers for examination. When daylight came the ship had vanished and now, of course, all shipping has been alerted to look out for her. The navy has sent two destroyers to patrol between Rathlin Island and Carrickfergus . . . the government know she's carrying arms and they are pretty certain they are for here so they are all out to catch her. The trouble is that neither Crawford nor her captain know this and we don't know where they are to warn them."

"And what is James doing now?" asked Ellen, single-mindedly.

"Oh, I thing he's at Larne with Wilfred Spender who drew up this plan tonight."

Well, thank God he's safely on dry land, thought Ellen, and immediately began to dread the thought of meeting him . . . what would she say? But Eric was busy telling her all the plans and she had to listen.

"It was Spender's idea to hold this parade to get all the

Volunteers into Larne area and then cordon the whole thing off. He even managed to persuade Mr. Bagwell, the manager of the Great Northern Railway, to agree to organise trains to be at the disposal of the U.V.F.—enough to hold thirty thousand men both coming and going! Only, I believe, at the last moment, Captain Craig and he decided it would be less obvious to do the transport by car, there being so many roads out of Larne. Hence, this call for the motor corps. I believe the ship must have turned up and we are to collect the guns. I'm sure that's what it is . . . I believe they have even managed to cut off all the telephones to and from Larne!" he told her.

"Goodness! To think I am in on the gun-running! It's too thrilling for words—I'm so glad you made me come. I would not have missed this for worlds!" said Ellen. "Uncle Charles will be wild." She ground the gears noisily as they came to the bottom of a steep hill and added mischievously, "And he'd die if he heard that!"

As they passed through Doagh she saw that there was not only one but many cars ahead of them and when they finally drew up in the main street of Ballyclare, fifteen minutes later, the line of cars stretched before and behind them as far as the eye could see. Excited faces looked out of every door and window: never before had so many cars been seen all at once—and at isolated Ballyclare, of all places! Small wonder that the entire population had turned out to see them pass. Few people had any idea what it was all about but when they saw the cockades in their hats, many people cheered them or called out to know where they were going.

There were Volunteers lining the streets at intervals and Ellen realised how necessary it must have been to lock up the police. This cavalcade could never have escaped notice! She said excitedly to Eric, "Gosh! I bet the police are sorry to be missing this! What on earth will they think is going on?"

"I bet they know jolly well what's going on and are thankful to have been saved the embarrassment of having to take action! They are on our side almost to a man. In any case, they couldn't possibly have arrested us all, even if they wanted to. Do you recognise the car in front of us?"

Ellen shook her head. "I don't think so—should I?"

"Well, it's the District Inspector's car! He's not driving it himself—that would be going a bit too far even for a prejudiced policeman! A friend of his is driving it and I'll bet it's not the only police car on this jaunt!"

After a short delay in Ballyclare an officer of the U.V.F. came along and gave them instructions for the route to Larne. They were to go in convoy and upon arrival in the outskirts they were to wait in darkness and silence for a sign, taking their cue from the car in front.

The half-hour drive to Larne took place in an atmosphere of mounting excitement. At every road junction more and more cars poured in to join the stream, horses and carts, pony traps, every imaginable conveyance, and it became clear that this was a manoeuvre of gargantuan size. Groups of Volunteers appeared at frequent intervals along the road, and an occasional motorbike despatch rider would snarl past them at high speed as they began the downhill run into the town.

A light drizzle began to fall and Ellen was thankful for the warm coat she had borrowed from Michael. Poor Michael! What wouldn't he give to be here wearing it himself! It was too dark to see much, but lights still shone here and there through the town below them and there was a gleam on the water that etched the harbour buildings in dim shapes beyond.

The whole convoy drew silently to a standstill and waited expectantly.

At first no one spoke, then, as the halt lengthened, one or two drivers climbed down and began to talk to each other. All were by now certain that they were here to collect the guns, which had so long been promised, and everyone was agog for the arrival of the ship. Word passed along the line that as soon as it was sighted all the cars were to light their lamps and proceed in triumphal procession down to the harbour.

This information threw Ellen and Eric into a bit of a tizzy, for on opening the front of their lamps they realised that they had no idea whatever of how to fix the wicks, nor had they any matches with them.

Eric went off to the man in the car behind and succeeded in borrowing some matches that he lit and held hopefully to the wick, with no result despite Ellen's shielding hands. After three tries he sighed ruefully, "I am beginning to have quite a fellow-feeling for the Foolish Virgins! Only they were able to go out and buy new wicks. Do you think if we got two sticks and rubbed them together it would be quicker in the long run?" he asked comically.

"Oh, Eric! What good is all your learning if you don't know any more modern method of keeping a light going than that?" exclaimed Ellen in mock despair. "Go and ask the wise virgin in the next car for some of his oil—and do be quick or he'll get suspicious at us not knowing what to do!"

So Eric went off to enlist help. After a rather baffling conversation, when the man asked him what oil he was using or was it acetylene, water and carbide and Eric had to confess that up till this moment he had always thought it was candles, his neighbour decided that he needed help more than advice and accompanied him back to the Argylle.

"Who's drivin' this car?" he asked, peering up at Ellen. "Not this young lad, I hope! 'Tis a good thing ye know more about drivin' than ye do about lamps!" Fortunately he did not wait for an answer as he bent over them. "They're bone dry! That's what it is. There should be a wee can of the mixture in that box by your knee, son. Yes, that's it." He filled the containers of both lamps and trimmed the wicks.

"There now! That ought to work for you, but don't light them yet. Imagine comin' out in the dark and not knowin' the first thing about lightin' the lamps! 'Tis easily seen you've not been drivin' long!"

Eric felt that some explanation was due after all his help so he said that their uncle, who owned the car was away, and they had brought it out so as not to disappoint the unit. They had, in fact, had very little previous experience in driving.

234

"You've done well to get so far—I hope you get home safely," he said dourly, turning up his coat collar against the rain and making as if to return to his own car, when a thought struck him and he glanced at the Argylle. A grin spread over his face.

"I suppose you don't know that there is a hood on your car? Or are you sittin' in the rain from choice? Come on, I'll give you a hand with it!" At this Ellen broke into helpless giggles. He paused and looked at her curiously.

"Aye . . . a nice boy you are, my lady! And a brave one, too, to come out with this bright lad to help you!" He nodded towards Eric, who was busy trying to find the sockets for the hood to fit onto the windscreen and added: "My girls will be mad with envy when they hear there was a young lady out drivin' tonight."

When the hood was in place Ellen felt that the least they could do was to invite him to shelter inside with them. He was delighted to accept, and for the rest of her life, Ellen was sure, the smell of wet tweed coats would remind her of this night.

They were all squeezed together on the front seat and he told her that his name was Irwin, that he had come all the way from Ballinderry himself but that there were others who had come from as far as Armagh, Enniskillen, and Londonderry, and how they had all been supplied with petrol and directions by Volunteers along the entire route. For nearly an hour he regaled them with tales of the U.V.F. and of his family—how they had farmed at Ballinderry since the last plantation and never would they, or any of their friends, yield to Home Rule.

Ellen was beginning to feel tired and cold. The wet had soaked through her coat and the wait seemed interminable. They had been there for nearly two hours. Supposing something had happened to the ship? The destroyers might have caught her . . . and what would they do then?

As she wondered, suddenly, far down the Lough, there was a blaze of light as a ship—*the ship*—put on all her lights. A great cheer went up that could be heard echoing up from the town, along the streets and up to the waiting cars still outside in the hills. And then, all at once, the headlamps began to go on. To his great joy and Mr. Irwin's pride, Eric's lamp lit with the first match! All over the hills long lines of twinkling lights shone out like the tentacles of an octopus and the town of Larne, like the body, shone all over as the householders lit lights in all their windows as well. It was a sight never to be forgotten—there must have been upwards of five hundred cars—and, down below, the glowing ship was gliding rapidly into the now brilliantly lit harbour, into the glare of the arc lamps, into the cheering, yelling mob of Volunteers waiting to unload her.

They were all wild with excitement. Eric hugged Ellen and Mr. Irwin hugged them both before hurrying back to his own car. The great venture had succeeded! Captain Crawford had brought his ship home and now it only remained to collect the guns and convey them back to the prearranged dumps throughout the country.

Slowly, with many halts, the cars moved down the hill into the town.

All the house doors stood wide open and many women were bringing out cups of tea to the waiting drivers. Ellen thought no tea had ever tasted so delicious as the one brought to her by a good lady clad in a dressing gown and curl papers.

Volunteers lined the streets and there were no less than three checkpoints before they reached the harbour, where the ship was being eagerly unloaded.

As it looked as if they would have a long wait before their turn came, Eric slipped off to see what news he could pick up, leaving Ellen to gaze in silence at the remarkable scene, at the little black ship lit up as bright as day. She could even see the name on her side. *Funny!* Eric had said it was *Fanny*—but this one was *Mountjoy*. That rang a bell, somehow. Oh, yes! She remembered now. It was a ship called *Mountjoy* that had broken the boom and raised the Siege of Derry in 1689. They must have changed this ship's name because they were breaking the Siege of Ulster! What a marvellous idea! No wonder everyone had cheered so!

She could see the men rushing back and forth like ants with their packages, loading them into the strange assortment of vehicles drawn up alongside. There was everything from hand-carts to pack horses, carts, carriages, bicycles, and—a superb sight —the Larne steamroller chugging majestically along with an immense trailer attached behind.

At one moment her heart did a somersault as she suddenly caught sight of James's tall figure striding along the quay towards her. She didn't know whether she was frightened or pleased, but he was evidently only trying to hurry some of the vehicles along, for she heard him saying "Hurry along! No time to waste. These have all got to be home and stored before daylight and we are two hours late already!" before he turned and went back towards the ship.

Eric had been gone sometime now and she only prayed that he would come back before it was their turn to go forward. In the darkness on the hill she had not worried at all about being discovered, but now, in the blazing light, with numerous acquaintances working on and around the ship, she felt as nervous as a cat on a tightrope.

At last is was her turn to go and she cast a despairing glance 'round for Eric, who reappeared miraculously and walked beside the car until they were close beside the ship. She hardly dared to look at it and huddled herself down in her seat as the dickey was swiftly folded down and packages strapped on top of it. More piled on the back seat. Two more were strapped on the mud guards. They were given the signal to go and Eric hopped up beside her.

Just as she pushed the gear forward she saw James come out of the crowd and, recognising the car, call out, "I say, Eric, is that Neill with you? Will you tell him . . ." She waited to hear no more but slammed the gear into place and the car leapt forward, scattering the workers as she careered out of the harbour. Someone called, "Steady on! That's a valuable cargo you've got!" She waved a hand in acknowledgment and slowed the car to a steadier pace as they approached the first of the three check-points again.

Soon they were out of the town, their lights quenched, feeling their way along in unaccustomed gloom.

237

Eric told her all the story of the *Fanny*, which he had gathered at the dock, and Ellen felt ready to burst with pride that James should have had a part in it.

In the end Captain Crawford had had to transfer the entire cargo at sea from the hunted *Fanny* to a collier from Glasgow called the *Clyde Valley*, which had then steamed past the British destroyers without arousing the smallest suspicion.

Once in the safety of Larne Harbour, Crawford had had the brilliant inspiration of hanging a cloth with the name *Mountjoy* painted on it over the old name and then, unmasking all their lights, sailed triumphantly in. "I gather they could hardly believe their eyes when they saw the lights go on in answer and realised that they were safe, everything was ready for them. The committee had wanted them to go to Belfast, but Crawford just sent a message saying he was going to Larne and they had to arrange accordingly."

"Oh, it's the most wonderful story!" cried Ellen. "And to think that we have actually helped . . . it's the most wonderful thing that ever happened."

They chattered on, in their excitement, for some time, until it began to dawn on them that they had not yet come to Bally-clare, although they had been driving for over an hour. The horrid suspicion arose that they must have taken a wrong turning while they were immersed in their talk. Goodness knows where they were now!

"Well, wherever we are, there are bound to be Volunteers at the crossroads and we must come to one some time, but we'd better hurry up a bit in case we've gone badly out of our way," urged Eric.

So Ellen rather gingerly trod on the accelerator and the big car leapt forward. It was terribly difficult as the night was really black and dark and she felt she was having to go faster than her reactions could cope with if something went wrong.

"Do you not think it would be safe to light the lamps again now?" she asked, and in that moment, as she turned to speak, they came to a sudden bend in the road. She jammed on her brakes and hauled the car around with all her strength. She got it safely around but it was lurching and bumping and making a noise like ten rubbish bins being knocked over.

"Oh, Lord!" groaned Ellen, pulling in to the side of the road. "I do believe one of the tyres has come off. How ghastly!"

And so it had. The speed and the sudden turn of the wheel had been too much; the car was down on the steel rim and a round white object flopped down in the middle of the road was the missing tyre.

"What on earth are we going to do now?" she asked, as they peered at the stricken wheel. "I don't know anything about mending a wheel, do you?"

"Oh, Ellen!" groaned Eric, in despair, "I should never have brought you out tonight—I never thought of this sort of thing happening! I do know how to change a bicycle tyre, but I don't even know where the tools are for this, and I seem to have lost the torch."

He searched frantically inside the car but the sudden lurch must have rolled it away; it was nowhere to be found. They tried every corner for tools but their unaccustomed hands could not find anything of use.

Finally Eric said "I'm afraid there's absolutely nothing for it—I'll have to walk on and try to get help at the next checkpoint, wherever that is. I can't leave you here by yourself . . . you had better come with me."

But Ellen thought not. "I couldn't possibly leave Uncle's car on the side of the road. No. I'd better stay with it. It can't be very far to the next cross—we haven't met one for ages and I can hide if anyone comes. At least I'll know if anything happens to her. It's the least I can do after knocking the wheel off!"

She climbed back into her seat. "Don't worry. I'm sure I shall be alright. But do hurry—we don't want to be stuck here when the dawn comes!"

Thus urged, Eric strode away into the darkness.

As the last sound of his footsteps died away, the stillness of the night became apparent, and with it the sudden realisation that she was completely alone in the middle of unknown country, with a stolen car laden with contraband rifles and ammunition.

The realisation sent a cold shiver down her spine. Supposing the police got out after all, and found her here—what on earth could she do? And then an even worse thought struck her. Supposing some Nationalist came along? Or worse, a drunken man . . . or a tramp?

By now she felt thoroughly frightened and the minutes dragged past on leaden feet.

She was much too cold and frightened to sleep. Would Eric never come?

Now the night did not seem still at all. There were all sorts of little rustling noises . . . and one in particular, a sort of regular scraping noise quite close beside her, that made her heart stand still. She held her breath and the sound stopped. Suddenly, with great relief, she realised that it was just the button of Michael's coat catching on the steering wheel with the movement of her breathing.

"What a fool I am!" She almost laughed, and then she caught her breath, for now she did hear something. Quite definitely there was someone coming along the road. She nearly cried with joy. It must be Eric coming back already! But no! There was only one pair of feet . . . and weren't they coming from the wrong direction? She wasn't sure . . . yes . . . they were . . . her heart pounded wildly. "Oh God, don't let them find me," she prayed silently as she slid out of the door next to the hedge.

Not drunk, anyway! she thought, as the sharp footsteps drew nearer, and she hardly knew which would be the worse. A drunk would not be likely to notice the guns but he might be much more unpleasant to deal with.

The footsteps were really very near now. There was something incredibly sinister about their steady rhythm. She was horribly scared and her mouth was as dry as a bone. They were almost alongside when they paused and she knew the stranger was looking at the car, walking 'round it, coming to her side!

She braced herself flat against the door and must have made a tiny sound, for a torch was suddenly flashed in her face and a voice exclaimed, "Good Lord! Ellen! What on earth are you doing here in that get-up?"

A voice she knew and loved . . . the one voice she wanted to hear more than any other. The relief was so great she pitched forward into his arms and clung to him, laughing and crying together, while he held her tightly to him. He pushed off her cap, and stroking her hair, murmured, "It's alright, darling . . . it's alright, don't cry . . . you're quite safe. Please don't cry. I love you and I can't bear you to cry."

He kissed her gently 'round the forehead, murmuring endearments. His tenderness nearly brought on another outburst of tears, but eventually she made a big effort, straightened herself, wiped her nose on the back of Michael's sleeve, and looking up at him, said, "Oh, James! Do you really?"

He looked at her in surprise. "Do I really what?"

She gave a watery giggle. "Love me, silly! You said you did just now."

He hugged her. "Of course I do, you ridiculous girl. I've loved you for ages—ever since I met you, in fact! Only I was never sure about you: whether you were serious or just flirting." He held her away from him and asked sternly, "Were you just flirting?"

"Oh, James!" He could hear the laughter in her voice as she leant against him. "How could you think so? . . . I adore you." She lifted her face to be kissed and for the next few minutes the entire police force could have come and taken the car away and neither of them would have noticed. There was a glorious privacy in the dark, and so many sweet nothings to be said, but at length they came back to their surroundings and began to ask questions.

He was lost in admiration of her courage in bringing out the car, and when she told him that Eric had been with her, he said, ironically, "Braver still! Of course now I understand about that extraordinary bit of driving down at the ship! I recognised the car and assumed Neill was driving. I really wondered if he had a 'drop taken,' the way you went off, mowing down half the Volunteers! What was the hurry?"

"James! I didn't! I was terrified you would recognise me."

"You don't seem at all terrified now," he said, in a quizzical tone, kissing her again. "But I admit you did look very frightened when I shone the torch at you. My poor sweet. I'm terribly sorry I scared you. I knew it was Charles's car and saw the wheel off. I thought it must have been abandoned and was worried about the guns being found when I suddenly saw a figure hiding. I thought it was a Nationalist snooping and meant to give him a good fright. You must forgive me for not expecting to find a beautiful maiden in distress!"

"Oh, it was such bliss to hear your voice . . . and I had been so afraid of not knowing what to say when I did meet you again . . ."

"Well, this made it not so difficult, didn't it?" He gave her another hug and said rather regretfully, "I suppose we had better get this car fixed before it gets light, though I much prefer helping you not to be frightened. Do you think you will be alright if I get this wheel on? Then we can get home and tell them the news."

He shone his torch on a box under the bonnet, which she had not noticed before, and took out some tools.

"You mean . . . about the guns?" she asked.

"Yes . . . that, too . . . here, hold the torch, please, while I undo this buckle. I thought we might tell them about getting married!" He looked up at her and she shone the torch mischievously in his face as she questioned, "Oh, are you getting married? I hadn't heard anything about that!"

He chuckled and took the torch from her. "No woman can ever hold a light straight."

He lifted the spare wheel down and leant it against the side of the car, then lay on the road and proceeded to push the jack in under the axle as he continued, "Yes . . . I'm surprised you didn't know! I have found the most wonderful girl . . ."—he paused as he screwed in the handle and Ellen had a moment of horrible doubt before he went on blandly—"she's English—but with good Ulster connections. No money, I believe. Poor dear—she can't help that! But beautiful . . . very beautiful," he repeated, savouring the words. Then he stood up. "In fact, she's the most beautiful girl in the world and certainly the bravest and cleverest and sweetest." He kissed her in between each adjective. "I do hope you will consent to be my wife, Miss Tristram, . . . dearest Ellen," he mimicked. "May I tell you how ardently I admire and respect you? But do you mind if I put this wheel on first?" He pumped up the jack.

Ellen was wreathed in smiles. She felt warm all over. Everything was perfect and she was wildly happy.

"Oh, James! I do love you! I've loved you for ages . . . only I was so afraid you weren't the marrying sort. Oh goodness, I am happy!" She seized the hand he held out for the spare tyre and kissed it warmly.

"Not the marrying sort?" he exclaimed in astonishment. "What sort of man is that? What on earth gave you that idea? I don't exactly shun the female company and I'm not quite a recluse!"

"Well . . . you took such a long time to ask me . . ." she complained from the pinnacle of happily-engaged security. "I thought you had decided it was perhaps safer to remain a bachelor."

"I thought it was a good deal safer to see how many other men you were encouraging before I ran the risk of being turned down myself!" he said with some asperity. "It takes an awful lot of confidence to ask a girl to marry you and it's not a thing I intend to do twice."

"But you should have known I was in love with you. I showed it a mile away . . . I felt I was always blushing and behaving like an idiot when I was with you!" she argued.

"How attractive it sounds!" he laughed. "Actually, I had noticed the blushes and I thought they were one of the nicest things about you. I almost proposed to you that time down in Galway, and then with the fire and all I felt it would be out of place. The next thing I knew you had got yourself an old boy friend and were flirting away like mad with him. It gave me quite a jolt, I can tell you. I thought I was 'home and dry' and then all at once I was only running second . . . or even third for all I knew!"

"Oh, darling!" she remonstrated, leaning against his shoulder as he stood up. "You know you were always first. Only suddenly you were so evasive and Desmond knows exactly how to turn a situation to his own benefit. Somehow he made it so difficult to avoid him—I didn't know what to do and you were no help at all!"

"There wasn't much I could do when I found you had cut my dance while I had been helping some fainting female onto a sofa . . ."

"At the regimental ball? Oh, James, how awful! Desmond told me you had gone home and I was so disappointed I went home, too. I couldn't bear the thought of dancing with him instead of you!" she said sorrowfully.

"The snake! It was he who told me you had gone home—though I suppose it was true by then."

"Yes, but I bet he made the most of it. And now I come to think of it, it was Desmond again who said you had gone off at the tennis match!"

He stared at her. "But I told Grania O'Neill to tell you I had been called away urgently and asked her to give you a lift home. Did she not do that?" he asked.

"I can't really remember now. I think she did offer me a lift but I suppose I said I was fixed up, meaning with you, and she must have thought someone else had told me. She's not the sort who would worry much, anyway."

"But, my darling, what on earth did you think then? And my letter can't have reached you for days!" he asked in concern.

Now it was Ellen's turn to be surprised.

"I didn't get any letter! I never knew what had happened until tonight, when I assumed that it must have been something to do with the guns . . . but I didn't know then that you were helping with them! I just thought you had walked out on me

244

again . . . and thought that maybe it was a habit of yours!" she said simply.

He was aghast. "But, sweetheart, I wrote telling you how terribly sorry I was! How dreadful! Old Kirk must never have bothered to post my letter—what must you have thought? What did you do?"

"Oh, needless to say Desmond was at hand with sporting car and helping hand! I decided I would never speak to you again and then I went and made such a fool of myself at the fete!"

He groaned. "No wonder! I only wonder you weren't ruder."

She burst into delighted laughter. "Oh, do you think I could have been? I was so ashamed of myself afterwards!"

He took her in his arms and kissed her long and luxuriously.

"Let us have no more recriminations. We obviously had no idea what marvellously honourable people we both really are! But I have had my punishment, for when I had recovered my nerve enough to try again I was so taken up with the gun-running and drilling I had no time to try to win you back."

She was immediately all compassion and sympathy, and they shared to the full the joy of being able to discuss all the feelings, which they had hitherto been unable to mention. At last they were roused from their absorbtion by the sound of voices coming up the road. This time it was Eric, with two Volunteers. They were more than a little surprised to find Ellen happily ensconced in the Argylle with one of their Officers and the car in perfectly road-worthy condition.

Eric was particularly deflated for he had had to walk over a mile before he found a crossing with its attendant U.V.F. The nearest tool-kit supply had been a farther two miles away, whence it had been fetched at top speed by bicycle, and during all this time Eric had been a prey to great anxiety on Ellen's behalf. Altogether he had had a wretched time and felt he had not cut at all the gallant figure that he had intended at the outset of the adventure.

However, these feelings were quickly forgotten in the relief of getting away again without discovery. James, it appeared, had seen the last of the guns loaded at Larne and the *Mountjoy* safely off to unload the rest at Donaghadee. He had then cadged a lift part of the way home in a trap and was walking the last stretch to where he had left his bike on the way out. So he was very happy to make over the care of the bicycle to one of the Volunteers when they dropped them off at their post and continue back to Kilwater with Ellen and Eric.

They had, indeed, gone considerably out of their way in the dark, and the first streaks of light were appearing in the east when they drove at last into the backyard.

There was no time to be lost in stowing the bundles of rifles in the airvent of an old disused greenhouse. Fortunately, with James's help, this was the work of only a few moments, and the Argylle also was returned to its garage, none the worse for its night's work, before the dawn broke fully.

They were all three ravenous, dirty, and bedraggled. But as James went off with Eric to have a bath before breakfast, Ellen could not resist going straight to her aunt's room in all the glory of her dirt and disguise. Lady Richardson's astonishment at this apparition so early in the morning can be imagined and she hardly knew which news was the more exciting, Ellen's engagement or the safe arrival of the guns. On the whole she thought the first piece of news brought the most unalloyed happiness, as the gun-running was marred for her by knowing how desperately disappointed her husband would be not to have been in on it—the climax of so much of his work for years. He would never forgive himself.

Great was the talk that went on over breakfast, the congratulations, the planning, the recounting of stories which had necessarily been kept secret until now.

Cynthia and Alice were, for once, so overwhelmed at the thought of being so close to the making of history and the romance of the engagement under such circumstances, that they could hardly eat for excitement.

Finally James announced that he must return to headquarters, to see if there was anything for him to do. But he promised faithfully to come back to join them all for dinner. In the hall he kissed his fiancée long and tenderly.

Then, holding her hands very tightly, he said, "I had a feeling, you know, that first day when I saw you on the *Patriotic* that your life was in some way going to be bound up with this country. I think it was that which first attracted me to you. You looked as if you had fallen in love with it!"

"And how right you were. I loved it from the very first moment and I'm so terribly, terribly happy that you want me to live here always. I don't know what Mama will say! But Aunt Marion is thrilled. And do you know, I have just had the most marvellous idea! When we go out calling after our engagement is announced—it would be an ideal opportunity for delivering the guns! Wouldn't it? No one would ever suspect us!"

She looked up at him with shining eyes and he looked down at her with that grey gaze which had first made her heart beat for him.

"Truly," he said, "I could not have found myself a more enchanting wife!"